Deathwork

Deathwork

Defending
the Condemned

MICHAEL MELLO

Foreword by Mark E. Olive

University of Minnesota Press
Minneapolis • London

Published by the University of Minnesota Press
111 Third Avenue South, Suite 290
Minneapolis, MN 55401–2520
http://www.upress.umn.edu

Library of Congress Cataloging-in-Publication Data

Mello, Michael.
 Deathwork : defending the condemned / Michael Mello.
  p. cm.
 Includes index.
 ISBN 0-8166-4087-4 (HC : alk. paper) — ISBN 0-8166-4088-2 (PB : alk. paper)
  1. Mello, Michael. 2. Lawyers—United States. 3. Defense (Criminal procedure)—
United States. 4. Capital punishment—United States. I. Title.
 KF373.M45 A3 2002
 345.73'0772—dc21

                  2002007388

Printed in the United States of America on acid-free paper

The University of Minnesota is an equal-opportunity educator and employer.

12 11 10 09 08 07 06 05 04 03 02   10 9 8 7 6 5 4 3 2 1

For two of my heroes,

Ellen Bruger

and

Richard Jorandby,

with love

and gratitude.

Contents

Foreword

Mark E. Olive

By the way, another thought has struck me about the lawyer: it would be a good thing if the man could spare some time for me, and wasn't too hasty. I think he should be like a doctor, who shouldn't give the impression that he has a great many things to do.

—Dietrich Bonhoeffer, *Letters and Papers from Prison,* 1951

Professor Mello had a great many things to do in 1985. The business of the state killing its citizens was booming in Florida, and Mike was steeped in stopping it. Every moment provided real opportunities for making a federal case out of something, meeting important-sounding people, and being heroic—just the stuff lawyers live for. Lives were on the line, and Mike had his hands full.

But Mike rarely gave his clients the impression that he had a great many things to do. Persons on death row are exactly like you. For example, they like some lawyers and dislike (most) others. Mike's clients loved Mike, like one loves a sibling or a parent or a friend. They loved Mike because Mike loved them, and showed it: he listened, explained, laughed, cried, and, most important, he showed up, without being hasty. He acted the way lawyers are supposed to act.

In *Deathwork,* Mike provides his journal of lawyering in the crucible torched by freshly minted legal claims and looming execution dates. Yet the value of this work is not just its quality chronicling of the great many things death lawyers do. Rather, *Deathwork* shines through its glimpses of the persons who are on death row. It is their humanity and extraordinary dignity that makes reading (and doing) *Deathwork* a privilege.

I don't agree with everything in *Deathwork* (most especially its Paul Bunyan yarns about my own work on death cases), but a measure of its power is that it made me think afresh about the machinery of death that arbitrarily plows people under in this country. Mike describes a system that accepts—indeed, that *takes as an acceptable given*—that, all other things being equal, African Americans have been and will be executed at a higher rate than Caucasians, based solely on racial considerations; a system that blindly allowed scores of defendants to be killed under a flagrantly illegal and unreliable death penalty statute in Florida; and a system that kills even likely innocent defendants by refusing to consider their claims because their lawyers did not raise them in a proper manner. To quote from Dorothy Day in her book *The Long Loneliness,* we have tolerated this "filthy, rotten system" far too long, and Mike's book urges us closer to the international norm of abolition.

You meet not just lawyers and judges here, thank goodness, but also real people, the remarkable people who are selected at random for our death chambers: Vietnam War veterans without a prewar blemish on them; severely mentally ill youngsters without medical care; denizens of turbulent, chaotic, and ravaged upbringings, literally tortured by "caretakers." These toss-of-the-dice characteristics—mental illness, upbringing, unspeakable trauma (and in many cases, all three)—started these folks down the bad luck path, and the worst luck struck like lightning.

The death row lives described in *Deathwork* reveal that, again, these individuals are exactly like you. They are not defined by—they *are not just*—the worst things that they have ever done. Are you? Mike shows the love and compassion these individuals have for one another and for their families, humanity blooming on death row the same way it blooms in your home. He shows how the clients genuinely fret over the lawyers' well-being, for goodness sake. And he shows the indomitability of human spirit—poetry, humor, spirituality, and grace—in the face of sometimes virtually certain death.

Two seemingly separate notions—that, on the one hand, there are *legal claims* to raise for death row inmates and, on the other hand, *there are real people,* people just like you, on death row—began to marry for death row lawyers in the early 1980s. When I first met Mike, he was full of the law and fervently believed in legal claims. Many of us did. Mike is a first-class legal scholar (sparkling, really), and he was right about the legal claims he raised; in any fair arena, they would have won. He discusses many of these claims in *Deathwork*. In court he presented these claims for clients with hundreds of footnotes, long strings of case names, and law review articles. Sadly, as Mike tells you, we buried a lot of those clients. There is not much life in a footnote.

There is, however, plenty of life in our death row clients and their families. It's a good idea to spend some time with them, to not be too hasty, and not just to be kind, but *to win*. They tell us the stories of life—stories about treachery, ambition, betrayal, greed, sacrifice, commitment, devotion, love—and in these stories we find a reason, not a fancy argument but a *reason*, for life.

Every good death penalty lawyer today knows this.

Mike slowly stopped doing legal claims and started doing claims that tell a true life story.[1] If you find an injustice in a case, you force sight into the blind eyes and sound into the deaf ears of clerks and judges. Law is, at best, an injustice delivery device: find the injustice, and the law ought to cover it. What else could law possibly be good for? I'll take a treachery or a redemption life story over a *Miranda* story any day. So will a judge—or a justice. Life begets life.

This book is full of life.

Tallahassee, Florida
2002

Note

1. When Mike first came to the Florida Office of Capital Collateral Representative, there was no software that would do footnotes well; we had to type them at the bottoms of pages, typewriter style. A simple edit in the body of a document, in the text, would throw off these "footers." Making the document look good again took time. Because we moved pretty fast in drafting and editing legal papers, it was hard to take the time for footnotes. Scharlette Holdman, whom you will meet in this book, tolerated this "lawyer crap" for a while. Finally, though, she told Mike, "No footnotes," a policy intended to quicken production and lessen "worthless" legalese. Mike seethed and threatened to quit. Ultimately, he complied, which is the custom around Scharlette. Other than this one note here (which is not lawyerlike), you will not find a footnote in *Deathwork*.

Author's Note

I would like to explain several aspects of this book. First, I do not include citation footnotes or endnotes. In most instances, I would be citing documents I helped create in the first place, and therefore citations seem to me unnecessary. This is in large part a collection of true stories written more for the laity than for academics; little numbers interlarded throughout the stories would have been unreasonably distracting.

Nonetheless, several books were indispensable to me as sources, and I want to acknowledge them here. David Von Drehle's brilliant book *Among the Lowest of the Dead: Inside Death Row* is the best treatment of America's modern experience with capital punishment, particularly (for my purposes here) the cases of Robert Sullivan and James Adams, and provides compelling portraits of Scharlette Holdman and Craig Barnard. Kent S. Miller and Michael L. Radelet's outstanding book *Executing the Mentally Ill: The Criminal Justice System and the Case of Alvin Ford* is the definitive work on the Alvin Ford case. *In Spite of Innocence: Erroneous Convictions in Capital Cases,* by Radelet, Hugo Adam Bedau, and Constance E. Putnam, provides the best treatment of the James Adams case. Ray Jenkins's book *Blind Vengeance: The Roy Moody Mail Bomb Murders* gives a masterful account of Judge Robert S. Vance. Doug Magee's *Slow Coming Dark: Interviews on Death Row* includes a haunting interview with David Leroy Washington. Anthony Amsterdam's essay "Selling a Quick Fix for Boot Hill: The Myth of Justice Delayed in Death Cases" (in *The Killing State: Capital Punishment in Law, Politics, and Culture,* edited by Austin Sarat) and Edward Lazarus's book *Closed Chambers: The Rise, Fall, and Future of the Modern*

Supreme Court are required reading for anyone interested in how the U.S. Supreme Court deals with death cases; Lazarus's chapters on Warren McCleskey's case were especially valuable to me. For excellent general treatments of capital punishment in the United States, see *America's Experiment with Capital Punishment: Reflections on the Past, Present, and Future of the Ultimate Penal Sanction*, edited by James R. Acker, Robert M. Bohm, and Charles S. Lanier; *The Death Penalty in America: Current Controversies*, edited by Hugo Adam Bedau; and *Cases and Materials on the Death Penalty*, by Nina Rivkind and Steven F. Shatz.

Close readers of my previous works will find several of these stories familiar. I briefly discuss the Ronnie Straight, Alvin Ford, Joseph Green Brown, and Stephen Todd Booker cases in my book *Dead Wrong: A Death Row Lawyer Speaks Out against Capital Punishment* (published in 1997). Michael Radelet and I published a *Law Review* article in 1986 on the James Dupree Henry case.

I do not include chapters here on two high-profile cases in which I was involved, those of Ted Bundy and "Crazy Joe" Spaziano. Bundy has been the subject of numerous books; I devoted a chapter in *Dead Wrong* to him, but the best treatment can be found in Von Drehle's *Among the Lowest of the Dead*. The "Crazy Joe" Spaziano story is not in this collection because I have recently devoted an entire book to his case, *The Wrong Man: A True Story of Innocence on Death Row*. My goal here is to tell the stories of more ordinary—and obscure—death row cases.

This book is in part a memoir of my years as a Florida capital public defender. Since leaving Florida in 1987, I have been involved in a few high-profile capital cases, including that of Theodore Kaczynski (the Unabomber). I do not examine those cases in this book. My book *The United States of America versus Theodore John Kaczynski: Ethics, Power, and the Invention of the Unabomber* focuses on the Unabomber case.

This book includes quotations from the private diary I kept during the time I was a Florida capital public defender. In fact, this book is grounded in my diary, my memory book during those chaotic years.

I resist the temptation to reiterate here my responses to Stephen Bright, David Dow, and other critics of my earlier book *Dead Wrong*. My reply, particularly to Dow, may be found in my article "Dead Reckoning: The Duty of Scholarship and the Ethics of Conscious Abstention from Death Row Representation," *Criminal Law Bulletin* 35 (September–October 1999): 478–504. I do want to be clear that all the arguments I address to Dow in that article apply with equal force to Bright. Similarly, I have elsewhere critiqued the recent version of the Florida Office of Capital Collateral Representative (CCR). My books *The Wrong Man* and *Dead Wrong* both address CCR's demise in some detail, and I see no reason to revisit this issue here.

This project has left me with numerous debts that I gratefully acknowledge. Mark Olive and Richard Jorandby reviewed the manuscript and generously gave me permission to use materials prepared in the litigation of several stories presented in this book. Mike Radelet allowed me to use a portion of our joint writing project on the James Dupree Henry case. Paul Perkins permitted me to use our work on the intertwined histories of the right to counsel, constitutional challenges to capital punishment, and the availability of habeas corpus. Mike Radelet and Mark Olive read and commented helpfully on the manuscript.

I do all my writing in longhand, on yellow legal pads, and Judy Hilts and Laura Gillen word processed the multiple generations of the manuscript with grace and good humor. Ted Sweet, Lee Cohen, Eric Fitzpatrick, Paul Perkins, and Brian Marsicovertere provided invaluable research assistance; I am especially grateful for their tracking down and obtaining for me Stephen Todd Booker's two books of poetry, *Waves and License* (1983) and *Tug* (1994). Emily (Kucer) LaPointe, Phil Meyer, and Doug Samuels read and commented helpfully on the manuscript.

Doug Armato, Carrie Mullen, Alison Aten, Kathryn Grimes, Robin Moir, Anna Pakarinen, Judy Selhorst, and the other folks at the University of Minnesota Press did a superb job with this book and its predecessor, *The Wrong Man.* They have proven that publishing can be a true pleasure. Laura Moss Gottlieb did an outstanding job on the index.

I am grateful to Vermont Law School for paying me to write and teach in one of the most peaceful and physically beautiful places on Earth, and to deans Kinvin Wroth and Stephanie Willbanks, and Sally Cooper in the business office, for providing financial support so I could complete the manuscript on time.

I am, as always, grateful to my bride Deanna. With her all good things are possible.

Finally, I would like to explain why I am dedicating this book to

Richard Jorandby, a man who has been indicted. Jorandby, public defender for Palm Beach County for twenty-eight years, was my boss from 1983 to 1985. He has also been my hero since that time. The criminal charges brought against him in July 2001, for corruption, are, in a word, hogwash. Those charges were manufactured by the Florida Department of Law Enforcement, the same hack agency whose secret, and bogus, police report kept "Crazy Joe" Spaziano on death row for crimes he didn't commit, as I discuss in *The Wrong Man*. No person who really knows the soul of Dick Jorandby can imagine him corrupt; he is one of the most honorable and decent men I have ever known, and he built his public defender's office into the best in the nation.

I dedicate this book to Dick because, without him, I would not be writing a memoir of deathwork. Without Dick, I would not have done deathwork; I would have gone to work for a corporate Wall Street law firm. I might have written a memoir about life on Wall Street, but I doubt it. I also doubt that you—or anyone else—would be interested in reading such a memoir. I know I wouldn't.

Introduction

The Justice of Man

Though the justice of God may well ordain that some should die, the justice of man is altogether and always insufficient for saying who these may be.

—Charles Black Jr., *Capital Punishment,* 1974

Legal cases are stories. Capital cases provide some of the law's most unsettling stories. For me, the legal machinery of death is a collection of stories.

There was the insane man the government wanted to execute.

There was the condemned person who was a juvenile when he committed his capital crime.

There are the innocent men: Nationwide, as of June 2002, one hundred death row prisoners have been freed since 1973. For every eight people executed, one has been freed after proving his innocence—*one in eight.*

There are the African Americans, and there was the Cuban refugee on Florida's death row.

There was the stone-cold killer.

There were the challenges to Florida's use of the electric chair.

There was the time my colleagues and I spirited a lawyer into Cuba to investigate the family history of one of our clients, a Mariel boatlift refugee.

There was the time my boss flew from South Florida to Tallahassee to argue for a stay of execution on behalf of our client, and his luggage landed in Jacksonville, and a friend in Jacksonville put my boss's suit in a cab to Tallahassee, so he wouldn't have to appear before the Florida Supreme Court dressed in blue jeans.

There were the times—frequent enough that they became rituals in my public defender office in Tallahassee—when, the evening after a client of ours was executed, everyone in the office would go to a local steak house to eat red meat and drink red wine.

There was the time a man was executed while his stay papers were still circling the Atlanta Hartsfield Airport, which was socked in by fog.

There was the time my office's computers crashed in the middle of the night during the Christmas holiday season, and assistants—full of holiday spirits—had to come in to the office to retype a brief in a landmark case.

There was the time I got lost in Jacksonville, dashing to file a stay application before the courthouse closed at the end of the day. We didn't make it, but it didn't matter, because the U.S. Supreme Court had already stayed the execution. Before we drove back to Tallahassee, we stopped at a drive-up liquor store, and we drank and sang all the way home.

There was the time we thought the Florida Supreme Court might stay an impending execution because a hurricane had just ripped through Tallahassee, where the court was located. As it turned out, our client didn't get the stay-due-to-hurricane; in Florida, death takes no breaks for hurricanes.

There were the logistical nightmares in the days before fax machines (my diaries refer to "zap mail," our term for shipping overnight via Federal Express) of getting our stay of execution papers to far-flung courts before a client's execution rendered those papers moot. Sometimes we didn't make it in time.

There was the time when Governor Bob Graham adopted themes in signing pairs of death warrants. One theme was serial killers: Ted Bundy and Gerald Stano had warrants signed the same day. On one day, Graham signed warrants on two men with the last name Thomas; that day, Ed Thomas's mother called my office in tears, because she'd just heard on the radio that a man named Thomas had been executed in Florida, and she'd thought Ed had a stay. He had; the man who had been executed was Dan Thomas.

There was the time an elderly Mafia hit man (who had gone soft in the head while on death row) was scheduled to be executed, and we called his "godfather" for help.

There was the time when I failed to persuade a state trial judge to stay my client's impending execution, and even so, my client's mother (who had been present in court during my unsuccessful oral argument) invited me to her home for Thanksgiving dinner.

There was the time a grateful volunteer lawyer, whom my office had helped, sent us a case of Chivas Regal scotch—which we cashed in at the local liquor store for a crate of bourbon, vodka, rum, wine, and cheap scotch. For the next six months, our office had a fully stocked wet bar.

Then there were the times when our work fighting death warrants kept us in our public defender office day and night for weeks at a time, and we brought in portable cots, slept in shifts, and lived on takeout Chinese food and pizza.

To my mind, these stories, and thousands more like them, show the real face of capital punishment in the United States. You won't find these stories in law books or Supreme Court opinions or the stump speeches of politicians. The reality of capital punishment is the sum of a constellation of stories about human beings in extreme circumstances.

This is a book for laypersons as well as for those trained in the law. Any idiot with a law degree can make the law sound mysterious, complex, and inaccessible. It is far more difficult to translate legal principles accurately into language that is comprehensible to readers who are not themselves graduates of the language lab that is law school. Telling the stories that I tell in this book requires some discussion of legal doctrine and procedures, but I try to present that discussion without resorting to unnecessary jargon or legalese.

Across the United States, 777 men and women have been executed by the government since 1977. There are currently more than 3,700 people living on death row; on average, one of these people is put to death each week, every week of the year. Each one of these cases is a story: a crime, a family, a death sentence. This book tells thirteen of these stories.

The stories selected for inclusion in this book had to satisfy four basic criteria. First, they had to be interesting as human stories: the senile hit man, the teenager who killed, the poet, the Vietnam vet, the insane man whose crime became a landmark case in the U.S. Supreme Court, the hard-as-steel con's con, the innocent man, the Cuban refugee.

My second selection criterion was that the stories be interesting *legally*. Each case illustrates at least one important feature of capital punishment as a legal system. Three of the cases explored in this book

(Alvin Ford's, James Hitchcock's, and David Washington's) resulted in landmark constitutional rulings by the U.S. Supreme Court.

Third, the stories could not be high-profile cases. I have in my previous writings discussed the infamous cases of accused serial killer Ted Bundy and clearly innocent man "Crazy Joe" Spaziano. Bundy and Spaziano represent the polar extremes of my life as a lawyer, but those cases are not typical or representative of the vast majority of my cases in Florida. Few death row prisoners are like the image of Ted Bundy that occupies the American imagination, and few (although more than you might imagine) death row prisoners are innocent. (Several prisoners discussed in these pages might well have been innocent; no fair treatment of the real capital punishment can exclude such cases.) For this book, I was seeking the more obscure—but also more typical—capital cases. Most people on death row are run-of-the-mill killers, indistinguishable from the mass of killers who are not sentenced to death. But as the poet Sam Hazo has written, "Obscurity equally has its own story to tell."

My fourth criterion is highly personal: these are some of my old cases that got under my skin, often for reasons I can't really identify to this day. All I know is that I just can't leave them alone.

Together, the case studies presented here provide a fairly comprehensive treatment of the death penalty as it exists as an American phenomenon today. That comprehensiveness, however, is somewhat inadvertent. It was my intention that each story/chapter be able to stand on its own; I never planned to cover a full range of possible death penalty–related topics, but that is very nearly the outcome.

In one respect, these stories are not at all typical. Approximately half of the stories I tell here end in execution. However, the success rates of the public defender's offices in which I worked were far higher than 50 percent. Of all our clients who had death warrants signed against them, we won stays in 95 percent of the cases. Thus the percentage of cases we "lost" is far smaller than the stories I tell here might suggest. The reason is both simple and complex. Whereas many lawyers' memoirs chronicle their brilliant wins, I tend to write about my defeats and the clients I lost. I write about the stories that haunt me. The few people whose cases I lost visit my dreams. They are restless spirits to me. I couldn't save their bodies, but by telling their stories, I can to some degree save their lives.

All the death row prisoners whose stories I tell in this book are dead men. Many were executed. One died of "natural causes" while still in prison, after fourteen years on death row. One is free. The rest live in prison, some on death row, some not. But they are all—even the one who was freed—dead. That is what a death sentence does to you. The actual execution is almost redundant.

This book isn't really a memoir. Most of it isn't, anyway. A memoir would tell the story of *my* life and, to some extent, this book does that. But my life as a death row lawyer in Florida is inseparable from the lives of the people I was trying to keep away from the executioner. This book tells the stories of others (their lives and their deaths, by electrocution), of prisoners I have known and represented.

Several unifying narrative themes are woven throughout and across the individual cases I discuss in this book: "legal technicalities" operate to execute far more people than they free; the brutal reality is that the U.S. Supreme Court doesn't really care about capital cases; matters of race and class warp capital punishment as a legal system; people, even lawyers and judges, make mistakes, and those mistakes cause innocent people to be sentenced to death and executed; the reality is that many death row prisoners had incompetent lawyers at trial; the fact is that police and prosecutors hide exculpatory information from capital defendants; the truth is that issues of legal ethics, and inherent attorney/client power imbalances, are present in virtually every capital punishment case. And, of course, I am something of a narrative thread here, because at one time or another I worked on behalf of all of the condemned men whose stories I highlight. Because I was a Florida capital public defender, these are Florida stories.

Notwithstanding the recurrent themes that cut across most or all of the stories I tell here, my overarching theme is *randomness*. The legal system decides who dies based more on chance and luck than on anything rational. Nowhere is this randomness clearer than in the so-called *Hitchcock* issue, which is a part of virtually every story told in this book. In the *Hitchcock* case, a unanimous U.S. Supreme Court struck down a particular jury instruction that had been given routinely in Florida cases. That jury instruction was given in virtually all of the cases explored in this book. Most of those prisoners who were still alive when *Hitchcock* was decided in 1987 won new sentencing trials. Those who had already been executed did not, of course, even though their juries received the same jury instruction later invalidated in *Hitchcock*. That is what I mean by *randomness*.

In a larger sense, however, I'm not sure these stories have a point. Vietnam veteran Tim O'Brien, in an elegant essay titled "How to Tell a True War Story," writes that "often in a true war story there is not even a point, or else the point doesn't hit you until twenty years later, in your sleep, and you wake up and shake your wife and start telling the story to her, except when you get to the end, you've forgotten the point again. And then for a long time you lie there watching the story happen in your head. You listen to your wife's breathing. The war's over. You close your eyes. You smile and think, Christ, what's the *point?*"

For four years in the early and mid-1980s, I worked full-time as a capital public defender in Florida. After that, I represented death row prisoners and national organizations in the Florida Supreme Court, the federal courts of appeal, and the U.S. Supreme Court. I have represented condemned prisoners in Texas, Georgia, Illinois, and Florida. In all, I have been closely involved in approximately seventy capital cases, including some high-profile ones: Ted Bundy, the Unabomber, "Crazy Joe" Spaziano, Paul Hill. My experiences with capital punishment as a legal system form the basis of this book. I'm not writing about capital punishment as an abstract issue of ethics (ethics as a branch of moral philosophy), theoretical public policy, or constitutional law. (As to the last of these, capital punishment is constitutional because the U.S. Supreme Court has said it is. Justice Jackson once said that the Court isn't final because it's infallible; rather the Court is infallible because it is final.) What I'm writing about is capital punishment *as a legal system*. That's how I've experienced it: up close and personal. I ended up doing deathwork by accident, if you believe in accidents. Deathwork surely wasn't the destiny I had in mind when I graduated law school in 1982. But it is my experience with capital punishment, on the ground, that qualifies me to write this book.

I oppose capital punishment as a system, and my opposition is based on experience, not politics, ideology, morality, ethics, or philosophy. I am not a pacifist, for instance. I do not believe that the state *never* has the moral right to take human life. I believe that the state *does* have the legitimate moral right to kill in some circumstances. One such circumstance is a just war, in which the state must kill in order to defend itself against its enemies. Examples of just wars include World

War II, the present U.S. war against al-Qaeda and militant Islam (not Islam in general, but *militant* Islam), and Israel's endless war against Arab terrorism. (I see the current U.S. war and Israel's war as the same war. I would expand the U.S. war to include Hamas, Hezbollah, Islamic Jihad, Fatah, and Arafat's Palestinian Authority.) From this it seems to follow logically that capital punishment cannot be immoral simply because it involves state-sanctioned homicide. In fact, I know of no persuasive argument based in theoretical morality or philosophy that capital punishment is wrong (I also know of no such argument against torture as an instrument of social policy). Of course, my practical arguments against capital punishment are, on some level, moral arguments as well: if the practical reality is that capital punishment is, as I believe it is, racist, class based, and guaranteed to result in execution of the innocent, then these are, in a way, moral claims as well. Lloyd Steffen is right in his assertion that the structural flaws in America's system of legal homicide constitute a moral as well as a practical indictment of the system. Still, I have heard no definitive *theoretical* moral argument against capital punishment. My concern in this book is with practical realities, not abstract moral or ethical claims.

To borrow some nomenclature from the antebellum debates over slavery: capital punishment may be justified if it is either a positive good or a necessary evil. I have never heard an argument that government-imposed executions are a positive good. With the exception of those sad souls who have tailgate parties outside the walls of prisons when executions are carried out, I think it is safe to presume that the death penalty is not a happy business or a positive good. Rather, capital punishment is, at best, a necessary evil. And that raises the twin questions: Is it necessary, and which side bears the burden of persuasion that it is or is not necessary?

It seems to me that the burden of persuasion rests with those who believe the government should be in the business of deciding that some of its people deserve to die. Capital punishment supporters should have the burden of proving that some important state interest is furthered by—and only by—giving the government the power of capital punishment. Opponents ought not need to prove why capital punishment is unnecessary. Supporters ought to be required to show why capital punishment is necessary.

Anthony Amsterdam makes this point well in his essay "Selling a Quick Fix for Boot Hill":

> I would like to set forth certain basic factual realities about capital punishment, like the fact that capital punishment is a fancy phrase for legally killing people. Please forgive me for beginning with such obvious and ugly facts. Much of our political and philosophical debate about the death penalty is carried on in language calculated to conceal these realities and their implications. The implications, I will suggest, are that capital punishment is a great evil—surely the greatest evil except for war that our society can intentionally choose to commit. This does not mean that we should do away with capital punishment. Some evils, like war, are occasionally necessary, and perhaps capital punishment is one of them. But the fact that it is a great evil means that we should not choose to do it without some very good and solid reason of which we are satisfactorily convinced upon sufficient evidence. The conclusion of my first point simply is that the burden of proof upon the question of capital punishment rightly rests on those who are asking us to use our laws to kill people with, and that this is a very heavy burden. . . .
>
> I submit that the deliberate judicial extinction of human life is intrinsically so final and so terrible an act as to cast the burden of proof for its justification upon those who want us to do it. But certainly when the act is executed through a fallible system which assures that we kill some people wrongly, others because they are black or poor or personally unattractive or socially unacceptable, and all of them quite freakishly in the sense that whether a man lives or dies for any particular crime is a matter of luck and happenstance, then, at the least, the burden of justifying capital punishment lies fully and heavily on its proponents.

I don't think capital punishment supporters can meet their burden of proof. One asserted justification for capital punishment is general deterrence: we punish (or execute) A to keep B, C, D, and so on from committing crime. Capital punishment does indeed deter crime, but so does life imprisonment. The issue is not whether capital punishment deters crime—it does—but rather whether it deters crime *any more significantly than does life imprisonment*. Fifty years of social science research have shown that capital punishment has no more deterrent value than does life imprisonment. General deterrence cannot carry the burden of proof that supporters of death as a punishment must shoulder.

In fact, I think that capital punishment can have and has had an *anti*-deterrent effect. Far from decreasing the incentives to commit capital murder, and far from sending a message that murder is wrong because, if you commit it, the government will kill you back, the death penalty actually can encourage and enable murder. This can happen in two ways. First, for some criminals, the possibility of execution is a reason *to* commit murder. Ted Bundy was one of these. After escaping from jail in Colorado in 1978, Bundy drove to Denver and then flew to Detroit, Michigan. But he didn't kill anyone in Michigan, a state with no death penalty. Rather, he headed for Florida—the state most in the news in the late 1970s as the capital of capital punishment. It was in Florida where Bundy next was found guilty of committing murder—the murder of a young woman in Lake City and a bloody rampage through the Chi Omega sorority house in Tallahassee that left two young women dead and several others badly beaten. Perhaps it was coincidence that Bundy—with literally the whole country to choose from—chose Florida. I think he went there because he had a death wish: if caught, he wanted the celebrity of a high-profile trial and execution. Florida gave Bundy his wish.

The second way in which capital punishment might encourage murders is through what Boston criminologist William Bowers calls the "brutalization effect." Simply put, Bowers found that, for some prospective criminals, the government's willingness to kill for its own ends is persuasive that killing is a legitimate way to solve problems. Some criminals follow the government's example. For some would-be killers, the government cannot itself kill while at the same time claiming credibly that killing is wrong.

Then there is specific deterrence or incapacitation: the idea that we execute A to ensure that A does not commit further crimes. Capital punishment certainly has an incapacitation effect of 100 percent: dead men don't commit crimes. However, life imprisonment without the possibility of parole achieves the same goal—separating the criminal from the rest of us, incapacitating him from criminality—without putting the state in the expensive and metaphysical business of deciding who deserves to die. Maximum-security prisons are as incapacitating as executions, even though there is a small risk of escape or murder in prisons. (Few people who commit murder in prison are in prison *for* murder; murderers are, as a group, the least likely group of prisoners to be recidivist murderers.)

Finally, there is retribution: the expression of society's (and the victim's) outrage and anger at heinous misconduct, and the related idea that some people simply deserve to die. As I've said, some crimes and some criminals simply cry out for capital punishment; that's what they *deserve*. The mass murderers of September 11, 2001, Timothy McVeigh, Charles Manson, Theodore Kaczynski, Adolf Eichmann, and Adolf Hitler leap to mind. If America's death rows were inhabited by thousands of Timothy McVeighs, I probably would not have devoted my professional life to fighting capital punishment. But McVeigh is the death row exception, not the norm. The stories told in this book are the norm. For every McVeigh on America's death rows, there are many more prisoners who are mentally ill or retarded, who were children when they committed their crimes, who never intended to kill anyone, or who are in fact totally innocent of the crimes for which they are scheduled to die.

So, if the supporters of capital punishment are to carry their burden of proof, they must do so on the basis of retribution. However, life imprisonment in a maximum-security prison is also strongly retributive. Some would argue, of course, that life imprisonment is not retributive enough; only execution is enough. Retribution is a credible argument—and, I believe, the only credible argument—in favor of capital punishment. I understand the urge for retribution better than you may think I do. A few days before Christmas in 1989, a racist coward with a grudge against the federal judiciary mailed a shoe-box-size bomb to Robert S. Vance, a federal appellate court judge. The bomb detonated in the kitchen of Judge Vance's home on the outskirts of Birmingham, Alabama. Judge Vance is the only person I have loved who was murdered. I served as his law clerk during the year following my graduation from law school in 1982. He was far more than a boss to me; in the years following my clerkship I came to rely on his wisdom and guidance and experience. By the time of his death he had become my friend and my father in the law. I was too distraught by his killing to attend the funeral; I bought the plane tickets, but I couldn't force myself to use them. I miss him and mourn him every day. I pray for him every night.

Before Judge Vance's murder, I thought I had an understanding of why people might support capital punishment. I was wrong. My intellectual understanding wasn't nearly enough. Since Judge Vance's murder, I have come to believe that there are only two kinds of people in the capital punishment debate: those who have lost loved ones to murder and those who have not. It took Judge Vance's murder for me to appreciate—on the most visceral of levels—why people might well demand death as a punishment.

I now date the events of my life as a death row lawyer based on before and after—before and after the day Judge Vance was assassinated. His killer, Walter Leroy Moody, now lives on Alabama's death row. Although I have spent a large portion of my life as a lawyer defending death row prisoners, when Moody is executed part of me will cheer.

Politicians often talk about capital punishment as a means of bringing "closure" to the families of crime victims. I've never understood what "closure" means; I think it's a psychobabble word that has gained currency through its repetition in the media. I've also never understood how the lack of finality of the capital appeals process can offer any sense of "closure" to the families of murder victims; whenever there is another appeal filed or court decision rendered or execution date set, the news media dredge up the case—and the victims feel the pain—again.

The families of murder victims are not monolithic. Some support the execution of the killers of their loved ones, and some do not. The survivors and the family members of the victims of the bombing of the Alfred P. Murrah Federal Building in Oklahoma City were evenly divided concerning the death penalty for Timothy McVeigh. The diversity of opinion among these victims reflects the feelings of the American public in general on capital punishment.

The murder of Judge Vance precipitated for me a crisis of conscience. The murder of a man I loved—and my human response to the crime and the criminal—forced me to reevaluate my long-standing opposition to capital punishment. So I honestly do believe that reasonable people can conclude that that extra measure of retribution, that amount beyond the punishment of life imprisonment, justifies capital punishment. However, before so concluding, supporters of capital punishment would be prudent to consider the costs of that extra measure of retribution. Before one decides that the extra retribution is worth the costs, one ought to know exactly what those costs are. This book is about some of those costs.

Two of the costs of capital punishment are intimately related: the financial burden and the omnipresent possibility that innocent persons will be executed. When a state tries to do capital punishment on the cheap, the risks that the innocent will be executed increase. That risk always remains—no matter how careful we are, no matter how much money we spend to try to ensure that innocent people are not sentenced to death and executed—but when corners are cut, that risk increases geometrically.

Innocent people are sentenced to death and executed in the United States. It is as inevitable as the law of averages and the fallibility of human institutions. Capital punishment is a government operation, and governments make mistakes because people make mistakes.

The various U.S. state governments make mistakes fairly frequently. As of June 1, 2002, one hundred people have been freed from death rows in the United States after having proved their absolute factual innocence. Under the same modern statutes, 777 men and women have been executed. Thus for every eight who have been executed, one who was innocent has been freed. Think about that ratio for a moment: *one in eight.*

It is very expensive to run a system of capital punishment that can decide, with reasonable accuracy, who deserves to die. At every stage—from pretrial investigation and motions practice to the bifurcated trial to the first appeal to the state postconviction litigation to the federal habeas corpus phases—capital cases are infinitely more complex than noncapital cases. Capital cases require more thorough fact investigation pretrial, and that is expensive; it requires the hiring of investigators specially trained to prepare for the sentencing stage, DNA and other forensic experts, and so on. The pretrial motions practice in a capital case is also far more complex and time-consuming and therefore more expensive than in a noncapital case: Defense lawyers are required—ethically required—to research and raise every possible constitutional issue, because if they don't, that issue is waived forever, and no defense lawyer wants a capital client to be executed on a technicality or because the lawyer neglected to raise an issue. Capital trials are longer and more complex than noncapital trials, in part because they often are really two trials: a traditional trial on guilt/innocence, and then, if the defendant is found guilty, a separate full trial on penalty. At the penalty phase of a capital case, the issue on the table is whether this particular person has forfeited his or her moral entitlement to live. The person's entire life is on trial, and thus the penalty phase often lasts longer than the trial on guilt/innocence.

The recent New Hampshire case of Gordon Perry illustrates what I mean. New Hampshire has not executed anyone since 1939; the state has not sentenced anyone to die since 1959. New Hampshire's capital punishment statute reserves the death penalty for certain narrow categories of especially heinous murder, including knowingly killing a police officer who is performing his or her duties as a law enforcement official. Perry's murder of Epsom, New Hampshire, Trooper Jeremy Charron seems to fit squarely within New Hampshire's existing capital statute. At the time of his death, Trooper Charron was only twenty-four years old. His apparently unprovoked murder justified a capital prosecution. If a state is to have capital punishment at all, it ought to have it for killings like this one.

Even though the Perry case seemed straightforward, it was enormously expensive for both the defense and the prosecution—and it didn't even go to trial. If it had gone to trial and resulted in a death sentence, the costs would have skyrocketed. New Hampshire has an excellent public defender system, and a significant portion of that system was diverted from its normal duties and into the Perry defense. A first-rate defense team was assembled, including an outside expert on litigating capital cases. The typical time spent investigating and preparing for a noncapital murder trial in New Hampshire is two hundred to three hundred hours. The Perry case consumed between three and four thousand hours over a period of fourteen months. One attorney spent more than half of his time, for a year, on the case. In all, the Perry case cost New Hampshire between seven hundred thousand and a million dollars in time and expenses. By contrast, it will cost the state approximately a million dollars to incarcerate Perry (who was only twenty-two years old at the time he pled guilty) for the rest of his life.

Capital cases also cost more than noncapital cases because everything about them is bigger, more complicated, and more bitterly contested. The pretrial factual investigation in the Perry case was exhaustive, as it needed to be, given the life-and-death stakes. Perry's lawyers researched and filed dozens of motions, and the prosecutors filed responses. In the end, Perry pled guilty and was sentenced to life imprisonment.

Had the Perry case gone to trial and then on to the penalty phase, the costs would have been tremendous. And that would have been only the beginning of the capital punishment assembly line for Gordon Perry and for the taxpayers of New Hampshire. After the trial and death sentence, there would have followed years of painstaking appellate and post-conviction judicial review, by the state courts and then by the federal courts. During all that time, the meter would never stop running: on defense lawyers' time, investigators' time, prosecutors' time, judges' time.

Consider, once again, the case of the infamous serial killer Ted Bundy. Even today, more than a decade after his execution, Bundy is still cited as the ultimate example of the need for capital punishment. We have to be able, the argument goes, to execute the Ted Bundys of the world. Execute him Florida did, and in a relatively short period of time (ten years from imposition to execution of the death sentence). Still, it cost the state of Florida approximately $6 million to get Bundy into the electric chair, millions more than it would have cost to incarcerate him for the remainder of his life. And that was cheap: Bundy was represented on his appeals pro bono by a powerhouse Washington, D.C., law firm, Wilmer, Cutler & Pickering. A partner in that firm once told me that he estimated the firm spent more than $1.5 million on the Bundy case in out-of-pocket expenses and lost opportunity costs. Thus the Bundy case cost around $7.5 million from the time the death sentence was imposed until Bundy's execution. And that was for a relatively easy case (the defendant was the notorious Ted Bundy, after all) in a state that had extensive experience with capital punishment as a legal system.

Add to all the costs mentioned above the high costs of housing and securing death row prisoners and of actually carrying out executions. Prisoners on death row are kept physically separate from the general prison population, and death row security needs are greater and more specialized. In addition, those who carry out the executions must be specially trained to handle all the tasks involved. All of these things cost money.

Of course, states can cut costs by, for example, underfunding capital case defense teams or being stingy in funding factual investigations.

But there is an inverse relationship between the resources devoted to defense teams and the risk of sentencing the innocent to death row and executing them.

Even when no one cuts corners on costs, the risk that an innocent person will be executed is always present. Again, the case of the murder of Trooper Jeremy Charron is illustrative. According to Kevin Paul, Gordon Perry's partner, Perry and Paul were sitting in a car parked near an Epsom, New Hampshire, swimming hole when Trooper Charron tapped on the car's window and asked to see the men's identification. Perry handed over his driver's license and vehicle registration, and then he shot Charron several times. Most of the shots were absorbed by Charron's bullet-proof vest, but one entered his side and ended in his chest. While Charron bled to death, Perry and Paul sped away. They were later apprehended by police.

This is the account that Paul gave to a jailhouse informant. Because, according to Paul's account, Perry was the actual shooter, Perry was arrested for capital murder. Paul was charged with second-degree murder, and, had Perry gone to trial, Paul would have testified against Perry in exchange for favorable treatment.

Here's the problem. Paul said Perry was the shooter, and Perry said Paul was the shooter. The physical evidence was at best inconclusive. The prosecutors had to decide which of the two occupants of that car they believed, because without turning one suspect against the other, they had no case for capital murder against either man. Paul was willing to turn state's evidence and testify against Perry in exchange for favorable treatment, so he got the deal.

Perry and Paul were the only living witnesses to what happened that night. Only they knew who really shot Trooper Charron. Circumstantial evidence suggested that Paul, not Perry, was the shooter. What if the prosecutors chose the wrong man? If Paul, not Perry, was really the shooter, then didn't he have the strongest incentive to turn state's evidence and testify against Perry? Thus it is possible that, in New Hampshire's first capital case in six decades, the man who actually shot the state trooper would have gotten off with a relatively light sentence, while his partner—who was technically guilty of felony murder but who didn't kill anyone—would have been put to death by the state of New Hampshire.

If this scenario sounds far-fetched, consider the case of Jesse Tafero.

When I was living in Florida and working as a capital public defender, this hauntingly similar case was playing itself out. Like the Perry case, the Tafero case involved the pointless murder of a police officer who had approached a car at a highway rest stop. As in the Perry case, the Florida car contained more than one adult occupant—in fact, there were three: Walter Rhodes, Jesse Tafero, and Sonia (Sonny) Jacobs (plus Jacobs's young child). As in the Perry case, in the Florida case one of the car's occupants (Rhodes) turned state's evidence in exchange for favorable treatment, and his testimony sent Tafero and Jacobs to death row. Hugo Bedau and Michael Radelet, the two leading scholars on innocence and the death penalty, have both concluded that Rhodes was the real killer.

One way out of the Perry/Paul paradox—in which each of the only two living witnesses blames the other for the killing—might be to adopt the Louisiana solution. Two Louisiana men, named Glass and Wingo, committed a felony that ended in murder. Both Glass and Wingo were charged with capital murder, even though only one of them could have done the actual killings. At their separate trials, Glass blamed Wingo, and Wingo blamed Glass. Both men were sentenced to death, and their executions took place two weeks apart.

States that only recently have instated or reinstated capital punishment, such as New York, like to think they will be different from Florida, California, Texas, and the other states that have tried to craft capital punishment systems that are fair and swift; only the guilty will be sentenced to die. But Illinois, Florida, Texas, Pennsylvania, and the others all thought they would be different; at least that's what they thought in the beginning of their experiments with legal homicide.

Like New Hampshire, New York has a relatively narrow death penalty statute. In four years, the much larger and more populous state of New York has sent only four people to death row. Like New Hampshire, New York has a very good public defender system. Like New Hampshire's capital statute, New York's is fairly recent (1995). The cost of New York's capital punishment system has been staggering. According to a 1999 article in the *New York Daily News,* in its first four years, "the total cost to taxpayers for prosecution and defense in death penalty cases has been estimated at $68 million. And by the time the first lethal injection is administered—which could be more than ten years from now—those costs could soar to more than $238 million."

Once the legal machinery of death is fired up, it takes on an inertia and a momentum all its own. It is all but impossible for a state to extricate itself from the politics of death once it has become involved. Narrow death penalty statutes tend to be broadened over time, as more and more categories and classes of criminals become death eligible; careful (and costly and cumbersome) procedures give way to calls for speedier and speedier executions.

As I have noted, some of the costs of capital punishment are quantifiable; capital punishment is enormously expensive, far more expensive than a justice system without the ultimate penalty permissible under the U.S. Constitution. But that is only the beginning. The inevitability that some innocent people have been and always will be sentenced to death and executed is a necessary cost of doing the business of government-sponsored executions. Capital punishment undermines and degrades the ethics and humanity of lawyers, the legal profession, and the law itself; the death penalty turns good people—judges, jurors, prosecutors—into killers. I hope to convey in this book some of this cost, in the hope that readers might better understand what the death penalty does to the people it touches. That has always been at the core of my opposition to state killing: what it does to people, and not just to the person who is killed. We are all part of the collateral damage of capital punishment.

Scholars and academics have identified and analyzed capital punishment's costs. Philosophers and theologians have debated the morality of death as a penalty. Criminologists have studied every aspect of the matter amenable to empirical research. Legal scholars have placed capital punishment jurisprudence under an exacting microscope. Wardens and prisoners have written memoirs. There have, however, been few views from the inside. I was on the inside, and I was there during the formative years of capital punishment as it currently exists in the United States.

In her classic diary of the Civil War, the incomparable Mary Chestnut wrote that she had, by chance or design, been present during what she called the "real show." By that she meant the events that, in historical hindsight, were crucial to meaningful understanding and appreciation of the historical moment covered by her diary. By similar fortuities, I happened to be present during what, looking back on it now, with more than a decade of hindsight, was a critical—I would argue the most pivotal—period of America's modern experience with capital punishment as a legal system. I was there for capital punishment's "real show." When I was, from summer 1982 to summer 1983, "death clerk" to Eleventh Circuit Judge Robert Vance, that appellate court (whose jurisdiction was composed of three active capital punishment states: Florida, Alabama, and Georgia) was receiving its first wave of federal habeas appeals from prisoners condemned in state court. Because the cases, and the constitutional issues they raised, were matters of first impression (that is, issues never decided before) for the Eleventh Circuit judges (for all federal judges, in fact), those judges took death cases deadly seriously.

Similarly, when I was a Florida capital appellate public defender (from summer 1983 to early January 1987), the Sunshine State and the nation as a whole were, for the first time in my lifetime, being forced to come to terms with the reality of capital punishment as a legal system—and with the realities of executions actually being carried out. During that time, executions went from being major media events to non-events. Florida led the nation in numbers of people on death row and numbers of executions; Florida also became the first serious capital punishment state to create a statewide public defender office to represent death row prisoners in state postconviction and federal habeas corpus proceedings. That new office, called the Office of Capital Collateral Representative (CCR), was created in 1985.

When it comes to capital punishment, Florida is a bellwether state. Wherever the rest of the nation is headed on capital punishment, Florida seems to get there first. Florida was the first state to enact a "modern" capital punishment statute in the wake of the U.S. Supreme Court's invalidation of all extant capital statutes in 1972. Florida has led the nation in the implementation of the death penalty since then. Florida was the first state to commit a nonconsensual execution (i.e., an execution for which the condemned prisoner did not volunteer) in a decade. Until 1986 Florida led in the number of executions since the modern resumption of capital punishment.

Equally important, the demographics of Florida's condemned population in the mid-1980s made it one of the first states where the lack of postconviction counsel for the condemned became a recognizable crisis of epidemic proportions. Moreover, Florida became a pioneer of sorts by crafting a legislative solution to its counsel crisis, setting up a publicly funded state agency to provide direct representation for the state's condemned. Before that, Florida experimented with the creation of a resource center to provide litigation support for members of the private bar who represented death row inmates pro bono; in August 1995, twenty states had created such resource centers, although the U.S. Congress withdrew all funding for the centers as of October 1, 1995. In addition, Florida's jury override system invites unique comparison between how judges and juries understand the same evidence and apply the same sentencing criteria.

In part because the state courts treat death cases so seriously, Florida has one of the most fully developed bodies of capital punishment jurisprudence in the nation. By March 2002, the Florida Supreme Court had rendered more than two thousand capital decisions, usually issuing one or more each week. The U.S. Supreme Court regularly uses Florida cases as vehicles for its fine-tuning of the constitutional jurisprudence of death.

Other states look to Florida's capital sentencing system as a model. Three other states, two with large death row populations (Alabama and Indiana), also permit judges to impose the death sentence notwithstanding a jury's recommendation of life imprisonment. Florida has also been a leader of sorts on the politics of death. In the period covered by these stories (1983–86), then Florida Governor Bob Graham showed his Democratic colleagues nationwide how politicians can use supporting executions to defuse arguments that they are soft on crime. When Graham was first elected governor, he was viewed as a liberal and a political wimp ("Governor Jello" was his moniker). But by signing death warrant after death warrant, Graham became a political powerhouse who readily won reelection and then parlayed his position into a successful run for the U.S. Senate. In 1992, Graham was on Bill Clinton's short list for a vice presidential running mate, according to *Newsweek*. Graham has played the politics of death with perfect pitch, and others have followed his lead—Bill Clinton and George W. Bush, to name two examples.

And Florida is, well, *Florida*. For reasons not really clear to me, the Sunshine State generates compelling death row characters who have fascinating stories. Perhaps more telling than the numbers I have cited is the raw, visceral enthusiasm with which many Floridians, at least many Florida politicians, embrace capital punishment. When Atlanta capital defense attorney Millard Farmer referred to Florida as the "buckle of the death belt," he was not talking about statistics. The Bundy execution in January 1989 resembled a tailgate party in its revelry, and the festivities did not begin in the 1980s. Historian Richard Kluger describes the scene at a 1952 Florida capital trial in his book *Simple Justice*:

> [Thurgood] Marshall and Jack Greenberg were greeted by a Saturday night torchlight parade of the KKK upon their arrival in Orlando, to defend a young black originally charged with beating up a white man and raping his wife near the town of Groveland. Marshall stayed at the home of a black resident and Greenberg at a white hotel, out of deference to local custom. Klan members circled Greenberg's hotel with trucks and torches throughout the night. . . . Though Marshall gave one of his finest courtroom performances, the all-white, all-male jury found the defendant guilty and doomed him to the electric chair. Marshall, stunned, came out of the courtroom fighting back tears, and promised the convicted man's mother, "Don't worry, darling, we're going to stick by you. We're going to keep on fighting for you." And he did. Twice he appealed the Groveland case to the Supreme Court.

Taxpaying Floridians appear willing to foot the bill for their death penalty despite economic recession. In a 1988 study conducted for the *Miami Herald*, David Von Drehle calculated, using the most conservative estimates available, that Florida had spent at least $57 million on a capital punishment system that had executed eighteen people—an average cost of $3.2 million per execution (this did not include the millions spent by volunteer defense lawyers); that is six times the average cost of keeping a person in prison until his or her natural death. Special cases can cost extra. A Florida prosecutor estimated that it cost the state $6 million to execute Ted Bundy; Bundy's law firm estimated that it spent $1.4 million in the first two years the firm handled Bundy's postconviction case.

Then there is the matter of Florida's malfunctioning electric chair. Several spectacularly botched electrocutions kept Florida's experience with capital punishment in the news as the millennium turned.

Florida's contribution to the 2000 presidential election kept the state in the headlines, of course. What didn't register on the media's radar screen was the similarity of *Bush v. Gore* to capital appellate litigation: litigating in multiple courts, state and federal, at the same time; expedited briefing and oral argument schedules; cliff-hanger court proceedings; sharp exchanges between the U.S. Supreme Court and the Florida Supreme Court.

This book had its genesis in a project undertaken by Michael Radelet in the summer of 1986. Mike had been asked to edit a collection of essays about capital punishment's impacts on the people whose professional and personal lives were touched by the death penalty as a legal system. It was not really a scholarly or academic project, and the contributors included several condemned prisoners, their counselors, and their advocates. At the time, I was working full time as a capital public defender in Tallahassee, Florida. During a six-week period in spring 1986, three of my office's clients had been executed: David Funchess, Dan Thomas, and Ronald Straight. Mike Radelet suggested I write about Ronnie Straight—not the case, but the man, and what the execution of the man had meant to me, not as Straight's attorney, but as a person.

When Mike invited me to write a personal essay for his collection, I thought I could knock it out in an afternoon at Juno Beach. After all, I had been writing about capital punishment—in court papers and articles published in scholarly law journals—for three years. But this turned out to be the hardest writing project I had undertaken up to that time, and I said so in the essay. I hated writing it, I hated editing it, and, when the collection, titled *Facing the Death Penalty,* was published in 1989, I hated reading it. It was too close to the bone, too personal.

In that essay, I made an assertion the truth of which I only dimly recognized at that time. I argued that death row defense lawyers do not litigate solely for the courts. They litigate to make a record of who our government executes and under what circumstances; they also litigate for historians, sociologists, and anthropologists.

I read somewhere that the two principal qualities of a public citizen are experience and reflection. Oddly, for me, my prereflective experience was far easier than reflection. I had the good luck to practice as a capital public defender in Florida during the crucial moment in that state's (and the nation's) modern experience with capital punishment: 1983–87. When I left Florida deathwork in 1987, and again when I left full-time law practice for full-time law teaching and writing in 1988, I thought my prereflective time was over, and, in a superficial sense, it was. When I became a full-time teacher, I certainly had the opportunity to reflect on the time I had spent in the Florida death wars.

When I was in the thick of the fight in Florida, I always thought that the first thing I would do when I finally had time to think and write would be to go back through the journals, correspondence, and other primary materials I had been keeping like a pack rat since I began deathwork in 1983. However, I devoted the early years of my teaching career to learning to teach and writing fairly traditional law review articles. When I get tenure, I thought, then I'll begin to draw upon my old journals and letters. I was granted tenure in 1990. My "tenure piece" was a traditional piece of legal scholarship exploring the historical and jurisprudential dimensions of the relentless dissents of U.S. Supreme Court Justices Brennan and Marshall in capital cases. It was a safe and essentially trivial project.

From 1988 to 1994, I managed (with three minor exceptions) to avoid writing any sort of interior memoir about my earlier time in Florida. Of course, my Florida experience influenced and drove my decisions about the subjects I did choose to write about. I wrote about capital punishment, exploring legal doctrine, theory, and history—everything except the source of why I cared about capital punishment in the first place: my time in Florida. By the mid-1990s, I decided it was time for me to undertake an appraisal of the ways I had chosen to live my life, which, for me, meant my work. Deathwork had been the emotional center of my life for so long that any examination of my life had to include an exploration of my relationship with capital punishment as a legal system. That in turn meant a return to my old corpus of primary source materials: the journals and correspondence from my time in Florida in the 1980s. Now, finally, I was forcing myself to reflect on capital punishment as the system I had lived with. Also, in a fortuity of timing, in the early 1990s the Thurgood Marshall papers became available to the public. Many of Marshall's papers concerned death cases, including my own cases.

I once heard about a comment attributed to a mountain climber who had reached the summit of Mount Everest. The effort had nearly killed the climber; his oxygen had run out, the weather was awful, and he barely managed to survive. An observer who was amazed that he kept going asked the climber, "Why did you climb Everest when you knew that you might die?" The climber replied, "I didn't climb Everest to die. I climbed Everest to live."

In doing deathwork in Florida, I lived. Except when I'm at the controls of an airplane, I've never felt more alive than I did in Florida. In writing about that work and the people who do it, I've lived. With my few real friends—all deathworkers in one way or another, whether they know it or not—I've lived; with some of these friends I've shared holy moments, and the bonds created in those moments are love and friendship, which I now believe are the same thing. These people offer me true company, because they hold dear the things I hold dear, and because they fight for those things by any means necessary, and because they understand that some things are worth dying for, and that death isn't the worst thing that can happen to a person.

For me, deathwork had about it an alluring magic as well as darkness and mystery. This, I think, is why I call what I did *deathwork* rather than *lifework,* although the latter term might be more precisely accurate, and it certainly sounds more upbeat. *Deathwork* captures the immersion I experienced in that moment of mystery that straddles existence and oblivion.

So, in the end, perhaps this book is a memoir after all. Here I tell the stories of death row. These stories—and many more like them—were my life when I was a capital public defender. These stories are my story.

This book is also a love letter to those deathworkers with whom I have been privileged to work, sometimes in close quarters: Mark Olive, Scharlette Holdman, Craig Barnard, Anthony Amsterdam, Henry Schwartzschild, Millard Farmer, Susan Cary, Clive Stafford-Smith, Tim Ford, David Kendall, David Reiser, Karen Gottlieb, Elliot Scherker, Jonathan Gaddess, Bryan Stevenson, Jim Liebman, Jack Boger, Steve Winter, Jerry Justine, Leon Wright, Steve "Bubba" Walter, Eloise Williams, Lee Curry, Richard Greene, Michael Radelet, Margaret Vandiver, Richard Jorandby, Marie Deans, and others. This book tries to describe their world—our world.

The Law's Machinery of Death

But the war in Vietnam drifted in and out of human lives, taking them or sparing them like a headless, berserk taxi hack, without evident cause, a war fought for uncertain reasons. . . . Certain blood for uncertain reasons. No lagoon monster ever terrorized like this.

—Tim O'Brien, *If I Die in a Combat Zone,* 1973

In this chapter I want to situate my capital punishment stories within a historical narrative context. I trace three intertwined historical strands: the campaign to use the courts to challenge the legality of capital punishment, the right to counsel, and habeas corpus. My focus is the state of Florida, where the history of capital punishment is as old—and as weird—as the Sunshine State itself.

1769–1922: The Bad Old Days of the Hangman's Noose and the Firing Squad

The framers of the U.S. Constitution clearly contemplated the validity of capital punishment. The Fifth Amendment speaks of deprivations of "life or limb" by the federal courts without "due process of law," a requirement extended to the state courts when the Fourteenth Amendment was enacted during Reconstruction.

Although the history of capital punishment in Florida prior to the twentieth century is incomplete, the available statutes, records (in particular the extensive archives compiled in Headland, Alabama, by Watt Espy), and commentaries make it possible to sketch the early historical development of Florida's use of the death penalty. The first recorded execution in Florida occurred in January 1769, when a convicted murderer was hanged in St. Augustine. From that time until 1924, there were 191 recorded executions in the state. Of these, 173 were hangings carried out under local authority, because executions in Florida during this period were controlled at the local level, by cities or counties. Over the same period, 18 other executions were carried out in Florida by military authority; 13 of them were by firing squad.

In 1822, Florida became a U.S. territory, and it became necessary for the territorial government to enact a criminal code. The First Legislative Council of Florida, meeting in Pensacola, passed "An Act for the Apprehension of Criminals, and the Punishment of Crimes and Misdemeanors." This act, which provided for the first sanctioned death penalty under Florida's territorial authority, designated three offenses as capital: murder, rape, and arson. The act used mandatory language, providing that any person committing the specified offenses "*shall* suffer death." Six years later, the legislature added twelve crimes to the list of capital offenses and, apparently for the first time, distinguished between crimes committed by white citizens and crimes committed by black slaves or freed people. Death was mandatory upon conviction of any one of five of these twelve offenses; the other seven were punishable, at the court's discretion, by death or a "lesser" penalty involving torture—whipping, branding, or nailing of ears.

Review of the statutory law extant in 1845 suggests that a jury decision for death was in effect a necessary condition for the imposition of the death penalty. Capital punishment was for the most part mandatory upon conviction of specified offenses. Capital sentencing was the jury's exclusive domain, in the sense that jury consent was a condition precedent to death sentences. The court in no instance possessed the discretion to increase a jury's "recommended" lesser conviction/sentence to death.

In 1845, there were ten crimes for which Florida imposed a mandatory death penalty on any person regardless of race:

Insurrection

Attempting to excite an insurrection or revolt of slaves

Murder

Rape

Arson

Slave stealing

Willful perjury which causes the life of another to be taken away

Sodomy

Willfully burning or making a hole in any ship valued above $200

Assisting in making a hole in any ship valued above $200

There were also twelve crimes for which Florida imposed a mandatory death penalty on any slave, free black, or mulatto:

Conspiring to insurrection

Conspiring to murder

Assault and battery of a white person with intent to kill

Poisoning with intent to kill

Manslaughter of a white person

Burning any dwelling-house, store, cotton-house, gin, mill, outhouse, barn, or stable

Accessory to burning any dwelling-house, store, cotton-house, gin, mill, outhouse, barn, or stable

Assault of white woman or child with intent to rape

Accessory to assault of white woman or child with intent to rape

Shooting at a white person with intent to kill

Willful or malicious wounding of a white person while attempting to kill another person

Aiding and abetting the willful or malicious wounding of a white person while attempting to kill another person

Additionally, there were five crimes for which Florida allowed for the death penalty upon any slave, free black, or mulatto, but also allowed the court discretion to impose alternate penalties if death was deemed inappropriate:

Robbery of the person	The alternate penalty was having one's ears nailed to posts and standing for one hour while receiving thirty-nine lashes on the bare back.
Burglary	The alternate penalty was having one's ears nailed to posts and standing for one hour while receiving thirty-nine lashes on the bare back.
Maiming of a white person	The alternate penalties available were (a) being whipped thirty-nine stripes and standing for one hour with one's ears nailed to posts, or (b) having one's hand burned with a heated iron in open court.
Attempt to commit any capital offense	The alternate penalties available were (a) being whipped thirty-nine stripes and standing for one hour with one's ears nailed to posts, or (b) having one's hand burned with a heated iron in open court.
Accessory to attempt to commit any capital offense	The alternate penalties available were (a) being whipped thirty-nine stripes and standing for one hour with one's ears nailed to posts, or (b) having one's hand burned with a heated iron in open court.

Thus, at the time that Florida's first state constitution was ratified, a jury's verdict of guilt of a capital crime meant that a death sentence was mandatory, except in limited circumstances. A jury's verdict of death was a necessary, and usually sufficient, condition of imposition of capital punishment. This was the functional equivalent of jury sentencing for capital offenses, at least for purposes of state constitutional doctrine.

The nexus between the jury's verdict of guilt and the jury's determination of sentence was recognized by the Florida State Legislature in 1868, when it enacted a statute providing that "no person whose opinions are such as to preclude him from finding the defendant guilty of an offense punishable by death shall be compelled *or allowed* to serve as a juror on a trial of such an offense." The Florida Supreme Court applied this statute in *Metzgar v. State,* holding that it was "proper to exclude from the jury in capital cases any person who, from scruples of conscience or some reason other than the want of sufficient proof, would refuse to find a verdict of guilty."

Indeed, the fact that mandatory capital punishment was a jury matter led to the demise of mandatory capital punishment systems in the United States. Mandatory sentencing obviously meant that the jury could avoid imposing the death penalty only by acquitting the defendant or finding him or her guilty of a lesser offense. This threat of jury nullification encouraged the states to replace their mandatory death penalties with discretionary capital punishment laws. Some twenty-four jurisdictions, including Florida, moved from mandatory to discretionary capital sentencing between the end of the Civil War and the beginning of the twentieth century.

In Florida, capital punishment became discretionary during the 1870s—apparently in 1872. By 1884, the Florida Supreme Court was able to state that "the law is positive. If a majority of the jurors recommend to mercy, by whatever motives they may be actuated (and these motives are not circumscribed) the court is bound to heed their verdict and pronounce sentence accordingly." This remained the law of Florida until 1972, when *Furman v. Georgia* invalidated all jurisdictions' capital statutes, including Florida's.

1923–62: The Advent of the Age of the Electric Chair, Executions "without a Hitch" (Except for the Lynchings), and Early Legal Challenges to Capital Punishment

It was in 1923, just eight years before Hollywood made the first film version of Mary Shelley's *Frankenstein,* in which a mad scientist uses the power of electricity to jolt the dead back to life, that the state of Florida began to electrocute people who had been tried and sentenced to death. Thirty-three years after New York botched the electrocution of William Kemmler, the electric chair was first presented in Florida as a "humane" alternative to hanging as a method of execution. During the 1923 session of the Florida State Legislature, a bill advocating the use of the electric chair was supported by the Florida Federation of Women's Clubs and endorsed by the Florida sheriffs at their annual convention. The bill passed the legislature, and electrocution was substituted for hanging as the method of capital punishment in Florida for all executions occurring after January 1, 1924.

The first five people executed in Florida using the electric chair were African American men, and so were five of the next six. For nearly two decades, county sheriffs acted as executioners, until a 1941 law created the position of executioner, for which compensation was available of up to three hundred dollars per electrocution. Executioners were all white men who wore hoods while carrying out their duties.

The Florida capital sentencing statute allowed juries uncontrolled discretion to impose death or permit mercy. Under this so-called mercy statute, all defendants convicted of capital offenses were to be sentenced to death unless the jury recommended mercy. A jury recommendation of mercy was binding on the trial court. The statute made no attempt to structure or guide the jury's process of deciding whether or not to recommend mercy; the jury could give or withhold a recommendation of mercy for any reason. The Florida Supreme Court interpreted the "majority" language of the statute to mean that at least seven members of the jury were required to vote for mercy. At least one man, an African American man from Columbia County named E. C. Daniels, died in the electric chair in 1959 because his jury deadlocked at six votes to six on a mercy recommendation.

Although the Florida Supreme Court heard appeals as a matter of right from judgments imposing the death penalty, capital cases did not receive automatic review by any appellate court, and appeals were restricted to challenges to convictions rather than to death sentences. There was no provision for appellate review of the sentencing decision. The Florida Supreme Court did not hear appeals for mitigation of sentence, reasoning that that court was "not a proper forum in which to seek a mercy commutation."

The capital punishment procedure created by the 1923 statute was fairly straightforward. Following conviction of a capital crime without a jury recommendation of mercy, the circuit court clerk prepared a certified copy of the record and sent it to the county sheriff, who then forwarded it to the governor. When the governor was assured that all was in order, he signed a death warrant setting the execution date for a specified period of time, usually a week. As soon as practicable following the signing of the warrant, and no later than five days prior to the week of the execution, the condemned was delivered to the state prison system, where he would be held in a special death cell next to the death chamber. The law provided that "the sheriff of the county wherein the conviction was had shall be ex-officio deputy executioner of such sentence of death and shall be present at the execution unless he be prevented by sickness or other disability." The statute also required the presence of "a jury of twelve respectable citizens" to serve as witnesses. However, the statute limited the ability of members of the general public to view executions by providing that "all other persons other than such jury, the counsel for the criminal, such ministers of the gospel as the criminal shall desire, officers of the prison, deputies and guards shall be excluded during the execution." For almost twenty years from the time the statute was passed, it was customary for the electric chair to be activated by the local sheriff or by a deputy. Following the execution, the statute required that the body be turned over to the dead person's family, but if the body remained unclaimed it would be "delivered to such physicians as may request the same for dissection, or shall be buried or disposed of as convicts dying in the State Prison are buried or disposed of." The superintendent of the state prison certified that the execution had taken place by returning the death warrant to the governor. Shortly after the enactment of the new statute, the Florida Board of Institutions oversaw construction of the electric chair at the Florida State Farm near Raiford. In August 1924, the state engineer reported to the board that the electric chair was operational. Within two months, the device was put to use.

The first person to die in Florida's new electric chair was an African American man from Jacksonville named Frank Johnson, who was also known as Luther Dorrill. Johnson had shot and killed a white Jacksonville railroad engineer during the course of a burglary in December 1923. Both Johnson and his companion in the burglary were convicted of first-degree murder, but the jury recommended mercy for the partner, who had apparently not been armed. Not having received a mercy recommendation, Johnson was electrocuted on October 7, 1924. Following the execution, the prison superintendent wrote to Governor Cary Hardee to tell him that the "execution was carried out yesterday without a hitch," and that there had been "a splendid representation of citizens as witnesses."

Despite the official move toward the electric chair as a means of capital punishment, the 1923 statute apparently did not cut down the gallows entirely. At least one, and perhaps two, state-sanctioned hangings occurred in Florida after 1924. Charles Browne was sentenced to death after fatally shooting a man during a 1923 robbery. The Florida Supreme Court reversed Browne's initial conviction, but affirmed the death sentence that the jury handed down following a second trial. After the sentencing judge ordered him to die in the electric chair, Browne challenged the manner of his execution. The Florida Supreme Court then remanded Browne's case to the trial court, holding that "the sentence should have been death by hanging as provided by the statutes as of October, 1923, when the crime was committed, and not by electrocution under the statute that became effective January 1, 1924." Browne was hanged in Deland in April 1927. The final official hanging in Florida apparently took place on August 17, 1929, when James Alderman was executed in Fort Lauderdale following a federal conviction for the murder of three people aboard a Coast Guard ship.

Although state-sanctioned hangings were abolished by the 1923 statute, that did not stop private persons from continuing the practice. According to statistics compiled by the National Association for the Advancement of Colored People, 178 people were lynched in Florida between 1889 and 1918. In the first two decades of the twentieth century, Florida's lynching rate was higher than that of any other state, and it was twice as high as the rates in Georgia, Mississippi, and Louisiana. Although lynching and other modes of private killings by vigilantes and mobs continued between the 1920s and 1940s, not a single person was convicted of lynching in Florida between 1900 and 1934.

It was not until the Scottsboro cases in 1932 that the U.S. Supreme Court recognized a constitutional right to court-appointed counsel in capital trials in state court. When the Supreme Court decided to grant new trials to the Scottsboro defendants, it looked to the history of the right to counsel and court-appointed counsel from the English common law to 1932. In 1836, England granted felony defendants the right to counsel in all matters. Before that, however, England granted the right only to those accused of misdemeanors. Lord Coke defended this anomaly in writings prescient of the rationalization the judge in the initial Scottsboro case used to deny the nine young men accused in that case a lawyer—that in a felony case, the court itself was counsel for the defendant. While the English rule was still in practice, most colonial governments in America recognized the defendant's right to counsel in all criminal matters. And even those that did not expressly recognize the right in their charters or constitutions either implicitly recognized the right as consistent with the English Declaration of Rights or expressly recognized it by statute. In the colonies, however, except in New Jersey and Connecticut, the right to counsel meant only that criminal defendants had the right to hire or retain lawyers. When the First Congress convened, James Madison proposed that one amendment that should be added to the Constitution was the guarantee that "in all criminal prosecutions, the accused shall enjoy the right to . . . have the assistance of counsel for his defence." There was little debate about this proposed amendment in the House or in the Senate, which raises the inference that the right to counsel expressed in the Sixth Amendment grants the very same right to retain an attorney in criminal prosecutions that was recognized by the majority of colonies in their own charters and constitutions. Thus, when the Bill of Rights was ratified, U.S. citizens who could not afford to retain or hire a lawyer had no real right to counsel, unless they lived in New Jersey or Connecticut, where counsel was granted even to those who could not afford to pay for it.

The U.S. Supreme Court did not limit the actions of the states in criminal procedural matters for the next eighty years after the Constitution was ratified. Even after the Fourteenth Amendment was added to the Constitution in 1868, the Court showed in a number of decisions over the next sixty years that it would not intervene in state criminal procedure matters. One such decision seemed to prevent the Court ever from reasoning that the Sixth Amendment's guarantee of the right to counsel applied to the states. In *Hurtado v. California,* the Court held that the right to indictment before a grand jury, although expressly contained in the Fifth Amendment, did not apply to the states. The Court reasoned that although the Fifth and Fourteenth Amendments contain due process clauses, only the Fifth Amendment expressly grants the right to indictment before a grand jury; therefore, because due process itself does not require the grand jury procedure, the Fourteenth Amendment could not be read to require that states recognize the right of their citizens to receive grand jury indictments.

Such reasoning clearly would prove an obstacle to the argument that indigent criminal defendants had a cognizable right under state and federal law to the assistance of counsel. The Fourteenth Amendment only provided for due process. Hence, the argument would go, given that due process itself does not require that counsel be provided to criminal defendants, and given that the Fourteenth Amendment contains no express provision for the right to counsel, defendants indicted under color of state law would not even be entitled to counsel, let alone have it provided for them.

Then came the Scottsboro case. Nine young African American men (Charlie Weems, Ozie Powell, Clarence Norris, Olen Montgomery, Willie Roberson, Haywood Patterson, Andy and Roy Wright, and Eugene Williams, ages thirteen to twenty-one) were arrested on March 3, 1931, for allegedly raping two white women (Ruby Bates and Victoria Price). Accused and accusers had all been riding the rails.

In a 1958 law review article, Frances Allen describes the case as starting in a freight train "slowly moving across the countryside of northern Alabama."

It was a time of economic distress and social unrest. As if in response to some common impulse, thousands of young people—no one knows how many—left their homes and communities to drift across the land by train and on foot, presumably in search of work, but, in reality, often without any defined or definable objective. In a gondola car of the train rode two groups of youths, one composed of Negroes, the other whites. Among the latter were two white girls. What occurred has ever since been the subject of sharp controversy. It is at least established that a dispute broke out between the Negroes and the whites. There was a fight and all but one of the white boys were thrown off the slow-moving train. Word was sent ahead, and when the freight train approached the village of Scottsboro, the Negroes were met by the sheriff and a posse. The charge was rape of the white girls. Fearing the violence of the community, the sheriff moved the defendants to the neighboring town of Gadsden. The militia was called to Scottsboro to maintain order. A few days later the defendants were tried, in three separate proceedings. Each of the three trials was completed in the space of a single day. All the defendants were convicted of rape, and the juries imposed the sentence of death on each.

The Scottsboro defendants appealed to the U.S. Supreme Court, arguing that they had received ineffective assistance of counsel. They were put on trial only six days after their indictment, and for all practical purposes they had no lawyer during their capital trial. The Alabama trial judge had "appointed all members of the bar" for purposes of arraigning the defendants, and he expected them to represent the "Scottsboro Boys"—as they were called—at the trial if no one else turned up to represent the accused. What this meant, of course, was that no lawyer had responsibility for the defense.

The U.S. Supreme Court opinion voiding the convictions and sentences and ordering a retrial was written by Justice George Sutherland, one of the "Four Horsemen" on the Court who were anathema to President Roosevelt's New Deal. For the Court, he explained why the right to counsel is a fundamental constitutional element of "due process of law":

> The right to be heard would be, in many cases, of little avail if it did not comprehend the right to be heard by counsel. Even the intelligent and educated layman has small and sometimes no skill in the science of law. If charged with crime, he is incapable, generally, of determining for himself whether the indictment is good or bad. He is unfamiliar with the rules of evidence. Left without the aid of counsel he may be put on trial without a proper charge, and convicted upon incompetent evidence, or evidence irrelevant to the issue or otherwise inadmissible. He lacks both the skill and knowledge adequately to prepare his defense, even though he have a perfect one. He requires the guiding hand of counsel at every step in the proceedings against him. Without it, though he be not guilty, he faces the danger of conviction because he does not know how to establish his innocence. If that be true of men of intelligence, how much more true is it of the ignorant and illiterate, or those of feeble intellect.

The 1932 Scottsboro decision did not require court-appointed counsel in all felony trials in state courts. The cases of the Scottsboro defendants were capital cases, and although a fair reading of the Court's opinion limited it to trials in which death was a possible punishment, it wasn't clear that the Scottsboro decision required counsel in all capital cases. The Court expressly limited its holding to cases involving capital defendants who could not afford to retain counsel and who could not be expected to carry out their own defenses. In one case, the Court explained:

> All that is necessary now to decide, as we do decide, is that in a capital case, where the defendant is unable to employ counsel, and is incapable adequately of making his own defense because of ignorance, feeble-mindedness, illiteracy, or the like, it is the duty of the court, whether requested or not, to assign counsel for him.

The uniquely hideous facts of the Scottsboro case—the farcical appointment of "all members of the bar" as counsel and the summary trials—had clearly made an impression on Justice Sutherland. "The defendants [were] young, ignorant, illiterate, surrounded by hostile sentiment, haled back and forth under guard of soldiers, charged with an atrocious crime regarded with especial horror in the community where they were to be tried," and were thus put in jail. Take away any one or more of these special conditions, and it became unclear whether the Supreme Court would still have regarded counsel as "fundamental" to "due process of law."

In 1942, the Supreme Court finally resolved the issue left open since Scottsboro and held that the right to counsel did not exist in all felony trials. Smith Betts, a farmhand in rural Carroll County, Maryland, was charged with robbery, a noncapital offense. Because he lacked the funds to hire a defense lawyer, Betts asked the court to appoint one. The Maryland trial judge refused, explaining to Betts that in Carroll County attorneys were appointed only in capital cases. At Betts's trial, the main dispute involved eyewitness identifications. Betts did the best he could acting as his own lawyer, but the judge who presided at the trial (there was no jury) disbelieved him, found him guilty, and sentenced him to eight years in prison.

The U.S. Supreme Court decided in Betts's case that there was no generalized right to counsel in noncapital trials. If "special circumstances" were present, however, then there was a right to counsel. Circumstances deemed "special" by the Court included "the age and education of the defendant, the conduct of the court or prosecuting officials, and the complicated nature of the offense charged, and the possible defenses thereto." And, of course, the "gravity of the crime."

These elements seem to have been lifted, somewhat, from the facts of the Scottsboro case. The Alabama trial court's behavior seemed an aberration—appointing all members of the bar to represent the defendants. Although the charges and defenses thereto did not seem complicated, the gravity of the crime, rape, was substantial, for at that time it was a capital offense. Yet the Court had been explicit in the Scottsboro decision about the limit of its holding; it applied only to capital defendants who could not provide for their own defense. The Court did not delineate the elements of the circumstances in its holding sufficiently to make the *Betts* decision its natural extension. Nor could it, for the Scottsboro Court was explicit that its holding applied only to capital offenses.

Betts threw the continued validity of the Scottsboro decision into doubt by raising the question, If a capital case did not present "special circumstances," then would the Scottsboro decision apply (requiring court-appointed counsel) or would *Betts* apply (not requiring counsel, because no "special circumstances" were present, even though it is a capital case)? In other words, did the Scottsboro decision establish a per se rule of right to counsel in capital trials where the defendants could not provide for their own defense? Or was the Scottsboro rule limited to cases with facts as howlingly unfair as the Scottsboro case? Furthermore, did the *Betts* "special circumstances" requirement apply equally across the board, to capital and noncapital cases alike?

In the years following *Betts*, the Court always found that capital trials did present "special circumstances." As a practical matter, the fact that a trial was capital represented a per se "special circumstance" requiring the appointment of counsel. In 1945, two capital cases raising "special circumstances" issues reached the Supreme Court, and in both cases the Court held, in votes of seven to two, that such circumstances were present. In 1961, the justices made clear that they were drawing a line between capital and noncapital cases: "When one pleads to a capital charge without benefit of counsel, we do not stop to determine whether prejudice resulted." The Scottsboro decision lived.

The bright-line distinction between capital and noncapital cases, however, was artificial. In case after case, the justices struggled to fashion a coherent definition of "special circumstances." This effort was not a happy one, as Justice Hugo Black, who dissented in *Betts*, seldom lost an opportunity to remind his brethren. By the early 1960s, the justices' frustration with the *Betts* "special circumstances" rule had increased to the point where overruling *Betts* became a distinct possibility. All the Court needed was the right case to use as a vehicle to reconsider *Betts*.

Enter Clarence Earl Gideon, a small-time Florida criminal who had been convicted of breaking into a Pensacola pool hall and stealing money from the pool hall's change machine. At his felony trial, Gideon had asked for a lawyer. Because Gideon's was not a capital case, the trial judge refused. The Florida Supreme Court affirmed. At this point, Gideon's case becomes the stuff of legends, best told by Anthony Lewis in his book *Gideon's Trumpet*. Gideon wrote and filed a petition in the U.S. Supreme Court asking the justices to throw out his felony conviction because he had been denied the right to counsel at trial. Gideon was wrong, of course; under *Betts* he wasn't entitled to counsel unless he could show "special circumstances." He probably couldn't. Gideon wasn't regarded as illiterate, and, in fact, he didn't do too badly as his own trial lawyer, especially as the presiding judge did the best he could to help Gideon make his case of innocence. But the very apparent *absence* of special circumstances made Gideon's case a good vehicle through which the justices could revisit the *Betts* rule itself. Here was a case lacking in special circumstances. If *Betts* remained the law, then Gideon would lose; for Gideon to win, *Betts* had to be overruled.

The Court invited Abe Fortas, of the Washington, D.C., law firm of Arnold, Fortas & Porter, to serve as Gideon's lawyer. The justices told Fortas to address the question of whether *Betts v. Brady* should be overruled. It was an invitation to Fortas, and his partner Abe Krash and his summer associate John Hart Ely, to take part in constitutional history.

In autumn 1962, Fortas's hand was strengthened significantly by the publication in the *Chicago Law Review* of a definitive article by law professor Yale Kamisar. The article would appear too late for Fortas to use it in his brief, but Kamisar, knowing about the Gideon case, telephoned Krash in September and offered to send him a copy of the manuscript. The offer was gladly accepted.

Kamisar's article filled an important empirical hole in Gideon's argument: What would be the practical, real-world consequences of the Court's overruling *Betts*? Rhetoric about "constitutional revolutions" notwithstanding, the U.S. Supreme Court has never been packed with revolutionaries. Only a few years earlier, in *Brown v. Board of Education*, the Court had sparked a social upheaval still very visible in 1962, when the Court granted review in Gideon's case. The justices might well have felt squeamish about making waves again.

Kamisar's article demonstrated that the consequences of the Court's overruling *Betts* would not be momentous. Kamisar showed that thirty-seven states already formally provided court-appointed counsel as a matter of right in all felony cases. In eight of the remaining states, a rule of court-appointed counsel existed de facto, notwithstanding the absence of statute or court rule. That left only five states that would be affected if *Betts* was overturned.

In its landmark ruling in *Gideon v. Wainwright*, the Supreme Court scrapped *Betts* altogether, including the capital/noncapital distinction that had proved so vexing. Justice Hugo Black, the *Betts* dissenter, wrote the Court's opinion in *Gideon*, stating that Clarence Earl Gideon did indeed have a Sixth Amendment right to court-appointed counsel in his noncapital trial for breaking into and robbing the change machine in a Pensacola pool hall. Henceforth, all felony prosecutions in state court required the appointment of counsel. Clarence Gideon's case did not affect the Scottsboro rule that counsel must always be appointed in capital trials; the *Gideon* decision simply extended the per se rule to include noncapital felony trials.

The right to counsel recognized in the Scottsboro decision was not the only federal constitutional right the Supreme Court extended to both state and federal criminal trials. The Scottsboro ruling was emblematic of what some have termed the Court's "revolution" in constitutional criminal procedure—the application of the procedural rights enumerated in the U.S. Constitution to state criminal trials.

Meanwhile, as the range of available constitutional criminal procedure rights expanded, so did the availability of habeas corpus to provide a federal judicial forum for vindication of those rights. The Court's decision in *Brown v. Allen* reaffirmed the cognizability in habeas of all federal constitutional claims presented by state prisoners, including, of course, the constitutional right to court-appointed counsel in capital cases recognized in the Scottsboro decision. As the Court recognized new rights, habeas kept pace and remained as a mechanism to vindicate those rights in federal court.

Many scholarly treatments of habeas corpus in the twentieth century begin with the infamous Leo Frank case. In 1913, Leo Frank, a New York Jew who was living in Georgia and managing a pencil factory there, was indicted for the rape and murder of a fourteen-year-old girl. The brutal nature of the killing—along with Frank's religion and northern origin—aroused violent local prejudices. In his dissent in *Frank v. Magnum* (1915), Justice Oliver Wendell Holmes described the atmosphere of terror and violence that permeated the courtroom and jury deliberations:

> The trial began on July 28, 1913, at Atlanta, and was carried on in a court packed with spectators and surrounded by a crowd outside, all strongly hostile to [Frank]. On Saturday, August 23, this hostility was sufficient to lead the judge to confer in the presence of the jury with the Chief of Police in Atlanta and the Colonel of the Fifth Georgia Regiment stationed in the city, both of whom were known to the jury. On the same day, the evidence seemingly having been closed, the public press, apprehending danger, united in a request to the Court that the proceedings should not continue on that evening. Thereupon the Court adjourned until Monday morning. On that morning when the Solicitor General entered the court he was greeted with applause, stamping of feet and clapping of hands, and the judge before beginning his charge had a private conversation with [Frank's] counsel in which he expressed the opinion that there would be "probable danger of violence" if there should be an acquittal or disagreement [i.e., a hung jury], and that it would be safer for not only [Frank] but his counsel to be absent from Court when the verdict was brought in. At the judge's request they agreed that [Frank] and they should be absent, and they kept their word. When the verdict was rendered, and before more than one of the jurymen had been polled there was such a roar of applause that the polling could not go on till order was restored. The noise outside was such that it was difficult for the judge to hear the answers of the jurors although he was only ten feet from them.

The jury convicted Frank, of course, and the trial judge sentenced him to death. When the Georgia Supreme Court affirmed, Frank filed a petition for writ of habeas corpus in federal court. Ultimately, a majority of the U.S. Supreme Court refused to second-guess the Georgia state courts. Holmes dissented in a blunt opinion:

Mob law does not become due process of law by securing the assent of a terrorized jury. We are not speaking of mere disorder, or mere irregularities in procedure, but of a case where the processes of justice are actually subverted. . . . Any judge who has sat with juries [as Holmes had] knows that in spite of forms they are extremely likely to be impregnated by the environing atmosphere.

Leo Frank almost certainly was innocent of the rape and killing for which he was convicted and, in the end, lynched.

In 1923, however, in another case involving capital juries intimidated by the threat of mob violence, the Court reviewed the convictions of five African Americans. African Americans had been systematically excluded from both grand and petit jury panels. The trial in question had lasted about forty-five minutes; it was, as the Court later observed, nothing but a mask for lynch law. Justice Holmes, writing for the Court, observed, "No juryman could have voted for an acquittal and continued to live in [the county]." The Court decided that federal relief was available:

If the case is that the whole proceeding is a mask—that counsel, jury, and judge were swept to the fatal end by an irresistible wave of public passion, and that the State Courts failed to correct the wrong, neither perfection in the machinery for correction nor the possibility that the trial court and counsel saw no other way of avoiding an immediate outbreak of the mob can prevent this Court from securing to the [defendants] their constitutional rights.

The year *Gideon v. Wainwright* was decided (1963) was also the year in which the Warren Court's expansion of habeas corpus reached its high-water mark. In 1966, Congress stepped in and scaled back the availability of habeas to state prisoners. It limited the discretion of federal judges to entertain habeas petitions "only on the ground that [the petitioner] is in custody in violation of the Constitution, laws, or treaties of the United States." Congress also created a presumption that any issue of fact determined by a state court after a hearing on the merits is correct, and required the petitioner to establish by convincing evidence that the state court's ruling was erroneous. The post–Warren Court contracted the scope of habeas further, as did Congress in the 1990s.

Into this history comes the history of challenges to the constitutionality of capital punishment. For nearly a century and a half, few seriously questioned the constitutionality of capital punishment. But on August 27, 1927, Massachusetts executed Nicola Sacco and Bartolomeo Vanzetti, two Italian immigrants who were considered to be political radicals. Caught up in the Palmer Raids and the Red Scare following World War I, Sacco and Vanzetti were likely innocent of the South Braintree robbery and murder for which they were executed (another man had confessed to the crimes). Sacco and Vanzetti lived on death row for six years while their claims of innocence and prejudice by trial judge worked their way through the courts. The final U.S. Supreme Court opinion, written by Justice Oliver Wendell Holmes, stated that in habeas corpus proceedings judicial prejudice is not a specific violation of the Constitution, and that absent such a constitutional violation the federal courts could not intervene into a state criminal trial.

The Sacco and Vanzetti executions caused some thinking Americans to wonder, not about the wisdom of capital punishment in principle, but about the way in which the penalty was being applied. Capital punishment was becoming a civil rights issue. It thus perhaps is understandable that the two preeminent national civil rights organizations—the American Civil Liberties Union, founded in 1920, and the NAACP, founded in 1939—began taking a hard look at who was being executed and under what circumstances.

Burton Wolfe, in his fascinating history *Pileup on Death Row*, writes that the national protest demonstrations against the Sacco and Vanzetti executions led the federal Department of Prisons, a division of the Department of Justice, to begin keeping track of executions in the United States. For the first time, Americans had available a realistic picture of death row demographics. Some interesting patterns emerged. For example, during the first six years that records were kept, 1930–35, southern states executed four times as many people as any of the other regions of the United States and sentenced twice as many African Americans to death as whites. These government statistics provided quantitative and disinterested support for something most southerners had known all along: capital punishment was predominantly a southern phenomenon. And in the South, the death penalty was disproportionately applied against African American men, especially African American men accused of raping white women.

In 1950, the racial demographics associated with the execution of rapists led the NAACP Legal Defense Fund, Inc. (LDF) to take on the defense of African American men accused of raping white women. Death wasn't the only issue on LDF's plate, of course. By the early 1950s, LDF's legal challenges to the *Plessey v. Ferguson* "separate but equal" doctrine and segregated public schools were chugging along toward the landmark 1954 decision in *Brown v. Board of Education*. Under the leadership of Thurgood Marshall, LDF and its allies crafted a brilliant strategy of undermining *Plessey* before finishing it off. Rather than waging a frontal attack on *Plessey*'s "separate but equal" doctrine, Thurgood Marshall brought a series of cases to the U.S. Supreme Court, arguing, in various factual settings, that "separate" could never be "equal." These early cases prepared the justices to overrule *Plessey* when the frontal attack did arrive, in *Brown v. Board of Education*. The cases prepared the justices—psychologically and emotionally, as well as legally and doctrinally—to accept Marshall's coup de grâce to *Plessey* in *Brown*. "Look," Marshall in effect said, "over the past few years we've been proving, in case after case, that in a wide variety of factual settings, 'separate' means 'unequal.' What we've been proving is that 'separate but equal' is a doctrine that isn't applied fairly. It just doesn't work. The court should reject it."

By the 1950s, the Florida legislature had clarified portions of the state's capital punishment statute. In that year, the legislature provided the Board of State Institutions with the authority to promulgate regulations that permitted representatives of the press to witness executions. Additionally, the revisions to the capital punishment statute relieved local sheriffs of the duty of performing executions. Instead, the legislature established that it was the responsibility of the first assistant engineer of the Florida State Prison "to execute and carry out the sentence of death by operating the switch or mechanism necessary to send the electric current through the body of the condemned person." In October 1941, the first executions under the new regime took place. Four men were electrocuted within a span of fifty-five minutes, and a newspaper reporter observed that the men were put to death by an executioner who, for the first time in the state's history, wore a hood to conceal his identity.

The Florida legislature again refined the capital punishment statutory procedures in 1959. Until that time, condemned inmates typically remained in county jails until the governor signed their death warrants, at which point they were moved to the death house at Raiford to await execution. Although condemned prisoners were sometimes turned over to the state prison system earlier, there was no express statutory provision governing the procedure. A bill passed in 1959 required that "the convicted person shall be delivered by the sheriff of the county to the superintendent of the state prison to await the death warrant." The current process of capital punishment in Florida still substantially reflects this aspect of the execution procedure.

Between 1924 and 1964, 197 men were executed in Florida. Of these, 43 had been found guilty of rape, and 154 were executed for murder. Despite their minority status in the population (approximately 11 percent), African American men constituted 95.3 percent of those executed for rape between 1924 and 1964 and 76.7 percent of those executed for murder during the same period. Similar disparities existed with respect to those awarded executive clemency between 1924 and 1964. During this period, the state granted clemency to 59 prisoners. Of these clemency awards, 44.3 percent were given to persons convicted of crimes against African Americans, and only 15.2 percent were given to persons convicted of crimes against whites. Additionally, among African American offenders who received clemency, 41.1 percent of the cases involved crimes with African American victims; only 3.4 percent involved crimes with white victims. Subsequent studies have consistently confirmed the correlation between race and Florida's imposition of capital punishment.

Concern about the racist application of Florida's capital punishment system manifested itself in various ways during the late 1950s and early 1960s. In several cases attorneys contended, unsuccessfully, that Florida's courts were racially discriminatory in their application of the death penalty in cases involving African American defendants charged with crimes against white persons. Additionally, a commission established in 1963 to study the use of the death penalty in Florida and recommend its retention or abolition noted the evidence of racial discrimination.

As these concerns about Florida's capital punishment system grew during the late 1950s and early 1960s, the execution rate declined. Only two executions occurred in 1960, and both of the condemned were African American men convicted of crimes against whites. Ralph

Williams was executed for the rape of a seventeen-year-old white woman, and James Brooks was put to death for killing a white clerk while robbing a Western Union office. In 1961, Florida executed two white men. One, Norman J. Manckiewicz, a decorated veteran of World War II, was electrocuted for the murder of a police officer during the robbery of a hotel in Miami Beach. The other, Robert Wesley Davis, was the last person Florida put to death for rape. Florida executed five men in 1962. Three were African American: Lee Jefferson, Johnnie Hill, and Samuel Johnson. The other two, Joe Smith and William Leach, were white men who were put to death for murdering a cell mate in the Union County State Prison. Florida executed only one person in 1963, a white man named Charles H. Lee who had murdered his estranged wife and his father-in-law.

1963–72: The Road to *Furman v. Georgia*

If Thurgood Marshall was the grand architect of *Brown v. Board of Education,* Anthony Amsterdam was the architect of *Brown's* capital punishment counterpart, the 1972 decision in *Furman v. Georgia,* which outlawed capital punishment as then administered in the United States and clearing every death row in every state. As the pre-*Brown* cases set the stage for *Plessey's* eventual overruling in *Brown,* so the pre-*Furman* cases set the stage for the *Furman* Court's rejection of capital punishment as then applied.

Sometimes individual justices of the Supreme Court send signals to the legal world outside the Court—lawyers and lower court judges—indicating that, although a majority of the justices are not quite ready to hear and decide particular constitutional questions, they are interested in those issues, and attorneys should persevere in asking the Court to decide those constitutional questions. One way in which a justice might telegraph such a message is to write a dissent from the denial of petition for writ of certiorari (plenary review). In 1963 such a dissent galvanized the nascent legal campaign to outlaw capital punishment.

In an Alabama rape case, Justice Arthur Goldberg, along with Justices William O. Douglas and William Brennan, signaled that the Court might be receptive to constitutional challenges to capital punishment for rape. Six justices voted against hearing the Alabama rape case, but Goldberg's dissent suggested that in the future the Court might be receptive to considering whether, in light of the worldwide trend against the death penalty for rape, executing rapists violates the "evolving standards of decency that mark the progress of a maturing society." Also, on behalf of the three dissenting justices, Goldberg wrote that the questions of disproportionality and "unnecessary cruelty" of death for rapists deserved the Court's full consideration.

Herbert Haines, in his indispensable book *Against Capital Punishment,* writes that the Goldberg dissent was an intentional signal to the lawyers who were then considering using the courts to abolish capital punishment for rape. That signal was received loud and clear at LDF and the ACLU. Borrowing a page from Thurgood Marshall's playbook in *Brown v. Board of Education,* LDF capital litigators, now led by Jack Greenberg, reasoned that the Court was not likely to strike down capital punishment on constitutional grounds "in one judicial stroke." Thus LDF "chose to attack the death penalty *indirectly.* They began working on a strategy that would attack the *process* by which convicted criminals were sentenced to die."

According to Haines, "There would be two parts to this strategy. One involved a concerted assault on racial discrimination in death sentencing and the other pertained to selected trial procedures in capital cases." The latter attack focused on three common features of capital trials at the time: (1) the exclusion of "death scrupled" jurors from sitting on capital juries, thus depriving capital defendants of the right to a jury composed of a "fair cross section of the community"; (2) the simultaneous determination by the jury of guilt and sentence in a single, unified trial; and (3) the absence of clear and objective standards to guide the jury's process of deciding who dies.

These challenges, and the appeals they generated, proved to be a successful strategy for convincing courts to put executions on hold until the lower courts, and eventually the U.S. Supreme Court, had a chance to consider and decide the various constitutional issues LDF was asserting in individual capital cases all across the country. By the mid-1960s, Amsterdam and LDF had won a virtual moratorium on executions in the United States. If a death row prisoner had a lawyer to file the legal papers mass-produced by LDF—called "last aid kits"— the condemned prisoner was entitled to a stay of execution. Wolfe quotes this explanation from Amsterdam in *Pileup on Death Row:*

> As papers came across my desk, I kept seeing cases of blacks sentenced to death in the South. I was constantly confronted

with the fact that in dealing with the death penalty, we were not merely dealing with a barbaric relic of civilization in its most savage days, but also with discrimination against blacks, the poor, the pariahs and outcasts of society. At the same time, as I looked at all the violence going on in our society, the death penalty came to symbolize to me the tendency to resort to violence instead of reason in seeking the solution to problems. This insight came to me while I was handling attacks on the death penalty on a case by case basis, on specific issues such as exclusion of black people and poor people from juries, loss of rights to counsel, and so on. This larger insight came together with a case by case study of discrimination against blacks in the South, often involving the death sentence. When I pulled all of that together, I knew that abolishing the death penalty altogether was the major job to be done.

But what if the death row prisoner didn't have a lawyer? LDF might be able to find him one. But what if LDF didn't even know of that prisoner's existence? What if LDF didn't know a person with a pending execution date even needed a lawyer? Such was the situation in Florida in 1966: the second-largest death row population in the nation (fifty-two condemned men) and not enough lawyers to file LDF's form papers to stay the executioner. Until 1966, Florida's death row prisoners were not at risk of imminent execution. The state had been governed, in succession, by three adversaries of capital punishment: Thomas LeRoy Collins, Cecil Farris Bryant, and William Haydon Burns. But in 1966 Claude Kirk Jr. was elected governor after making campaign promises to enforce the death penalty. Kirk was determined to keep his promises.

Thus Florida became one of the principal crisis states for Amsterdam and LDF. If Florida began executing people, the entire, shaky national moratorium on execution would be in jeopardy of coming apart. Much of the moratorium's power was grounded in perception: Amsterdam and LDF had persuaded various judges and governors in the capital punishment states that the U.S. Supreme Court would countenance no executions until the Court had sorted out the challenges to the constitutionality of capital punishment as a legal system. The moratorium thus was in part a self-fulfilling prophecy: if Florida broke ranks, then other states might as well.

The Florida Supreme Court would let executions proceed, even though the prisoners sent to their deaths lacked lawyers to raise the very constitutional claims that were getting stays for others in many other states. This was, after all, the same Florida Supreme Court that had refused to give Clarence Earl Gideon a lawyer in his felony robbery trial. It wasn't until the U.S. Supreme Court reversed in *Gideon v. Wainwright* that the Florida Supreme Court joined the rest of the nation in providing court-appointed lawyers to citizens on trial for noncapital felonies. Given that the Florida Supreme Court didn't think defendants had a fundamental right to lawyers at felony *trials,* the justices could hardly be expected to extend *Gideon* to require counsel for habeas corpus proceedings in federal court.

Thus the capital counsel problem in Florida had several elements: a large (and undefined) death row population, too few lawyers to represent each individual prisoner, a governor intent on signing death warrants on an unknown quantity of prisoners, and a state supreme court willing to let unrepresented people be executed.

Florida had carried out its final two pre-*Furman* executions on May 12, 1964. Emmett Clark Blake was a white man who was electrocuted for a murder committed in 1962. The case of the other man executed on that day, Sie Dawson, vividly illustrates the potential for the seriously weird in Florida's pre-*Furman* capital punishment system. Dawson was an African American man with one leg and an IQ of 64 who had allegedly murdered the wife and child of his white employer. After police officers threatened to turn him over to a lynch mob, Dawson confessed to the slayings. Afterward, however, Dawson consistently maintained that he had been present when his employer committed the killings. Despite the fact that the state had no eyewitnesses and premised its case on inconclusive circumstantial evidence, and notwithstanding that Dawson recanted his confession at trial, a jury made up exclusively of white males convicted him of the murders and sentenced him to death.

Similarly disturbing was the case of Freddie Pitts and Wilbert Lee, two African American men sentenced to death for a murder that took place in Port St. Joe in 1963. Although Pitts and Lee confessed to the murder and pled guilty, it later came to light that the police had obtained their confessions with threats and beatings. After a white man admitted that he had committed the murders, the local sheriff responded, "I already got two niggers waiting for the chair in Raiford for those murders." The case remained in court for many years, and the two men were ultimately granted a new trial. Although they pled innocent, Pitts and Lee were convicted and sentenced to death by an all-white jury in March 1972. Their death sentences were reduced to life in prison later in 1972 by the *Furman* decision, and they remained incarcerated for three more years after that, until Governor Askew granted them both full pardons in 1975. The *New York Times* editorialized that many observers felt that the Pitts and Lee case was "the saddest, most blatant miscarriage of justice in Florida's history. . . . For some, it has embraced all that was notoriously and traditionally grievous in Southern society—the racism, the poverty, the bigotry given silent but forceful sanction by government and law."

Capital punishment was a politically contentious issue in Florida during the mid-1960s, as it was nationally. Governor William Haydon Burns, whose tenure lasted from 1965 until 1967, refused to sign death warrants during his administration. By 1967 Florida had fifty-two prisoners awaiting execution, the second-largest death row population in the country, and capital punishment was part of the "law and order" debate in that year's gubernatorial election. During his successful campaign for governor, Claude Kirk Jr. made an issue of his predecessor's failure to employ the death penalty as a deterrent to crime. During the campaign, Kirk visited the Florida State Penitentiary at Raiford, shook hands with the death row inmates there, and, according to one newspaper account, "with a courteous smile told them, 'If I'm elected, I may have to sign your death warrant.'" Governor Kirk made good on his campaign promises by signing several death warrants and by ordering fifteen African American condemned prisoners to prepare for clemency hearings as a step toward the resumption of executions.

As Governor Kirk was attempting to move forward with executions, Miami attorney Tobias Simon was working to stop them for good. Simon, a cooperating attorney with the NAACP Legal Defense and Educational Fund and chairman of the state chapter of the American Civil Liberties Union, prepared a creative lawsuit that ultimately brought executions to a halt in Florida for ten years. Skeptics called it "Simon's frolic." Concerned for death row inmates who lacked legal representation, Simon filed a class action lawsuit in habeas corpus on their behalf. Simon argued that death row inmates represented "a class of persons whose constitutional objections to death case procedures and execution itself could be joined and resolved in one proceeding." Nevertheless, using habeas corpus in conjunction with a class action to overturn a large number of illegal convictions or sentences simultaneously was highly unusual, and many observers were surprised when U.S. District Judge William McRae ruled on April 13, 1967, that the argument was compelling enough to warrant a temporary stay of all executions in Florida. Four months later, Judge McRae decided that the propriety of a class action depended on whether or not death row inmates had effective access to the courts, and he consequently ordered a full factual inquiry to examine that question.

As a result of McRae's order, Simon worked with Anthony Amsterdam, principal architect of the federal constitutional challenges to the death penalty, to interview death row inmates at Raiford and compile a statistical profile of them. Of the thirty-four inmates who had already lost their direct appeals to the Florida Supreme Court, half had no lawyers or means to hire counsel. Of the forty inmates interviewed, thirty-seven were entirely destitute and the other three reported financial assets of less than one hundred dollars. Additionally, IQ tests clearly revealed that the prisoners' mean intelligence was below average. Apparently persuaded by these findings, Judge McRae continued the prohibition on executions in Florida while he considered arguments that the state's capital punishment system was unconstitutional.

The situation in Florida was substantially replicated at the national level. By 1967, litigation over the constitutionality of capital punishment in the United States had created a national moratorium on executions. Similarly, as Michael Meltsner notes in his book *Cruel and Unusual,* the essential effect of McRae's ruling was to prevent "the execution of any death sentence in Florida pending the outcome of the Supreme Court litigation testing the constitutionality of capital punishment." Observers in Florida and across the United States would wait five years before the U.S. Supreme Court resolved that question—in a way.

LDF's strategy resulted in a moratorium on executions in the United States from 1967 to 1972, while the courts sorted through the legal challenges to capital punishment. Also, on the road to the 1971 and 1972 cases in which the Supreme Court squarely addressed, for the first time, the legality of capital punishment itself, the Court revolutionized the death-deciding process in state capital trials: in 1968 the

Court struck down the "Lindbergh Law," which made defendants subject to capital punishment only if they exercised their right to jury trial. Also in 1968, the Court, in *Witherspoon v. Illinois,* case, sharply limited the ability of state courts to exclude from capital cases potential jurors with moral doubts about the death penalty.

At issue in *Witherspoon* was an Illinois statute that provided: "In trials for murder it shall be a cause for challenge of any juror who shall, on being examined, state that he has conscientious scruples against capital punishment, or that he is opposed to the same." The Court granted certiorari to decide "whether the Constitution permitted a State to execute a man pursuant to the verdict of a jury so composed." The state's only justification for the challenged jury-selection technique was that "individuals who express serious reservations about capital punishment cannot be relied upon to vote for it even when the laws of the State and the instructions of the trial judge would make death the proper penalty." The Court noted, however, that, as in Florida, the jury is given "broad discretion" to decide whether death is the proper punishment and that jurors' views on the death penalty "play an inevitable role in any such decision." Justice Stewart explained:

> A man who opposes the death penalty, no less than one who favors it, can make the discretionary judgment entrusted to him by the State and can thus obey the oath he takes as a juror. But a jury from which all such men have been excluded cannot perform the task demanded of it. Guided by neither rule nor standard "free to select or reject as it (sees) fit," a jury that must choose between life imprisonment and capital punishment can do little more—and must do nothing less—than express the conscience of the community on the ultimate question of life or death. Yet, in a nation less than half of whose people believe in the death penalty, a jury composed exclusively of such people cannot speak for the community. Culled of all who harbor doubts about the wisdom of capital punishment—of all who would be reluctant to pronounce the extreme penalty—such a jury can speak only for a distinct and dwindling minority.

Witherspoon, therefore, has been said to stand for the limited proposition that "the state cannot challenge a venireman [a member of a panel from which a jury is drawn] for cause merely because he said he was 'opposed to capital punishment' or indicated that he had 'conscientious scruples' against inflicting it. No defendant can constitutionally be put to death at the hands of a tribunal so selected."

Early the next year, the Court's decision in *Witherspoon* was further clarified when, in *Boulden v. Holman*, the Court addressed an Alabama statute providing that a fixed opinion against capital punishment was sufficient to support a challenge for cause by the state. *Boulden* effectively eliminated any assumption about the potential juror's ability to consider the imposition of the death penalty regardless of the juror's opinions. Justice Stewart, quoting from his opinion in *Witherspoon*, made it quite clear that "unless a venireman states unambiguously that he would automatically vote against the imposition of capital punishment no matter what the trial might reveal, it simply cannot be assumed that that is his position."

The rule, then, after *Witherspoon* and *Boulden*, appeared to be that a challenge for cause will not be supported unless the venireman unambiguously states that he or she is opposed to the death penalty and will under no circumstances vote for its imposition. Anything less is insufficient, and the execution of a person pursuant to a jury so composed is unconstitutional. It would seem to follow, therefore, that in a capital case, because of the possibility the accused may be sentenced to death, exclusion of jurors in a manner that violates *Witherspoon* and *Boulden* at the outset would be unconstitutional. To reason otherwise would be to say that the state could select the jury and conduct the trial, and only if the defendant is found guilty and sentenced to death is there a constitutional problem. The accused whose jury fortuitously recommends life would have the identical procedure deemed constitutional. Although this logic may appear to be only the musings of an inexperienced law student, the Florida Supreme Court thought that was just what the U.S. Supreme Court meant.

Witherspoon and *Boulden* set the stage for the U.S. Supreme Court's confrontation with the legality of capital punishment itself. After at least two false starts (*Boykin v. Alabama* in 1969 and *Maxwell v. Bishop* in 1970 provided the Court with opportunities to address the larger issue of capital punishment's constitutionality, but in both cases the justices ducked, basing their decisions on narrower, case-specific procedural grounds), the Supreme Court finally decided the big issues. It was the culmination of Anthony Amsterdam's and LDF's constitutional attack on capital punishment.

In 1970 the court granted review in *McGautha v. California*. Amsterdam and LDF raised the full range of their procedural challenges to capital punishment, arguing that the unitary trial and the absence of sentencing standards offended the Fourteenth Amendment's guarantee of "due process of law." The Supreme Court issued its decision in *McGautha* in 1971. Amsterdam and LDF had lost by a vote of six to three.

The moratorium on executions appeared to be over. Now that the Court had spoken, LDF prepared for a bloodbath. In mid-May 1971, an emergency conference was held at Columbia Law School. According to Haines, Amsterdam told the conferees that "the central conclusion" to be drawn from *McGautha* and its companion cases was that "the Supreme Court could not be expected to take any favorable action on the death penalty anytime soon."

LDF still had its Eighth Amendment "cruel and unusual punishment" angle to present to the Supreme Court; it would be a relatively simple matter to repackage its "due process" challenges as Eighth Amendment challenges. But if the procedural challenges had a chance of persuading the Court to outlaw capital punishment itself, it seemed that the concept of "due process of law" would provide the justices with the best constitutional hook. And LDF had lost the due process claim in *McGautha*. But then, less than two months after *McGautha* was decided, the Court agreed to hear four cases to decide the Eighth Amendment challenge to capital punishment as a legal system. Two of the cases involved murder and two involved rape. This package of four cases became known as *Furman v. Georgia*.

The Supreme Court heard oral arguments on *Furman* and its three companion cases on January 17, 1972. Amsterdam argued *Furman* brilliantly. Still, there was little reason for optimism. LDF's best arguments had been shot down in *McGautha,* and two new Nixon appointments to the Court didn't help LDF's odds.

Then the constitutional hurricane hit. On June 29, 1972, the Supreme Court announced its decision in *Furman*. Amsterdam and LDF had won, five votes to four. The very procedural challenges to capital punishment that the Court had rejected one year earlier in *McGautha* had carried the day in *Furman*. The legal system of capital punishment as it then existed was history. Every capital statute was invalidated. Every death sentence of every person on every death row in every state was reduced to life imprisonment. In a stroke, 629 condemned people were no longer subject to execution.

In *Cruel and Unusual*, Meltsner writes that the news of the *Furman* decision struck LDF's New York headquarters "like an earthquake.... That evening, while a rock band called 'The Eighth Amendment' played in the library of their headquarters on Columbus Circle, [LDF] staffers celebrated into the wee hours." Meltsner describes the scene as the news first came in: "Within minutes the story began to appear on every major wire service ticker. Calls jammed the [LDF] switchboard. Lawyers and secretaries produced transistor radios. General disbelief. Numbness. Tears in people's eyes. Slowly smiles replaced gaping jaws; laughter and embraces filled the halls. 'This place looks like we just landed a man on the moon,' [staffer Douglas] Lyons shouted into a phone."

June 29, 1972, is a singular date in the history of American jurisprudence. But, although *Furman* marked the end of one era of capital punishment and the courts, it also marked the beginning of a new, in many respects more complicated, era. *Furman* didn't outlaw capital punishment per se; only two justices, Thurgood Marshall and William Brennan, would have gone that far. The three other justices in the *Furman* majority only voted to eliminate the capital punishment legal system *as it was then applied*. Thus seven justices seemed to leave open the possibility that states could retool and restore capital punishment as a legal system, and that such new statutes could pass constitutional muster. In fact, the primary procedural defects in the death penalty statutes struck down in *Furman* appeared easy to correct: replace the unitary trial with a bifurcated trial, at which guilt and sentence would be decided in two separate proceedings, and provide the sentencing jurors with standards (statutorily listed aggravating and mitigating circumstances, for example) to guide their consideration of whether a particular defendant has lost the moral entitlement to live.

The *Furman* holding, which resulted in vacated death sentences for all 629 persons on death rows nationally at the time of the decision, was handed down in a short per curiam opinion that stated, without elaboration, "The imposition and carrying out of the death penalty in [the cases before the Court] constitutes cruel and unusual punishment in violation of the Eighth and Fourteenth Amendments." Each of the nine justices wrote his own separate opinion, and no justice in the five-person majority joined any other.

In a 1983 law review article, Robert Weisberg has written that *Furman* "is not so much a case as a badly orchestrated opera, with nine characters taking turns to offer their own arias." However, "in the manner of literary criticism, one can extract unifying 'themes' in the *Furman* opinions." The individual opinions suggest that the central concern of the three crucial justices was that the statutes at issue in *Furman* lacked sentencing standards. Justice Douglas wrote, "We deal with a system of law and justice that leaves to the uncontrolled discretion of judges or juries the determination whether defendants committing these crimes should die or be imprisoned." Given this absence of guidance, it is not surprising that the penalty is applied "selectively to minorities whose numbers are few, who are outcasts of society, and who are unpopular, but whom society is willing to see suffer though it would not countenance general application of the same penalty across the board." Justice Stewart also stressed the randomness of the penalty: "These death sentences are cruel and unusual in the same way that being struck by lightning is cruel and unusual. For, of all the people convicted of rapes and murders in 1967 and 1968, many just as reprehensible as these, these petitioners are among a capriciously selected random handful upon whom the sentence of death has in fact been imposed." Justice White reached the same conclusion based on his experience as a justice. Because Justices Brennan and Marshall would have declared the death penalty unconstitutional per se, the holding of the case must be found in the Douglas/Stewart/White opinions. The Court has in subsequent opinions noted that "a fair statement of the consensus expressed by the Court in *Furman* is that where discretion is afforded a sentencing body on a matter so grave as the determination of whether a human life should be taken or spared, that discretion must be suitably directed and limited so as to minimize the risk of wholly arbitrary and capricious action."

The *Furman* decision struck down ninety-eight death sentences in Florida; all of those sentences were commuted to life imprisonment. Ninety-seven of those ninety-eight were off death row for good. The lone exception was Bennie Demps, whose case I discuss in chapter 11.

1972–76: Modern Times

Many lawmakers around the nation revisited the capital punishment issue extensively during the months preceding the 1972 *Furman* decision. Florida led the way; indeed, Florida's efforts to rehabilitate its capital punishment statutes predated the decision in *Furman*. At the time, the crimes punishable by death in Florida were premeditated murder, certain felony murders, bombing or machine-gunning in public places, homicide caused by a destructive device, rape of a female of the age of ten years or more, "carnal knowledge and abuse" of a female child under the age of ten years, and kidnaping for ransom. During February 1972, Governor Reubin Askew issued an executive order that stayed the execution of any death sentence until July 1, 1972, providing time for the resolution of pending litigation and for legislative consideration of the entire capital punishment question. The governor noted in the order that he had unsuccessfully asked the 1972 Florida legislature to declare a moratorium on further executions and to authorize the appointment of a commission to examine the entire capital punishment system in Florida.

The following month, perhaps anticipating the U.S. Supreme Court's imminent *Furman v. Georgia* decision, the Florida legislature revised the state's capital punishment statute. The amendment, which was to become effective on October 1, 1972, had two significant aspects. First, it provided that if capital punishment were held unconstitutional, then all persons previously sentenced to death would be required to be resentenced to life imprisonment with no eligibility for parole. Second, the amendment established a bifurcated trial system in which a defendant convicted of a capital crime was given a separate sentencing trial to determine whether the punishment would be death or life imprisonment. This provision was never used, because *Furman* intervened between the statute's passage and its effective date, and because the Florida Supreme Court later ruled that *Furman* eliminated capital punishment for all extant felonies in Florida.

Three months after passage of the statutory amendment, the U.S. Supreme Court decided *Furman v. Georgia*. As a result, all of the ninety-eight people then on death row in Florida had their sentences commuted to life imprisonment. Seventy-three of them had been sentenced to death for murder, and twenty-five had received death sentences for rape.

On July 17, 1972—eighteen days after *Furman* was decided by the

U.S. Supreme Court—the Florida Supreme Court held that *Furman* had eliminated capital punishment and capital felonies from Florida law until new legislation might revive them, and that, until that happened, persons thereafter convicted of "capital" offenses were to be punished by life imprisonment. Two weeks later, the U.S. Court of Appeals for the Fifth Circuit agreed that *Furman* invalidated Florida's death penalty. Two months later, the Florida Supreme Court resolved any lingering question of the status of Florida's death row inmates in the wake of *Furman*. *Anderson v. State* involved forty prisoners whose direct appeals were still pending before the Florida Supreme Court. The *Anderson* court resentenced the forty prisoners to life imprisonment, with the possibility of parole remaining open. Three weeks later, the court, as a matter of equal protection, provided the same resentencing for those inmates who at the time did not have appeals pending.

Only five months after the *Furman* decision, the Florida legislature met in special session to consider a new capital punishment statute. The state Senate passed a bill at the special session, by a vote of thirty-nine to one, that required the trial judge to impose a life sentence if the jury refused to recommend a death sentence. However, if the jury recommended death, the trial judge had to agree before the sentence could be imposed. The state's House of Representatives passed a bill at the special session that gave sentencing responsibility to a three-judge panel. Faced with this discrepancy, the House and the Senate compromised and produced a capital punishment statute that created a bifurcated sentencing procedure of the type first recommended by a special commission in 1965.

The Florida legislature passed the new Capital Punishment Act on December 1, 1972, and when the governor signed the measure into law a week later, Florida became the first state in the country to reinstate the death penalty after *Furman*. All of the stories told in this book involve death sentences imposed under this new statute.

Florida's post-*Furman* statute attempts to guide the courts' capital punishment decisions by establishing a procedure to be followed in determining what penalty should be imposed upon a conviction for first-degree murder. The statute provides that the court shall conduct a separate sentencing proceeding before the jury, unless the defendant waives his or her right to this proceeding. Many trial procedures have been imported into this penalty phase. The statute provides that evidence probative of sentence may be presented "regardless of its admissibility under the exclusionary rules of evidence, provided the defendant is accorded a fair opportunity to rebut any hearsay statements."

The statute also enumerates aggravating and mitigating circumstances to guide the jury in its deliberations. The jury then renders an "advisory sentence to the court." The statutory language is clear that the jury's recommendation is not binding: "Notwithstanding the recommendation of a majority of the jury, the court after weighing the aggravating and mitigating circumstances" enters a sentence of life or death. If the sentence is death, or if the judge imposes a life sentence despite the jury's recommendation of death, the court must set forth in writing its findings as to the aggravating and mitigating circumstances. Death sentences are subject to automatic review by the Florida Supreme Court.

The Florida capital punishment scheme enacted in 1972 has survived to the present day at least in part because it survived the initial legal challenges to its constitutionality. On July 16, 1973, the Florida Supreme Court upheld the constitutionality of the new capital punishment statute by a vote of seven to two. The court read *Furman* as allowing some degree of discretion in the capital sentencing process and concluded that the discretion allowed in the Florida statute is sufficiently reasonable and controlled to withstand constitutional scrutiny. Three years later, on July 2, 1976, the U.S. Supreme Court agreed, holding that the Florida capital sentencing statute complies with the guidelines of *Furman* and does not violate the Eighth Amendment. With the major legal obstacles removed, it seemed that Florida was once again free to execute prisoners convicted of capital homicides. But because there were still a few constitutional bugs in the system, executions have occurred in fits and starts in the many years since 1976.

Postmodern Times: Capital Punishment Today

Capital punishment today is a wasteland of broken promises and shattered dreams. The U.S. Supreme Court has largely abdicated to the states the duty to operate the legal machinery of death in a fair and constitutional manner. At the same time, the Court and Congress have gutted habeas corpus and erected a forest of procedural barriers to federal consideration of constitutional claims raised by state death row prisoners. Thus litigating for life itself has devolved into a lethal game of "gotcha." The result, as Robert Weisberg predicted nearly twenty years ago, is a wholesale "deregulation" of death as a punishment.

Today, every year is a banner year for executions. In 1999, for instance, there were ninety-two executions in the United States, up thirty from the year before, and the most since 1952. More people live on America's death rows today than at any other time in our history—more than thirty-six hundred people. Thirty-eight states and the federal government authorize executions.

Since the U.S. Supreme Court put its constitutional seal of approval on capital punishment in 1976, 777 men and women have been executed as of this writing. The South leads the nation both in numbers on death row and numbers of people executed. The three states with the highest execution rates—Texas (245), Virginia (82), and Florida (51)—are all in the South. Texas sets the standard, both in terms of numbers of executions and in terms of downright creepiness. Because of the Bush brothers (the present governor of Florida and the former governor of Texas, now president of the United States), there is a connection between capital punishment in Texas and Florida. On four consecutive nights in May 1997, Texas executed four men, one per night. This was a modern record. The press covered the executions as if reporting the results of a ball game. "At this rate," a *Washington Post* reporter wrote, "Texas will easily shatter its own record of 19 executions set in 1995." Three weeks later it did. "Texas Puts 2 to Death, Tying Record" was the June 3, 1997, headline on a story in the *New York Times,* a story buried on page A24. The executions of Dorsey Johnson-Bey and Davis Losada were the third and fourth in Texas that week. They marked the first double execution in the state since January 1997, and the third multiple execution in the nation since executions resumed in 1977. Texas had four more executions scheduled for that week, and at least eleven planned for that month.

But even by Texas standards, the December 8, 1999, execution of a man who required oxygen and continuous medical care to live (following a drug overdose) was notable in its weirdness. Two days prior to his scheduled execution, Martin Long, forty-six years old, was found unconscious in his cell by death row guards. According to news reports, Long had hoarded and then "ingested an overdose of anti-psychotic drugs." He was placed on life support.

On the day before his scheduled execution by lethal injection—a state-mandated drug overdose, in a manner of speaking—Long was taken off the respirator that had supported his breathing and upgraded from critical to serious condition. He remained in intensive care, or, actually, he would have remained in intensive care for another two or three days, were it not for his scheduled execution.

According to one newspaper account, Long's doctor in Galveston was asked by the state "to sign an affidavit saying Mr. Long could be safely transported to Huntsville [for execution], a request he said he refused." However, the doctor "did sign an affidavit stating that Long's health had improved, that he suffered no seizures, and was responding to questions—but that transporting him could be risky without appropriate medical care." So, Long was transported—on oxygen and with continuous medical care—by airplane from Galveston to Houston, a twenty-five-minute trip. He was then executed. Long's case wasn't even the first time such an execution had been carried out in recent years; something similar occurred in Oklahoma in 1995.

The Long case had no impact on the pace of executions inside or outside Texas. Another Texas execution was scheduled the next night, and two more for the next week. On the night Long was executed in Texas, convicts were executed in Oklahoma and Indiana. All in all, 1999 was a busy year for the executioner.

Twelve days into the twenty-first century, Texas carried out its two hundredth execution since capital punishment resumed in that state in 1982. In the year 2000 Texas set a national record for executions in a single year. Garry Dean Miller, who was executed on December 4, 2000, was the thirty-eighth person put to death by the Lone Star State that year, breaking the record of thirty-seven set by Texas in 1997.

In 2001, Texas lost its edge. Oklahoma executed eighteen people in 2001, one more than Texas. However as Associated Press reporter Michael Graczk noted in the December 28, 2001, edition of the *Dallas Morning News,* "Texas will likely execute more people in 2002 than any other state, again becoming the nation's most active death penalty state."

2

Death Clerk

I'm going to hell for my role in these capital cases.

—My diary, near the end of my clerkship with Judge Vance

After a poor showing on the LSAT, I wasn't able to get into my first few choices of law schools, and I ended up going to Case Western Reserve Law School in Cleveland, Ohio. As it turned out, I loved it there, but the tuition was $8,500 per year. I knew that I couldn't accumulate that sort of debt load and still practice the kind of public interest law I wanted to practice upon graduation, so I worked like a demon during my first year at Case, hoping to transfer to the University of Virginia in Charlottesville, where, because of my status as a Virginia resident, tuition would be $1,500 per year. I was fourth in my class at the end of that year at Case, wrote onto the *Case Western Law Review,* and then graded on. I then applied to and was accepted by UVA, where I wrote onto the *Virginia Law Review.*

I didn't much like law school at UVA, except for my work as an articles editor for the *Virginia Law Review*. I was told that I was only the second write-on transfer student to serve at that post, and my way had been paved by the first, Gary Francione, a pioneer then and now. Mostly, I found law school at UVA to be elitist and disorienting. I went to law school to become Clarence Darrow, and I came out not having a clue about what I wanted to do with my law degree. I did a summer clerkship with a large urban firm, and I thought: I can do this, and the money is swell. I graduated law school with an offer from the Wall Street superfirm of Cravath, Swaine & Moore. That's what UVA graduates were expected to do. But first I would clerk for Eleventh Circuit Judge Robert S. Vance in Birmingham, Alabama. My clerkship would bring me into close contact—up close and personal—with capital punishment.

A year before I clerked on the Eleventh Circuit, the court did not exist. In 1981, the U.S. Congress divided the Fifth Circuit into the Fifth Circuit and the Eleventh Circuit. The old Fifth Circuit was the legendary court that implemented *Brown v. Board of Education* and desegregated the South in the 1960s. The new Eleventh Circuit comprised the states of Florida, Alabama, and Georgia. Most cases that come before the Eleventh Circuit Court are heard by panels of three judges chosen at random from among the twelve who serve on the court. The full (en banc) court hears cases only rarely.

Judge Vance was an old warrior from the Alabama racial politics of the 1960s; he was George Wallace's principal political nemesis in the Alabama Democratic Party. I had mixed feelings about living for a year in Birmingham, the scene of so much violence against the activists of the civil rights movement. The memories of those confrontations were everywhere in the city. I ate lunch in Kelly Ingram Park near where Bull Connor's police dogs and firehoses had been unleashed against the peaceful desegregation demonstrators.

Judge Vance hated capital punishment, and while he was interviewing me for the clerkship, he spoke proudly of his ruling that had cleared Alabama's death row. As an intermediate appellate court judge, however, he was bound by the U.S. Supreme Court's decisions upholding the constitutionality of death as a punishment. I don't recall which of us originated the term, but in conversation Judge Vance and I sometimes referred tongue in cheek to the Eleventh Circuit as the "death court." The characterization fit, with the qualification that the Eleventh Circuit is now one of a growing number of death courts. Other federal circuits have become or are about to become death courts as well. These circuits are now experiencing what the Eleventh Circuit first encountered in the 1980s.

Two of the three states that make up the Eleventh Circuit, Florida and Georgia, remain at the leading edge of capital punishment and its resultant constitutional challenges. Georgia cases provided the principal vehicles for testing the constitutionality of the death penalty, facially and as applied systemically: *Furman v. Georgia* in 1972, *Gregg v. Georgia* in 1976, and *McCleskey v. Kemp* in 1987. Florida was the first state to enact a "modern" capital punishment statute, and it led the nation in the implementation of the death penalty in the modern era. Equally telling is the raw enthusiasm with which many Floridians, at least many Florida politicians, appear to embrace capital punishment.

Judge Vance was on the front lines of capital punishment in the modern era. By my count, his name appears as author of twenty-five published capital habeas opinions. He voted to grant interim or permanent relief (such as retrials, resentencings, evidentiary hearings, or stays of execution) in eleven of those cases and to deny relief in fourteen. Vance also voted in eighty-one capital habeas cases in which he did not write opinions, voting to grant some form of relief in thirty-four cases and voting to deny relief in forty-seven cases.

Partly by chance and partly by design, I served as Judge Vance's death clerk. On the first day of my clerkship, the judge called me and his two other clerks into his office. He pointed to three stacks of files, and said, "I need one of you to be responsible for the civil rights cases, another for the death cases, and the third for the business cases. Pick a pile." I wasn't quick enough to snare the civil rights cases, and I sure didn't want the business cases. So I picked the capital pile, and that was that.

It soon became clear that my tender sense of fairness was more easily offended than was Judge Vance's; to be more precise, I found at least one (and usually more than one) reason that every death sentence that came before the court was "unfair" and thus, in my naive view, unconstitutional. Sometimes the judge agreed; usually he did not, and we spent long afternoons deconstructing concepts such as "fundamental unfairness," as opposed to garden-variety unfairness, and error of federal constitutional magnitude, as opposed to prosaic error that was benignly harmless. The U.S. Constitution does not require a perfect trial, the judge told me more than once; it requires only a fundamentally fair one, or at least one that is not fundamentally *un*fair. Capital habeas cases consumed approximately half of my clerkship workload, but my time as Vance's death clerk became a defining experience of my professional life.

Judge Vance and I disagreed, sometimes loudly, on the scope of his power to supervise the capital punishment systems of Georgia, Florida, and Alabama, as well as on his ability to follow his own sense of justice in deciding these cases. His views were textured, grounded in his experience. I opposed capital punishment in the abstract before my clerkship, but the truth is that I had never before thought much about it. My time with Judge Vance forced me to think about and worry about the death penalty. That led to my focusing on capital postconviction in my work as a litigator and now as an academic, as evidenced by my postclerkship career projectory.

When my clerkship began, I was certain (as only a newly minted and zealous recent law school graduate can be) where Judge Vance was ambivalent. I saw black and white where he saw neither. As I grow older, I appreciate and cherish the lessons Judge Vance taught me about seeing nuances and shades of gray.

Looking back at it now, I cringe at how much of a pest I must have been to Judge Vance. I didn't understand why he didn't push the envelope more in death cases. It certainly wasn't for lack of personal courage—he had literally put his life on the line when he fought racism during the George Wallace era in Alabama. And death cases always seemed to me to be civil rights cases. I knew Vance loathed capital punishment, and I knew that he agonized over these cases. Why, then, didn't he do more? The answer is that he tried to do a lot, but whenever he did, he was resoundingly reversed by the Supreme Court. In Vance's first foray into the thicket of capital punishment, he tried to clear Alabama's death row in one fell swoop. He wrote an opinion for the court invalidating the Alabama death sentence of John Louis Evans. That opinion, had it withstood review in the U.S. Supreme Court (which it did not), would have invalidated virtually every extant death sentence in the state.

Although it can never be proved, I am convinced that if any single case explains Judge Vance's capital habeas jurisprudence, it is *Evans v. Britton*. John Louis Evans III was an Alabama death row inmate who was challenging the facial constitutionality of Alabama's 1975 modern capital statute. Judge Vance was an Alabamian, born and bred, and *Evans v. Britton* was one of his first capital cases. His opinion in *Evans v. Britton* stood for the unremarkable proposition that a citizen cannot, consistent with the U.S. Constitution, be convicted and condemned pursuant to an unconstitutional statute—in that case Alabama's 1975 capital statute. The opinion's implications reached beyond Evans's own case. Had the court's opinion remained in force, all Alabama death row inmates condemned pursuant to the 1975 statute would have been entitled to retrials as to guilt/innocence as well as to sentence.

The lower court's decision in *Evans v. Britton* was reversed by the Supreme Court, however. In that reversal, I believe, resides an important key to explaining Judge Vance's subsequent capital habeas jurisprudence. The only hard evidence of *Evans*'s influence on Vance is that he never again cast his vote in favor of recognizing constitutional issues that would grant relief to classes of death row inmates.

The core basis of my conviction that the *Evans* decision was important to Judge Vance is more impressionistic. As mentioned above, I interviewed with Vance for a clerkship position before the Supreme Court reversed *Evans*. He clearly was proud of his involvement in the case, and he was relatively (and comfortably) expansive about his role in reviewing capital cases. I began working for Vance shortly after *Evans* was reversed, and he then and thereafter spoke the language of judicial restraint. That change in rhetorical stance was subtly reflected in his post-*Evans* capital opinions. *Evans* was the fulcrum of the change.

Evans was convicted of capital murder pursuant to a statute that precluded the jury from considering lesser included offenses in capital cases. The statute gave juries only the option of convicting defendants of capital offenses or acquitting them. Subsequent to Evans's trial, but before his case reached the federal court of appeals, the U.S. Supreme Court in *Beck v. Alabama* found Alabama's capital statute unconstitutional. The Court in *Beck* held that the sentence of death could not be imposed, consistent with the Constitution, unless the jury was permitted to consider a lesser included noncapital offense, at least when the evidence would have supported a verdict of less than capital murder. In *Beck* the state conceded that, on the evidence presented in Beck's case, but for the preclusion clause Beck would have been entitled to an instruction on the lesser included noncapital offense of felony murder. Although in some cases defendants might profit from the preclusion clause, the Court reasoned that "*in every case* [it] introduce[s] a level of uncertainty and unreliability into the fact-finding process that cannot be tolerated in a capital case."

Evans was convicted and condemned under the statute subsequently held unconstitutional in *Beck*. Alabama argued, in essence, that any constitutional error was harmless in Evans's case. The state contended that Evans adduced no evidence at trial that would have required instruction on a lesser offense even if such instruction were not prohibited. Against his trial attorney's advice, Evans testified on his own behalf at trial. He told the jury that he had shot the victim. He further informed the jurors that he had "no intention whatsoever of ever reforming in any way," and that he would return to a life of crime if released from prison. Release from confinement in the near future was unlikely, given that Evans was wanted for a number of crimes in different states as a result of an armed robbery spree. Finally, Evans told the jurors: "I would rather die by electrocution than spend the rest of my life in the penitentiary. So, I'm asking very sincerely that you come back with a positive [death] verdict for the state." The jury obliged.

The opinion of Judge Vance's court, rejecting the state's harmless error arguments, was a study in brevity, common sense, and sensitivity to the practical realities of lawyering and trial tactics. The court found that it could not conclude that Evans's trial pursuant to Alabama's unconstitutional capital statute was harmless beyond a reasonable doubt, reasoning that "the peculiar nature of the offensive statute would infect virtually every aspect of any capital defendant's trial from beginning to end." Putting itself in the shoes of Evans's trial lawyer, the court recognized that "every decision concerning trial strategy, the selection of evidence to use and its presentation, the argument of counsel, objections, requests for charges, all were inevitably influenced by the brooding omnipresence of the unconstitutional edict—Evans must either be sentenced by the jury to die . . . [or be] set free." As to the state's contention that harm to Evans was sheer speculation because he did not undertake to prove a lesser offense, the court countered that "it offends the most fundamental notions of fairness for the state to tell Evans that there is no lesser offense and then later urge that his death sentence should be upheld because he failed to present evidence which would prove a lesser included offense." The court declined to "speculate as to whether if tried under a constitutional statute Evans will adopt some different strategy or whether he can present evidence of some less serious offense." The court concluded that Evans was entitled to a retrial on the issue of guilt or innocence as well as penalty.

The Supreme Court reversed, unanimously, as to Judge Vance's determination that Evans's conviction, as opposed to his sentence, could not stand. Accepting the state's harmless error argument that the Alabama statute's preclusion clause did not prejudice Evans in any demonstrable way, the Court held that Evans was not entitled to a retrial because his own evidence negated the possibility that a lesser included offense instruction might have been warranted. The Supreme Court concluded that Judge Vance misread *Beck v. Alabama,* which, according to the *Evans* Court, held that due process requires that a lesser included offense instruction be given only when the evidence warrants such an instruction. Because in Evans's case "the evidence not only supported the claim that [Evans] intended to kill the victim, but affirmatively negated any claim that he did not intend to kill the victim," Evans was not entitled to a lesser included offense instruction.

The Court emphasized that Evans was challenging only the facial validity of Alabama's capital statute, stressing—unfairly, given the state of the record and the procedural posture of the case—that Evans "did not allege that he had been prejudiced by the Alabama death penalty statute's preclusion clause, but instead argued that the statute was unconstitutional on its face and that his conviction therefore must be set aside." The Court noted that Evans "suggest[ed] no plausible claim which he might conceivably have made, had there been no preclusion clause, that is not contradicted by his own testimony at trial." In a footnote to its opinion, the Court observed, "In another case with different facts, a defendant might make a plausible claim that he would have employed different trial tactics—for example, that he would have introduced certain evidence or requested certain jury instructions—but for the preclusion clause." The Court made clear, however, that such a claim was not available in *Evans:* "That is not this case, since the defendant here confessed that he shot the victim and then pleaded guilty to capital murder."

Judge Vance remained involved in the *Evans* case until its end. Alabama scheduled Evans's execution for April 22, 1983, at 12:01 A.M. central standard time. Two and a half hours before the scheduled execution, District Judge Cox (then of the Southern District of Alabama) temporarily stayed the execution. At 12:25 A.M. on April 22, an Eleventh Circuit panel, which included Vance, refused to vacate the temporary stay. The state then brought its arguments to the U.S. Supreme Court, which dissolved the stay. Chief Justice Warren Burger complained that "this case falls within a familiar pattern of literal 'eleventh hour' efforts to frustrate judicial decrees after careful and painstaking judicial consideration over a period of years."

The Supreme Court's opinions in *Evans* were notable for their aggrieved tone. The justices were unhappy with federal trial judge Cox for issuing the stay and with Evans's lawyers for seeking it in the first place. Anthony Amsterdam has accurately pointed out that the Supreme Court was saying that the stay was "ignorantly entered by a [trial] judge selected for his ignorance and made a tool and fool by some designing lawyer who had lain in ambush for the opportunity." The Court ignored the Eleventh Circuit altogether. As Amsterdam notes, the Court refused to "face up to the awkward fact that the decision which it is reviewing and undoing is *not* the [trial] court's decision to issue the stay but the [Eleventh Circuit] Court of Appeals' decision that the stay was proper, given the [trial] court's discretion. If the [trial] court receives at least the Court's condescending pity as a new camper, the court of appeals is excommunicated entirely from the camp of players to be considered."

The Supreme Court entered its final order in the case, dissolving the stay, at 7:01 P.M. on April 22, and Evans was pronounced dead at 8:44 P.M. According to Evans's lawyer, who witnessed the execution, the electric chair malfunctioned and, in effect, Evans was burned to death.

The above narrative of Evans's final litigation fails to capture the frenetic energy of the events as I experienced them. Here is an excerpt from my diary for Thursday, April 21, 1983:

> U.S. Supreme court, on appeal from state court, denies *Evans* stay; Judge Vance tells me at 5:15 p.m. about it: says the next step for him is federal district trial court in Mobile, Alabama. Came into office at 10:20 p.m.: heard on Ann's radio that *Evans* got a stay from federal trial Judge Cox from Mobile at 9:30; the State of Alabama is in Atlanta, trying to dissolve Judge Cox's stay. 10:37: Eleventh Circuit is deciding the issue and will rule tonight. 10:39: a judge sounding like Eleventh Circuit Judge Lanier Anderson called Judge Vance at the office and I said he's at home: Judge Anderson said, "You know this *Evans* case is in the Eleventh Circuit?" 11:50, at home: "Eleventh Circuit upheld Judge Cox's stay."

On Friday, April 22, I wrote:

> 8:00 a.m.: Radio says Alabama "frantically" petitioning the U.S. Supreme Court to dissolve the *Evans* stay; Judge Vance, Roney and Anderson were the emergency Eleventh Circuit panel last night: they see it as the abuse of the *habeas* writ case; *Evans* law-

yers raised two issues: *Lockett* and *Profitt* "jury instruction on endangering many people"; federal trial Judge Cox in Mobile, Alabama did not understand it: they had conference call last night, with the parties on Judge Cox's phone: it was Anderson that called last night; Judge Cox just doesn't understand the legal issues and needed more time–*that's* why they upheld the stay— not to get to the merits of any of *Evans* constitutional claims; Judge Vance thinks *Evans* lawyers waited too late to go into court: "good chance" panel will dissolve it; his opinion on Tuesday was "sweeping"; read the entire record. 8:30 a.m.: Birmingham newspaper says *Evans* was executed at 8:30; I called the newspaper: they said it's on TV and Public Radio; Supreme Court denied the stay at 7:30; nothing on commercial radio yet. 8:47; radio interrupts baseball game: "executed 25 minutes ago"; eyewitnesses report that they had to electrocute him twice before they killed him. 9:30 a.m.: They did it *three* times; the station alternates between baseball and news of *Evans* execution.

A perceptive intermediate court judge digesting the Supreme Court's opinions in *Evans* might have drawn two lessons. First, classwide claims brought by death row inmates ought to be viewed with suspicion. Second, and similarly, federal courts ought to be reluctant to grant habeas relief that would result in retrials as opposed to resentencings. Whether these were the lessons that Judge Vance gleaned we cannot know, but what we do know is that he never again cast a vote that would have had the effect of removing a large class of people from death row in a single stroke. Vance was a law-abiding judge, and he chose his battles well. This was not a battle with the Supreme Court he could win.

On my first day of work for Judge Vance, I was assigned the task of drafting an opinion affirming the denial of resentencing relief in the case of Ivon Ray Stanley, a mentally retarded African American man from rural Georgia who followed along while Joseph Thomas committed the murder for which both men were sentenced to die in Georgia's electric chair. Stanley and Thomas had robbed, beaten, and buried alive an insurance agent named Clifford Floyd. I don't think Thomas or Stanley intended Floyd's death to be as horrible as it was; they were incompetent killers, not torturers. Stanley's mental retardation, and the fact that he was following Thomas's lead, suggested to me that Thomas was by far the more culpable of the two men. However, because Floyd's death occurred during the course of the felony of robbery, the felony murder doctrine made both men equally guilty of capital murder.

In his federal habeas corpus case, Stanley's counsel argued that the defense lawyer at trial had been ineffective in failing to investigate mitigating evidence. This was an uphill battle, because some mitigating evidence did trickle in before the jury. First, there was evidence that Stanley had at least a learning disability; he was a slow learner, and he had been placed in an educable mentally retarded class in school. A state sheriff read into the record the results of a psychological evaluation conducted on Stanley when he was fourteen years old. That evaluation concluded that Stanley had an IQ of 62 (counsel had previously informed the jury that "imbecile" was defined as a person with an IQ of zero to 65); his test scores "suggest[ed] a history of culture deprivation. . . . The test results and observation indicated he was an educatable mentally retarded youngster"; and it was "therefore recommended that he be placed in the exceptional child class designed for educatably mentally retarded youngsters as soon as possible to avoid any further experience that he has undoubtedly incurred throughout his school history." Finally, during the penalty phase of the trial, Stanley's mother read into evidence a letter he had written to her:

> It says, "Dear Mother, I just sending a letter to let you know I am going to hope," I think it is—I don't know whether it is—it is R-O-O-K, room that is room, July 6, 1976. "Hay Mother, I having" let me see. "Hay Momma, I have seen the lawyer, mother, and he say this carries the chair and, mother, I don't know—don't know, what to go to—what now, I don't know what to do now about it, Momma. I didn't murder no one and rob no one and kidnap no one. To mother, and mother, I not lying to you. God knows it, but no one believes me, Momma. I don't know what to do. I don't know, I want—want to go to no chair for nothing I didn't do. Tell me what to do, say, hay Momma, are you coming to see me when I go, Momma, hay, Momma, you' have told me, told us to be good and you will, we won't have to go to jail. I been good," I think way, he got this W.A.Y., it say, "Momma." It is the same thing he got down there. W.A.Y.
>
> No, it says, "Momma, don't worry. I sorry, Momma. I didn't

do it, believe me, and Mary, and Cat, you good to Momma and Senator, too, be a sweet baby for me, Cat, Sheriff, pray for me, I didn't do it because no one believes me, Momma."

"I want to come home and, Momma, he told them I robbed him and I—won't make them believe it. Id didn't do it. Tell me what to do."

"Hay, tell T.C. to come and I go to Court and tell him I say hay and come, too."

So some mitigating evidence came in at trial, but that was only a small fraction of what was available had Stanley's trial attorney bothered to look. Postconviction counsel produced the testimony of five members of the Stanley family and a family friend to the effect that if called they would have testified that he had never been in trouble, was obedient, helpful, and cooperative, and was not violent. His mother stated that he had difficulty in school and indicated that he was a slow learner. Stanley himself testified at the habeas hearing on his own behalf. He stated that his lawyer had once asked him about people who could testify about his character, that he had given the lawyer names of some people, but it never came up again. He also introduced into evidence a letter from the pastor of his church that noted his good character, as well as a high school report that indicated that his character was thought to be excellent in every respect.

The oral argument in *Stanley* was held shortly before I started working for Judge Vance, but I listened to the audiotape about two dozen times while I was drafting Vance's *Stanley* opinion. ("Drafting" is exactly what it was; the judge wrote his own opinions, and our job as law clerks was to translate his analysis into drafts, which he then virtually rewrote; that's why his opinions had such similar analytic and writing styles down through the years.) The *Stanley* oral argument tapes were painful to listen to because Stanley's habeas lawyer's palpable condescension toward these benighted judges from the Bad Old South obscured Stanley's quite powerful challenges to the legality of his death sentence. Stanley's trial *was* atrociously unfair.

The judge instructed me to draft opinions in *Stanley* and *Thomas*. The court intended to uphold Stanley's death sentence and to send Thomas's case back down to the federal trial court for an evidentiary hearing. Why was Thomas, the really bad actor in the Thomas/Stanley killing, sent back for an evidentiary hearing in the district court while Stanley, the retarded follower, was not? Part of the answer is simply that Thomas had a better habeas lawyer. But the *legal* difference between Thomas's and Stanley's cases in the Eleventh Circuit was a technicality of habeas: Stanley had already received an evidentiary hearing in Georgia *state* court, on his ineffective assistance claim, and Thomas had not. Never mind that the "hearing" in *Stanley* was presided over by a state judge whose boredom with the hearing shone through even in a cold appellate record. The fact was that Stanley had received some sort of hearing in state court, and Thomas hadn't. That lethal procedural technicality, in the end, was what decided that Ivon Ray Stanley would die and Joseph Thomas would live.

It ended up taking me three months to draft the opinion in *Stanley*. I highlighted the place in the *Stanley* record where his mother read the letter written by her son. I tried to recast *Stanley* as a civil rights case, given that Stanley was an African American. Before President Carter appointed Robert Vance to the federal court in 1977, he had been leader of the non–George Wallace wing of the Alabama Democratic Party and the architect of the "Freedom Democrat" challenge at the 1964 Democratic National Convention. During my year as Judge Vance's clerk, my sanctimoniousness about *Stanley* could not have made his life easier. He always listened patiently to my arguments, and he didn't fire me even when I once stormed out of his office over the case.

The *Stanley* opinion I was drafting would be horrible for Ivon Ray Stanley and for many other death row prisoners raising similar claims. The opinion I was drafting for Thomas, Stanley's codefendant, was just the opposite. Not only would it be good for Thomas himself, but it would make "good law" for other condemned prisoners. That's what I told myself, anyway: the bad I was doing in *Stanley* was balanced by the good I was doing in *Thomas*. The *Thomas* precedent would win stays of execution for many prisoners litigating for their lives.

My argument for the invalidation of Stanley's death sentence focused on an issue called HAC. Modern capital statutes include laundry lists of "aggravating circumstances"; a sentencer must find at least one aggravating circumstance to exist in a case before a death sentence may be imposed. HAC is shorthand for the "heinous, atrocious, or cruel" aggravating circumstance mentioned in virtually all capital statutes. In Florida, that circumstance has been found in 80 percent of death cases. Thus invalidation of the HAC circumstance would affect many capital cases.

In 1982, when I was clerking for Judge Vance and working on the *Stanley* opinion, the stakes were high. The Supreme Court was considering a case, *Zant v. Stephens*, that presented the question of whether a capital jury's finding of an invalid aggravating circumstance rendered the death sentence invalid. Thus, *if* the omnipresent HAC was unconstitutional, and *if* the Court were to hold in *Zant v. Stephens* that an invalid aggravating circumstance rendered the death sentence invalid, large numbers of death sentences would be subject to reversal.

I argued hard with Judge Vance about the HAC issue in the *Stanley* case. He responded that he would not "play God." I replied with a memo:

To: Judge Vance

From: Michael Mello

Re: On Playing God

Our conversation yesterday gave me much to think about. These are my reactions.

This may surprise you, but, at least in my present position, I share your hesitancy about adding more levels of intricacy to the already arcane game of death penalty litigation. When I am practicing law, I will use the game for all its worth, but I am now acutely aware that I am *not* practicing law. I would not have pushed this issue as hard as I have if I didn't genuinely believe in its overriding importance.

The [HAC] issue, it seems to me, goes to the core of the law of death. So long as [HAC] remains as vague as written, there is a gigantic loophole in the entire edifice erected by the courts to protect those charged with offenses carrying the ultimate penalty. And I'm not talking about arbitrariness as an abstract principle, as an artificial line used by the courts to give an empty appearance of consistency. The evil of arbitrariness is that it gives the sentence the *legal* authority to give play to its racial or class prejudices. The problem with [HAC] is the problem with the statutes condemned in *Furman*: when the *law* gives the jury unlimited discretion, it is predictable that that discretion will be exercised against groups that juries don't like anyway: the poor and racial minorities.

I have given much thought to why the penalty so bothers *me*, on an abstract, gut level. It is in part because of this race and class element. Death cases are really civil rights cases. In a sense, given the reality of who lands on death row and who doesn't, capital cases are the ultimate in civil rights litigation. It is the ultimate form of discrimination.

You may be right that juries ignore the law anyway. But in this case the jury instruction *does*, I firmly believe, make a difference. Are you willing to say that a reasonable juror could not have been misled by this instruction? This jury might not have sentenced to death had it known that it must find serious physical abuse to do so. The presence of *mental* torture, combined with the evidence of *physical* torture, suggests that the jury might very well have been misled into assuming that psychological torture is enough.

Finally, I don't see this opinion as playing God and I can't see that your colleagues would either. *Most* of the recent death cases have come out while certain dispositive issues were pending in higher courts.

The death row prisoner lost *Zant v. Stephens* in the U.S. Supreme Court in 1983. Still, the challenges to HAC continued on a case-by-case basis. Beginning in 1988, the Court eventually took a dim view of HAC's legality. By then, however, Ivon Ray Stanley had been dead for years.

Judge Vance was determined that every death row prisoner, no matter how awful his crime, would receive his day in federal court. No case better illustrates his approach to capital cases than Ted Bundy's. This is so in part due to who Vance was and in part due to who Bundy was. I believe that Vance considered the existing habeas statute to be in need of legislative reform so as to limit state prisoners' access to federal court. Until Congress acted to "reform" the habeas statute, however, Vance was unwilling to do so by judicial fiat. He took habeas seriously. Thus, although it may be a bad idea as a matter of public policy, until Congress decided otherwise, state prisoners would have a statutory right to access to the federal courts—*all* prisoners, even Theodore Bundy. Virtually everyone wanted Bundy dead. But Eleventh Circuit panels, including Judge Vance, demanded that even (especially) Bundy was entitled as a U.S. citizen to his day in federal court.

Prior to his execution in January 1989, Bundy was perhaps the most universally hated death row inmate in the United States. He was despised by the public, by the media, and even (if secretly) by some death penalty abolitionists who felt uncomfortable explaining why Bundy ought not be killed.

The public and political pressures to speed along Bundy's execution were intense. Successive Florida governors used Bundy for political gain, and the state courts provided the palest illusion of postconviction due process. Had the Eleventh Circuit shirked its responsibility, few people would have noticed and fewer would have cared. However, the court stayed Bundy's execution and subsequently remanded the cases for evidentiary hearings. Judge Vance sat on the panels that took both actions, and his stridency during oral argument revealed his bedrock determination that even Bundy should receive the hearing due him in federal court.

In my book *Dead Wrong,* I argue that at the postconviction stages of litigation Bundy received for the most part the appearance rather than the reality of fair judicial process. I maintain that view. Still, of all the governmental entities that sat in judgment of Bundy (state executive, state judicial, federal judicial), the Eleventh Circuit performed its job the best by far.

There were actually two Bundy cases in Florida, proceeding on different litigation tracks. In one case, Bundy had been convicted and sentenced to death for the bludgeoning murders of two sorority women, Lisa Levy and Margaret Bowman, in the Chi Omega chapter house at Florida State University in Tallahassee. In the other case Bundy was convicted and condemned for killing twelve-year-old Kimberly Leach in Lake City. In May 1986, seventeen days after the U.S. Supreme Court denied direct review in the Chi Omega case, Florida's Governor Martinez signed a death warrant on Bundy for that case. The execution was scheduled for July 2, 1986.

The month leading up to the scheduled execution was a blur of frantic legal activity, aptly characterized by Bundy's lead (and pro bono) counsel as "litigating at the speed of light." During that period, Bundy's lawyers unsuccessfully sought postconviction relief, including a stay of the execution, from the state trial court, the Florida Supreme Court, and the federal district court. The federal trial court denied an indefinite stay without even bothering to obtain the fifteen-thousand-page state court record in the case upon which Bundy's constitutional claims were based. The record was in the trunk of the prosecutor's car during the few hours that the district court had the case under consideration. The trial court granted a twenty-four-hour stay so that Bundy could live long enough to appeal these rulings. An Eleventh Circuit panel including Judge Vance stayed the execution indefinitely, less than fifteen hours before the rescheduled execution. The court put the case on an expedited briefing and oral argument schedule.

Meanwhile, during the summer of 1986, Bundy's lawyers had filed a petition asking the U.S. Supreme Court to grant plenary review in the Kimberly Leach case. On October 14, 1986, the Court denied review. Seven days later, Governor Martinez signed a death warrant as to the Leach case, setting the execution for a month in the future. The lawyers repeated the same frenetic drill as in the Chi Omega case, seeking stays from four courts in three weeks and being denied stays by three courts (the Florida trial court, Florida Supreme Court, and federal trial court) in *one day*. Again, an Eleventh Circuit panel that included Judge Vance stayed the execution, this time less than seven hours before Bundy was to have been electrocuted. The prosecutors unsuccessfully petitioned the U.S. Supreme Court to dissolve the stay. Thus, by mid-1986 both Bundy cases were in the Eleventh Circuit, both on expedited briefing and oral argument schedules.

The oral argument in the Chi Omega case sizzled. Judge Vance dominated much of the argument. He seemed mystified that the district court could have denied habeas relief (and a stay) without making even the pretense of looking at the records of the state court proceedings, and that the prosecutors could have led the district court into such a glaring error. Vance blistered the prosecutor:

> I can't understand your behavior. . . . This case is going to be reversed and sent down there [to the district court] because of a stupid error. If you had called it to the attention of the [district] judge at the time, it could have been corrected in four days. It's wrong. It's clearly wrong, counsel. It's not arguable by an attorney of integrity.

Later in the argument, Vance moderated his frustration a bit and allowed that "maybe the court has been a little too harsh on you personally, counsel."

In 1987 the Eleventh Circuit remanded both cases to the respective federal trial courts for evidentiary hearings on the issue of Bundy's mental competence to stand trial. Again, the proceedings were to be expedited. The district judge in the Chi Omega habeas case, who was new to the federal bench (and whose error reportedly had been termed "stupid" by Judge Vance in the *Bundy* oral argument), appeared determined to proceed with extreme deliberation; events in that judge's court progressed at a snail's pace. By contrast, the trial judge in the Kimberly Leach habeas case moved at hyperspeed. He held the evidentiary hearing on Bundy's competency to stand trial issue and unceremoniously ruled from the bench against Bundy. The Leach case was appealed to the Eleventh Circuit while the Chi Omega case languished in limbo in the federal trial court.

The Eleventh Circuit again expedited briefing and oral argument in the Leach case. In mid-1988, the court affirmed the trial court's denial of habeas relief.

In December 1988, Bundy's lawyers petitioned the U.S. Supreme Court to review the decision of the Eleventh Circuit. The Court conferenced on Friday, January 13, 1989—not a good sign. At a few minutes past 10:00 A.M. on Tuesday, January 17, 1989, the Court released its order denying certiorari in the Kimberly Leach case. Within minutes, Governor Martinez signed a seven-day death warrant. This time the execution, scheduled for January 24, 1989, at 7:00 A.M., was carried out. The Supreme Court denied a stay at 10:00 P.M. the night before the execution. The vote was five to four. The Chi Omega case was subsequently dismissed as moot.

I have described the Bundy case here both because it illustrates Judge Vance's approach to capital cases and because it demonstrates how, at oral arguments, Judge Vance could be rough on lawyers. He was as hard on defense counsel as he was on the prosecutor in *Bundy*. He had no patience for lawyers he thought were "trifling with the court," as he put it. In one case, Vance said that the attorney arguing before him was "offensive to the court, unethical, a disservice to the legal profession."

After my clerkship, I orally argued only one case before Judge Vance. The case was a big one, and it was before the full (en banc) Eleventh Circuit. The other judges hammered me with questions, but Vance, bless his heart, remained silent during the oral argument (and in the end, he voted my way).

Near the end of my clerkship with Judge Vance, I applied to work for about seventy-five different capital public defender organizations. I got one interview, with the West Palm Beach, Florida, Public Defender's Office. At that interview, I was cross-examined in some depth about my role in Judge Vance's capital decisions, especially *Stanley*.

Craig Barnard, my future boss, was particularly troubled by my role in *Stanley*; he had been having lunch when the *Stanley* decision had been issued, and he'd been called out of the restaurant to hear the bad news. The entry in my diary for the day of my interview begins: "Interviewed with Craig Barnard, Richard Burr, and Richard Jorandby; talked mostly about cases I had worked on for Judge Vance, and they especially disliked the opinion I'd drafted in *Stanley*; Craig said my opinion in the *Stanley* companion case, *Thomas,* was 'wonderful': their concern was that I wouldn't be enough of an 'advocate' after my clerkship (ho, ho, ho: ask Judge Vance)."

Craig asked me how I would feel seeing my *Stanley* opinion being cited by prosecutors and courts in support of the execution of my clients. I told him I'd feel like crap, but I also told him that I knew all the ways around *Stanley*. I didn't tell my interviewers that I'd already had experience trying to navigate around the *Stanley* minefield. I'd seen drafts of Eleventh Circuit opinions that cited and relied upon *Stanley*. About one, I wrote in my diary, "The opinion relied on my *Stanley* opinion, which was quite depressing."

I would spend a good bit of my time as a capital public defender trying to get around the *Stanley* precedent. In a December 1983 diary entry, I wrote, "Oh my God, [Alpha Otis] Stephens is going to be killed based on the opinion I wrote in *Stanley*." In February 1984: A colleague "wondered why I didn't resign [as Vance's clerk] in protest rather than write the *Stanley* draft opinion for Judge Vance—not a pleasant chat, because it was a good question." In March 1984: "The Eleventh Circuit relied on my *Stanley* opinion for Judge Vance in ruling against us in Jim Hitchcock's case." In July 1984: "At the death penalty conference at Airlie House, Virginia; I've been asked to be on a panel with Joe Nursey and George Kendall; I asked them whether they'd have a problem sharing a panel with me, because of my role in *Stanley*."

In any event, my future employers seemed unimpressed with my rationalizations about *Stanley*. To this day, I believe I got my first job in deathwork because, during the interview, I was able to recite from memory all the lyrics to a particular Monty Python song.

When I was offered the job, I accepted on the spot. I couldn't believe my good luck; in the world of capital litigation, West Palm Beach was at the center of the universe. This was so because of the work of one man: Richard Jorandby, the elected public defender for Palm Beach County.

Dick Jorandby was a bedrock conservative Republican. His office was filled with photos of Ronald Reagan and Richard Nixon, and he quoted the gospel according to Barry Goldwater. In his book *Among the Lowest of the Dead*, David Von Drehle says that "all Jorandby's stands—anti-Communist, pro–free enterprise, low tax, small government—derived from his faith in individual freedom under a government of laws. Where he parted company with most of his fellow conservatives, however, was when the tenets of his faith were pushed into the field of criminal law."

When it came to the death penalty, Jorandby was three decades ahead of conservative Republicans. Jorandby saw capital punishment as a government operation—the IRS with the power to kill you. In the year 2000, some prominent conservatives (such as George Will and Pat Robertson) had begun to make this connection. Jorandby had made it in the 1970s, and he made this insight the cornerstone of his life as a lawyer.

Jorandby combined an iron will with a field commander's breadth of vision and a chess player's guile. A prominent fixture in Florida's conservative circles, he tirelessly devoted his life to ensuring that every citizen accused of crime, no matter how guilty, would be guaranteed the best possible legal aid. While other public defenders' offices were being slaughtered by budget cuts, ours survived—in fact, our capital appeals division thrived and became the best in the nation. This was because of Dick Jorandby's political acumen.

In the November 2000 election, the people of Palm Beach County voted Dick Jorandby out of office. But that was the season of the butterfly ballot and inadvertent votes for Pat Buchanan for president, and so I can only hope that the votes against Jorandby were cast in error. Jorandby's electoral defeat was unfortunate. His subsequent indictment for corruption was part of a shameful and self-serving campaign by disgruntled, greedy, and cowardly former employees and a police agency known for its ineptitude. Dick Jorandby created the best capital appeals division in the nation. He was an ideal boss, because he provided his assistants with independence, resources, and the knowledge that he was behind us even when the going got tough.

One of Jorandby's most inspired decisions was to hire Craig Barnard to be creator and coach of his capital appeals unit. Almost nothing rattled Craig. In spite of the onslaught and chaos of death warrants, briefs, oral arguments, and deadlines, he remained serene, puffing on his pipe in his office overlooking the intercoastal waterway. He was the mastermind of our team.

Richard Greene, a graduate of the University of Texas Law School, was our guide through the maze of Florida politics. Richard Burr was a master at tugging the heartstrings. His manner was self-deprecating, that of the southern gentleman—Jimmy Stewart with a law degree. Jorandby, Barnard, Greene, and Burr—they were the team. I was the kid. I felt like a schoolboy working at the Manhattan Project.

We called ourselves "the conspiracy," an ironic reference to the views of some prosecutors, politicians, and judges that there was a vast, tight-knit network of anti–capital punishment lawyers around the nation, directed by LDF in New York, who were implementing a coordinated, clever master plan of using the courts to abolish capital punishment by making it unworkable. In fact, this vast "conspiracy" consisted of about a dozen lawyers around the country—each far too independent, stubborn, and idiosyncratic ever to be part of any conspiracy—most of whom were always treading water to keep their death row clients alive.

In 1985, the Florida State Legislature, governor, and attorney general endorsed the creation of the Office of Capital Collateral Representative (CCR), a new statewide public defender office to represent everyone on Florida's death row who didn't have a lawyer. Virtually everyone on Florida's death row was a candidate. The legislature, governor, and attorney general were all passionately in favor of capital punishment and against the postconviction judicial process that can result in delays of a decade or more between the imposition and execution of death sentences. The idea was that if all condemned prisoners were given lawyers, the chaotic and time-consuming system of postconviction appeals would become more routinized and efficient, and thus delays between sentencing and execution would be reduced.

From the mid-1970s until the creation of CCR in October 1985, the only institutionalized mechanism for locating pro bono lawyers for Florida death row inmates was a small, nonprofit community organization called the Florida Clearinghouse on Criminal Justice. The Clearinghouse, which received no government funds and relied for financial support on contributions from private citizens, religious groups, and foundations, consisted of a director, Scharlette Holdman, and a one- or two-person staff. Neither Holdman nor any of her staff were attorneys. The primary responsibility of the Clearinghouse was to attempt to recruit and assist volunteer counsel for condemned inmates whose convictions and sentences had been affirmed by the Florida Supreme Court. Although Holdman described the nature of the recruitment work as "pretty informal," David Von Drehle describes it this way in *Among the Lowest of the Dead*:

> All day, every day, Holdman sat at her telephone in her shabby office at the FOG Building, chain-smoking Benson and Hedges cigarettes with one hand and dialing with the other. Quite a sight she was: Hair frizzed, feet bare, body rocking in a cheap swivel chair, face lost in a cloud of smoke. She called the heads of local bar associations and asked for recommendations. She called managing partners at big law firms and inquired about their pro bono programs. She got rosters of various liberal organizations and cross-indexed them with the state legal directory, targeting potentially friendly lawyers for calls. She haunted law conferences, scouting for likely prospects. Holdman spent so much time on the telephone in search of lawyers that one Christmas her secretary gave her a cushion for the receiver to prevent cauliflower ear.

In Florida, as I've mentioned, an execution date is set by the governor's signing of a death warrant. During the 1980s, the number of death warrants signed increased dramatically at the same time the pool of available volunteer counsel decreased. Between 1979 (when Florida inmate John Spenkellink became the first person subjected to nonconsensual execution in the modern era of capital punishment) and December

1983, the Florida governor signed sixty-five warrants. Fifty-one (78 percent) of those cases required volunteer counsel. Six warrants were issued in 1979; twenty were issued in 1983. Of the six inmates scheduled for execution in 1979, five (83 percent) were continuously represented by volunteer counsel; all six had counsel at the time their warrants were signed. By 1982, when twenty-three warrants were signed, fifteen (65 percent) were without counsel at the time their warrants were signed.

During the summer of 1985, after CCR had been created but before the new agency opened its doors on October 1, I applied for a job there. As very few Florida attorneys with real capital appellate experience wanted to work at CCR, I guess I looked attractive. After two years working with Craig Barnard, Richard Greene, and in Dick Jorandby at the West Palm Beach Public Defender's Office, at least I had some experience. Craig was one of the best teachers in Florida or anywhere else. CCR offered me a job as a senior assistant, at a salary of thirty thousand dollars per year.

There was a wrinkle, though. In 1983 I had committed to work for Jorandby and Barnard for three years. When I asked them to let me leave a year early to work at CCR, they would have been well within their rights to hold me to my three-year contract. After all, they'd invested two years in training me; now, just when they were beginning to see some return on their investment, I was asking to abandon ship. West Palm Beach had its own capital clients to consider. By summer 1985 I was one-half of the full-time capital appeals division.

Throughout the spring and summer of 1985 I went back and forth on whether to stay at West Palm Beach or go to CCR. In August, I wrote in my diary:

> I understand and appreciate that Craig wants me to stay, but it seems to me that my fight now is with CCR in Tallahassee—here, we have three full-time people working on about a dozen cases, from one appellate district—CCR, which at the moment solely consists of Mark Olive and soon Steve Malone as well, will be responsible for *everyone* on Florida's death row who doesn't otherwise have a lawyer, which just about means everyone on Florida's death row who has had cert. denied from Florida Supreme Court direct appeal—and we should expect that many, possibly most,

pro bono lawyers in capital cases will dump their cases on CCR, once CCR is operational, because most of those pro bono lawyers took the cases in the first place only because of the desperation in Scharlette's situation, and, more recently, under moderate pressure from the Florida Bar. Craig thinks we will lose *Aldrich*, *Ford*, and *Hitchcock* within the next year; . . . maybe I *should* stay at West Palm Beach rather than go to CCR, and leave Craig and Dick Burr and Jorandby hanging: CCR will be a madhouse, but it feels like the madhouse I should be at, where I can do the most good for the greatest number of death row people.

Dick was graciousness and decency personified. In the end, he and Craig left the decision up to me. I decided to go to CCR—decided to go for a range of reasons, some of which I'm proud and others of which I'm not so proud (for example, I *enjoyed* the adrenaline rush of litigating cases under death warrant). From the day CCR opened its doors, the agency became the front lines—in the Western Front, World War I sense—and it was the front not only in Florida but nationally as well. Capital punishment states from Texas to California to Pennsylvania were watching Florida's experiment in creating a state agency to provide legal aid to death row prisoners. CCR was the first entity of its kind in a state serious about carrying out executions.

CCR thus had no models; we would be making it up as we went along. Actually, that was part of the agency's attractiveness to me in the summer of 1985. Until CCR became operational in October 1985, the West Palm Beach Public Defender's Office had been the front lines, the epicenter of the newest and most sophisticated litigation strategies and constitutional theories. Thereafter, that center of gravity shifted to CCR in Tallahassee. I went to CCR because, to paraphrase Willie Sutton, that's where the cases were. CCR was where the action would be, and I didn't want to miss any of it. I was twenty-eight years old when I started working at CCR.

At West Palm Beach, my two supervisors and I had a dozen cases. I was lead counsel in three—the cases of Joe Spaziano, Butch Sireci, and Nollie Lee Martin. At Craig Barnard's suggestion, I took these three cases with me when I relocated to CCR in Tallahassee. Plus, I became responsible for thirty or so other capital cases. I had been practicing law for two years.

On September 30, I packed all my stuff into my blue 1972 VW Beetle (nicknamed Bluebird by my father). My significant other and son would remain in South Florida until Ruthann could find a legal aid or legal teaching job in Tallahassee. If I had any real foreboding about the legal and political hurricane I was driving into, speeding up I-95 with the windows open and rock and roll blasting from the boom box on the seat beside me, I don't really remember it today.

As I drove, I heard a radio news report that Governor Bob Graham had signed twenty-eight-day death warrants on two men whose names I didn't recognize at all. Both would be CCR clients. One of them was Robert Preston, my brand-new client. Two weeks later, the governor signed two new warrants on two other CCR clients. Two weeks after that, two more warrants. And that became the pattern. At any given time—except over the Christmas holiday and during the three weeks in August when the Florida Supreme Court justices took their summer vacation—four CCR clients would be under death warrant.

"Office of Capital Collateral Representative" sounds more like the name of an insurance underwriting outfit than a death row defense agency, a perception not discouraged by CCR's location in the Independent Life Insurance Building on South Pensacola Street (motto on the window: "There's No Substitute for Life Insurance"). Such camouflage was not accidental. The protective coloration was useful because our Tallahassee office was a political lightning rod. From the office it was an easy walk to the Florida Supreme Court, the state legislature's chambers, the law library at Florida State University, and the Hilton bar.

Everyone at CCR in those days worked extraordinarily long hours and shared a deep commitment to the office's mission. The strength of CCR came from the quality, sweat, and sense of duty of the people who worked there. David Reiser, a former law professor, was a fast-talking New Yorker with a brilliant legal mind. Tim Schroeder could take a mess of raw biographical facts and craft them into a powerful narrative of a person's history that sang with humanity. But what made the office work in the early years was the presence of two certifiable geniuses: Scharlette Holdman and Mark Olive. Precision and soul—that's what they had: precision and soul.

Mark Olive was the Joe Dimaggio of Florida deathwork: brilliant, brave, quirky, and original, moving gracefully, never overdoing it, making everything look easy. He never quit, and, because he led by example, we never quit either. Mark brought a unique combination of quietude and intensity to his work. At oral argument, he was unflappable. Once, when he was making an argument seeking a stay of execution from the Florida Supreme Court, he used the word *vignette*. One of the justices apparently thought he meant *vendetta*, and he began yelling at Olive for suggesting that the court had a vendetta against death row prisoners. Had it been me, I would have defined the word *vignette* for the jurist. Mark didn't miss a beat; he assumed, correctly, that the other judges would soon explain the meaning of the word *vignette* to their confused colleague. Mark then apologized for *his* mistake and continued the argument.

The Omar Blanco case is vintage Mark Olive. When Governor Bob Graham signed Blanco's death warrant, Blanco was no more to me than a name on an unread case file piled upon many other unread case files. The death warrant changed all that. It was signed on January 7, 1986. Execution was scheduled for four weeks hence.

Blanco was borderline retarded, a fact we needed no IQ test to ascertain. He had dropped his wallet—including photo ID—at the murder scene, and his getaway vehicle was a bicycle. His being retarded was not enough to win him a stay of execution, however. In 1989 the U.S. Supreme Court ruled that executing the retarded does not violate the Constitution. In 2001 the Court decided to reconsider the matter. Also in 2001, the Florida State Legislature enacted a statute prohibiting execution of the mentally retarded; with the addition of Florida, fifteen states and the federal government had acted to ban execution of the retarded. Still, at least thirty people put to death in the modern era have met the generally accepted definition of retardation (an IQ of less than 70), and at least two hundred retarded prisoners currently live on America's death rows.

The 2001 Florida statute does not apply to prisoners already on death row at the time the law was enacted. Further, the statute does not set a specific IQ level as a definition for retardation. It merely sets out criteria for evaluating a defendant. Whether Omar Blanco might meet those criteria is anyone's guess.

Omar Blanco was convicted and sentenced to death for the murder of John Ryan. The only witness to the offense was thirteen-year-old Thalia Vezos. According to her testimony, she was in bed studying on January 14, 1982, when she saw someone at her bedroom door. The person had a gun, spoke Spanish, and said, "Shhh." He did not threaten her, and he was leaving her room when her uncle confronted him. The uncle said, "What the hell are you doing in my house?" There was a struggle over the gun, and shots were fired as Thalia's uncle "tried to fight the man for the gun." The person was facing Thalia as the struggle began. The shots came very rapidly, two or three occurring in the hall, and three or four more as the victim moved across the bedroom and fell on Thalia. All but one of the shots occurred from within two or three feet of the victim, and that one was probably from a distance greater than an arm's length—three feet. Thalia Vezos ran next door.

Forty-five minutes after the offense took place, Omar Blanco was about a mile away, riding a bicycle. According to the police dispatcher's call, the suspect who committed the crime was "a Latin male with a dark complexion, about 5'10" in height, mustache, black curly hair, and wearing a gray jogging suit or a light green jogging suit. Traveling on foot." Officer Curtis Price stopped Blanco, a Latin male without a mustache who was riding a bicycle, and arrested him when Blanco could produce no identification. Blanco had made no effort to evade the officer. He was handcuffed and taken to the scene of the offense, where he was questioned without first receiving a *Miranda* warning. Blanco's "form" was identified at the scene by a neighbor who had reported seeing a *woman* in a jogging suit walking away from near the scene.

Police officers later testified that they found a man's purse with a wallet in it in Thalia Vezos's bedroom. Inside the wallet were papers apparently belonging to Blanco, including an identification card with his photograph. After the photograph was compared to Blanco, he was transported to the police station.

Blanco's lead attorney, Mark Olive, initiated a factual investigation into every aspect of Blanco's personal history and background. The only problem was that that history seemed to end, for us, in the waters between south Florida and Cuba in the year 1980. Omar Blanco had been one of the 125,000 refugees Fidel Castro forcibly evicted from Mariel, Cuba, in 1980. President Jimmy Carter had hurt Castro's feelings in some way, and Castro retaliated by opening his prisons and mental hospitals and depositing their contents in Mariel. Castro in effect told the United States, "You want 'em? Come and get 'em."

While Carter dithered, the highly organized Cuban American community mobilized a flotilla of small pleasure crafts to bring the Mariel refugees over the ninety miles of water separating Cuba from Miami. The Mariel boatlift worked, sort of. When the boats returned to U.S. waters with the refugees, they were met by officials from the Immigration and Naturalization Service and the Coast Guard. Some of the boats were confiscated and the refugees were incarcerated. Eventually, most of them found sponsors in the United States and were released from custody. Most made reasonably smooth transitions into American life in south Florida. Some became petty criminals. At least two ended up on Florida's death row: Omar Blanco and Pedro Medina. When Medina was executed in the spring of 1997, the electric chair malfunctioned and his face mask burst into flames. Eleven years before Medina's botched electrocution, Omar Blanco was scheduled to die.

Mark Olive knew that to win a stay for Blanco we needed to extend our investigation to Cuba. We needed to get one of CCR's lawyers into Cuba. Our problem, however, was that it was illegal under U.S. law to travel directly to Cuba, and spending money in Cuba was a violation of the Trading with the Enemy Act. Courts and bar associations take a dim view of lawyers who violate the criminal laws of the United States.

Still, necessity being the mother of invention, Mark found a way—a perfectly legal way. We wouldn't send him directly to Cuba; we'd fly him from Miami to the Yucatán, and then—via an airline without a name—into an area outside Havana. He would enter Cuba with no money (to avoid breaking the law by spending any), through a remote airport, far away from the cities and the Cuban security people who patrolled them.

Cuba has no embassy in the United States, so we made the arrangements for Mark's trip through the Cuban Interests Section in Castro's shadow embassy in Washington, D.C. Our intrepid and flat-broke lawyer was to be met at the tiny Cuban airport by an escort with a car who would transport him to the hamlet where Omar Blanco was born and reared. Of course, as it turned out, no one was there to meet him, so he hitchhiked to Blanco's hometown, where he was welcomed like the Prodigal Son. He received warm food and good wine and affidavits from Blanco's family and village priest.

The information Mark Olive brought back from Cuba, combined with the information contained in Blanco's trial record, persuaded the state trial judge to order an evidentiary hearing. That was the good news. But there was a catch: no stay of execution. That was the bad news. The hearing would take place under death warrant. Despite the crushing time pressures, Mark and Scharlette Holdman put on a hell of an evidentiary hearing. It was enough to win Blanco a stay of execution, but not enough to win him a retrial or resentencing, at least not in the state courts.

Over the next couple of years, Blanco lost in the Florida Supreme Court. A second death warrant was signed on him. That scheduled execution date was stayed by a Miami federal trial judge, Alcee Hastings, who ordered a new evidentiary hearing. Hastings, the first African American appointed to the federal trial bench in south Florida, was rock solid on issues of civil rights and capital punishment. From the perspective of Blanco's lawyers, Hastings was a smart judge with a sensitive heart and a sympathetic ear. The only problem was that he was about to be impeached and removed from office by Congress.

Death row lawyers are often accused of delaying capital cases, but in *Blanco*, Mark pressed Judge Hastings for a quick ruling. He wanted a ruling while Hastings was still on the bench to rule. Hastings did rule, and he ordered a new sentencing trial for Blanco. Shortly after Hastings decided Blanco's case, he was impeached by Congress on charges of corruption—charges on which he had been acquitted by a Miami jury.

The prosecutors appealed Judge Hastings's ruling to the Eleventh Circuit. A conservative panel of judges resoundingly affirmed Hastings's *Blanco* decision.

Before his retrial, the Florida prosecutors offered Blanco a negotiated plea of life imprisonment. His new lawyers urged him to take the deal, but these new lawyers didn't know their client, and he refused the plea. Tragically, Blanco's new lawyers never bothered to ask Mark Olive to speak with his former client. I believe that, had they done so, Mark could have convinced Blanco to take the plea. He could have done it with one simple argument: "Look, Omar, are you *really* going to make me fly back to Havana and tell your mother that I let you turn down a plea bargain that would have saved your life?" Because that conversation never happened, Blanco was resentenced to death. As of this writing, he remains on Florida's death row. His death warrant could be signed at any time.

Mark Olive and Scharlette Holdman made the CCR of the mid-1980s a dangerous law firm—dangerous to the powerful, the dishonest, and the deceitful, and dangerous to the prosecutorial state that had created CCR and that paid our salaries. It's hard to find the words to describe what made CCR dangerous, but I do know that it had little to do with levels of funding or resources. We were a hungry army. Perhaps it was a matter of attitude. What Olive and Holdman brought to CCR, in addition to skills and experience, was a fearless will. I asked Mark once what it was that stopped executions from occurring. He told me that it wasn't good facts (although those helped), it wasn't good law (although that helped), it wasn't even having an innocent client (which didn't help at all, it just made the state actors more determined not to admit they had made a mistake). What stopped executions was will: an iron determination that *this killing will not happen.*

Sometimes stopping an execution requires taking risks, and taking risks requires courage—what Plato defined as wise endurance. Taking *wise* risks isn't being reckless; it's the difference between Oskar Schindler and Evel Knievel. For a deathwork law firm, living safely is dangerous—dangerous and deadly to its clients.

My memories of CCR are like the jagged shards of a shattered mirror. There were times when we brought in portable cots so we could steal a few hours of sleep as we lived in the office for days at a time, existing on take-out pizza and Chinese food. Late one night, I calculated my hourly salary since I had started working at CCR. It came to ninety-seven cents per hour.

We felt soaring highs and crashing lows with brutal speed. Once, I was reveling in the adrenaline rush that accompanies an especially good oral argument in the Florida Supreme Court. Then I got a phone call from my client's brother, asking about retrieval of the body following execution. Wham.

Conversely, terror could turn to laughter in the blink of an eye. That happened once at a point when one of our clients, Ed Kennedy, was scheduled to die in a few days. Before he became our client, while serving a sentence for murder, Kennedy had escaped from Florida's maximum-security prison and, in the course of the escape, had killed two white peace officers, Floyd Cone and Robert McDermon, with their own weapons. He was recaptured and tried for these two murders, found guilty, and sentenced to death.

Ed Kennedy was a quiet soul, and I came to like him very much, but his case never really had much in the way of legal issues. His trial lawyer was inexperienced and pretty inept, but not bad enough to matter constitutionally. Kennedy was black, however, and there had been only two other black families in the small Massachusetts town where he had been raised. We sent an investigator to the town in hopes of finding evidence of racism. We found none; in fact, of Kennedy's two black childhood friends, one had gone on to become a doctor and the other a lawyer.

Kennedy loved New Orleans jazz, and he loved to paint. He painted mostly landscapes from his native New England: tugboats in Boston Harbor, the fall foliage. That meant that he had a powerful visual memory. It also meant that, when he painted, his mind's eye never saw the prison bars that defined his existence for the seventeen years before his death.

In June 1985, in the period after Kennedy's first death warrant was signed, we were scrambling to finish the stay papers for filing in the state trial court in Jacksonville. Mark Olive was in Jacksonville, chatting up the judge and his law clerks, while they waited for the papers to arrive. We also had a stay application pending in the U.S. Supreme Court, but Washington was fogged in, and our papers were in a holding pattern above National Airport.

At noon on the day before the execution was scheduled to take place, my cocounsel David Reiser and I got in a car to drive the Kennedy stay papers from Tallahassee to Jacksonville. At every exit on I-10, we stopped and called the office to see if the U.S. Supreme Court had ruled. None of us had slept in days. David was driving, and I was navigating. Then I fell asleep. I must not have been doing much of a job navigating, because it took David a while to notice I'd nodded off. He woke me up by screaming that we were lost somewhere in Jacksonville. He pulled into a gas station, and I found a phone and called the judge's office. The judge himself answered the phone and gave me directions to his courthouse. He also told me that it was 4:40 P.M., and that his office closed at 5:00—sharp.

We tore into the parking lot at 5:05. The courthouse was dark, and Mark Olive was sitting on the courthouse steps. He informed me, with homicidal calm, that we were late. Then he broke into a broad grin. The U.S. Supreme Court had issued a stay. Our stay papers had landed at National Airport after all.

So there we were, in the city of Jacksonville with a car full of useless stay papers and time on our hands. So we decided to get blasted. We bought Wild Turkey and rum, and as David drove us all back to Talla-hassee, Mark and I drank and we all sang, loudly. Mark and I got very drunk. And why not? Ed Kennedy had a stay. It was a Friday night. We could sleep it off on Saturday and come to work on Sunday. Three of our other clients had active death warrants at the time.

What I most remember about Ed Kennedy, though, is a letter he wrote me. I framed it, and it now hangs on my law school office wall. In 1992, Kennedy got a new death warrant and a new execution date. This date was real, and we both knew it; as I've mentioned, his case never had any real constitutional issues to speak of. He wrote to me a few days before he was to be electrocuted. The letter arrived while he was on Phase II of deathwatch, which means that he mailed it from the very lip of the grave.

Dear Mr. Mello

I received your letter the other day and it was very nice to hear from you again.

I appreciate your concern very much and I know that you can see what the Federal Courts are doing with my appeal.

I know that you are angry about this but the best way that you can use that anger is to use it in a way that will turn it into a positive force rather than a negative one.

I would like to see you teach your law students what they are doing to me and others like myself, I believe the best thing that you can do is make people aware of just what these Courts are doing, this is the best thing that I believe that you can do to fight this thing.

Take Care
Your Friend
Ed

Ed Kennedy was put to death on schedule, at 7:00 A.M. on July 21, 1992, in Florida's three-legged, solid-oak electric chair. He was forty-seven years old. He never married. He had no children.

An odd thing happened outside the death house the morning Ed Kennedy was killed: a rainbow appeared. Rainbows are extremely rare in north Florida; I don't know why. In my four years in the Sunshine State, I had never seen a single rainbow. But, just moments after Ed Kennedy was pronounced dead, and as the witnesses to his execution filed out of the bunkerlike death chamber, a radiant rainbow appeared in the misty dawn sky.

I don't want to make too much of this rare Florida rainbow. It wasn't a telegram from God telling us to keep up the good fight. Rainbows are naturally occurring phenomena; they're caused by light refracting through atmospheric vapor (or something like that). Still, I like to think of Ed Kennedy's rainbow as a symbol of renewal, redemption, and hope. And now, whenever I see a rainbow, I think of Ed Kennedy and New Orleans jazz and paintings of landscapes. I don't think of his death when I see rainbows; he'd hate it if his memory spoiled rainbows for me. Rather, rainbows make me think of his life and of the people he touched with his love.

Because of our staggering caseload at CCR, I lived in fear of making mistakes. And I made mistakes. The worst was failing to file a notice of appeal in the Tommy Zeigler case. Zeigler had a death warrant at the time.

This was a major disaster—the single worst mistake anyone at CCR had made in the office's early years. Filing a timely notice of appeal is a jurisdictional prerequisite to taking an appeal to the federal court of appeals. Failing to file the one-sentence boilerplate notice within the required thirty days deprives the appellate court of jurisdiction: the appellate court is jurisdictionally banned from entertaining the appeal. A lawyer's failure to file a timely notice of appeal constitutes per se ineffective assistance of counsel. In the Zeigler case, my failure to file the timely notice of appeal—of the federal trial court's denial of Zeigler's first (not successive) habeas corpus petition—meant that he was jurisdictionally barred from appealing. The death warrant thus created the possibility that Tommy Zeigler would become the first Florida death row inmate to be executed on a first warrant, as well as the first to be executed without ever having an appeal from the denial of his first federal habeas corpus petition.

Despite my error, this story had a happy ending. I persuaded Steve Winter, of LDF in New York, to take Zeigler's case and to argue that CCR was ineffective for failing to file the notice of appeal. Winter successfully obtained a stay and then a full appeal in Zeigler's case. (In his book *Fatal Flaw*, Phillip Finch argues that Zeigler was innocent.)

The Florida State Legislature set the size of the CCR staff and the office's budget with the expectation that CCR would handle about thirty cases in its first year of operation. Instead, the office handled about five times that many cases. Even though CCR attorneys were routinely working sixty- to ninety-hour weeks, and some private attorneys remained available as volunteers, CCR was having trouble keeping up with the increase in Florida's death row population. CCR's crushing caseload raised serious ethical dilemmas—dilemmas that have led courts and commentators to find that staggering caseloads can result in inefficient representation.

The creation of CCR did mean the end of the pernicious practice of signing death warrants on unrepresented death row prisoners. Technically, because CCR represented everyone on death row at risk of a warrant, no one on death row was "unrepresented." Further, the adoption of time limits for filing state postconviction motions eliminated the need to sign warrants to get those cases moving in the postconviction process.

However, the sheer numbers of CCR clients had the same effect as when warrants were being signed on unrepresented people. Virtually all of our resources were devoted to clients under warrant. The result was that we were always dashing from court to court, trying to plug the leaks in a dam that always threatened to burst and drown us along with our clients.

Despite the caseload, CCR did not fulfill expectations and speed up the execution process, at least in its early years. In its first year and a half of existence, only three executions occurred in Florida. CCR or CCR-assisted volunteer counsel won retrials or resentencings in several cases. Further, stays of execution were usually obtained in state court, far earlier in the postconviction process than had been true previously. Ironically, once CCR had become operational and had succeeded in preventing a string of executions, some legislators complained that CCR had violated the legislative intent behind its creation.

When I began doing deathwork in summer 1983, there had been only one Florida execution in seventeen years, that of John Spenkellink. Of course, I knew the odds. I'd done the math—we all had. Still, we hadn't lost yet. It was still possible, for me at least, to imagine winning the war for judicial abolition of capital punishment as a legal system. The other side had the resources and the power those resources could buy, but there are ways a tiny army can defeat a large army—ways, indeed, to use the larger army's strengths against it. Lee and Jackson, Mosby and Stuart, Longstreet and Forrest had taught that lesson all across the Virginia of my childhood. And our side had the best generals: Anthony Amsterdam, Craig Barnard, Mark Olive, Scharlette Holdman.

Given the amount of work and soul and emotional energy that capital postconviction litigation requires, CCR's caseload was overwhelming. I have never worked so hard in my life, and I never will again. The office's lawyers, support staff, and investigators routinely worked eighty-hour weeks and fifteen-hour days, and longer hours were required in (frequent) crises. During an especially frenetic five weeks in 1986, one CCR lawyer seldom left the office except to shower. Three people represented by CCR were put to death during that period. Fierce commitment to the clients, and not nearly enough time in the day or night to fulfill that commitment, was the essence of the job.

David Von Drehle wrote in 1997, in his foreword to my book *Dead Wrong,* that his seven years of studying capital punishment had taught him that "the guts of our American death penalty are not to be found in prison. Death row—with its prisoners, wardens and pastors—is a dull, slow hell of waiting and despair. . . . [The] real death penalty enterprise is a bustling, frantic mill of investigation, litigation, brief drafting, strategy, oral and written argument, a Rube Goldberg contraption kept clanking perpetually by the fuel of caffeinated lawyers and their cousins, the poll-driven politicians."

The stories that follow are not capital punishment in the abstract. These stories—and thousands like them, on death rows from Florida to Texas to Virginia to Illinois to Missouri to Nevada to California—are the real capital punishment.

3

The Aging Hit Man:
Anthony Antone

Tony was a good boy. Give him my regards.

—Florida "Godfather" Santo Trafficante, shortly before
the execution of Anthony Antone

One of the primary tasks assigned to new lawyers is to research and
write memos of law. Soon after becoming a Florida public defender, I
was given the job of researching and writing a memo on whether we
might be able to argue successfully that executing the insane is a violation of the U.S. Constitution. One of my office's clients, Alvin Ford,
would be a perfect test case to raise this issue.

I did the research and wrote the memo. The memo explained why,
although there was a U.S. Supreme Court decision squarely in our path,
I thought the claim had a fair shot at success. Ford would not need to
raise the issue for some months, however. In the meantime, another
death row prisoner, Anthony Antone, was scheduled to die. Antone
wasn't as crazy as Ford. More important, Antone wasn't our client.

The Crime

Anthony Antone never killed anyone. Antone was sentenced to death
on August 27, 1976, for his role as a middleman in a gangland-style
execution. The "hit" was allegedly carried out on orders of the organized crime family with which Antone was affiliated. The murder was
committed on the morning of October 23, 1975, when Detective Richard Cloud, a suspended Tampa police officer, was killed at the front
door of his home. Antone's conviction was based on the assertion that

he was the mastermind of this execution slaying, and that he directly hired the two men who carried out the murder. One of the men Antone hired, Ellis Marlow Haskew, was the primary witness for the state.

According to David Von Drehle's account in *Among the Lowest of the Dead*, "Police concluded that a mobster named Victor Acosta had ordered the murder, and that Anthony Antone, as Acosta's lackey, had hired the two gunmen." Acosta and the man who pulled the trigger committed suicide. The second hit man, Ellis Haskew, "turned state's evidence. That left Antone—who had neither planned the murder nor pulled the trigger—as the odd man out, the last bad guy vulnerable to prosecution. Cutting deals with the prosecution is like musical chairs: The slowest man loses."

So Haskew's testimony sent Antone to death row. In that testimony, Haskew recounted the following about this murder. Upon discharge from Florida State Prison in May 1975, Haskew returned to Tampa to live and to establish contact with Antone. In September 1975, Haskew helped Benjamin Gilford to escape from prison, after which he and Gilford went to the Bradenton, Florida, area to live. Immediately after Gilford's escape, Antone advised Haskew by telephone that he was looking for someone to perform five "installations"; Haskew testified that by "installations," Antone meant murders. Haskew and Gilford then traveled to Tampa to meet with Antone, who personally informed Haskew that another man wanted five people killed, including Richard Cloud. Haskew accepted $1,750 in "front money," which was used in part to purchase a used Oldsmobile. In late September 1975, he went to Antone's house and was given a .32 caliber automatic with an attached silencer to test. Although Antone previously had tested the gun himself, he wanted Haskew to check the effectiveness of the silencer. Haskew fired the gun twice into a rattan couch in Antone's home. After the testing, Antone repacked the silencer with the kind of fiber used in air conditioning filters, which he stored in a shed behind his house.

In addition to supplying Haskew with the gun, Antone gave Haskew a picture of Cloud and drove Haskew by Cloud's home. Approximately ten days before Cloud's death, Antone asked Haskew to complete his assignment, because Cloud was due to testify before a grand jury about matters concerning Antone's friends. Haskew made final preparations for this murder by constructing a cardboard box to conceal the weapon, retesting the gun, which required more packing fiber from Antone, and obtaining ammunition from an outside party. On October 23, 1975, Haskew and Gilford drove past Cloud's home and noticed that only Cloud's car was there. They circled the house, and Gilford left the vehicle. While Gilford entered the house, Haskew drove around the block. When he returned to pick Gilford up, he saw an ashtray fly out of the front door after Gilford. Haskew recalled that Gilford later explained that Cloud had thrown an ashtray or a plant at him as he fired at Cloud. Antone visited Haskew at his apartment later that day, gave him $200 to get Gilford out of town, and drove Haskew to Gandy Bridge to dispose of the murder weapon in Tampa Bay. Haskew made several trips between Tampa and Miami in the ensuing days and received about $9,000 from Antone in several installments. It was also established that Antone personally received at least $750 for this contract murder.

On February 25, 1976, at approximately 8:30 A.M., Haskew was arrested in Miami. Although he initially denied involvement with the Cloud murder, later that day he admitted his participation and agreed to cooperate with law enforcement authorities. Haskew fully implicated Antone as the person who hired him and Gilford to murder Cloud. He also explained a telephone code arrangement he had made with Antone that would enable Antone to determine the number from which Haskew was calling. Upon receiving the code, Antone would return the call to that number from a telephone booth. In cooperation with the police, Haskew called Antone at approximately 8:30 P.M. that same day and used the code to have Antone return the call to a pay phone in the police building in Miami. Antone had been placed under surveillance at the time and was observed leaving his house and going to a pay phone booth nearby. A recording made of the return call from Antone was later introduced into evidence.

Approximately an hour and a half later, Antone was arrested at his home and taken to the office of the Federal Bureau of Investigation. While at that office, Antone complained of chest pains and discomfort. He was taken to the hospital, where he was subsequently placed in the coronary care unit. At approximately 1:10 A.M. the following morning, with the approval of the attending physician, an FBI agent entered Antone's hospital room. The FBI agent later testified that "Mr. Antone told me that he was a hundred percent Sicilian and Sicilians do not fink."

In the afternoon of February 26, 1976, a search warrant was issued for Antone's residence. The warrant sought from the premises "certain evidence, to wit: .32 caliber projectiles, couch, cushions, couch stuffing, and counterfeit currency." The affidavit in support of the warrant stated the following: (1) Richard Cloud was shot and killed on October 23, 1975, and evidence from the crime scene indicated that the shots fired were from a .32 caliber automatic pistol; (2) Ellis Marlow Haskew had been arrested and had admitted being present at the murder of Cloud by Benjamin Gilford, and that Gilford used a .32 automatic pistol given to Haskew by Antone; (3) prior to giving the pistol to Haskew, Antone tested the weapon by firing it into a couch in the den of his residence, and the fired projectiles were still in the couch, floor, or surrounding walls; (4) at the time of Antone's arrest, the arresting officer had seen a couch on those premises; and (5) Haskew had informed the affiant that Antone kept counterfeit money on the premises, and this appeared to be confirmed in a recorded conversation between Haskew and Antone.

Early that evening, a search of Antone's premises was conducted in accordance with the warrant. A bullet was recovered from a rattan couch that, when compared with the bullet removed from Cloud's left leg, was found to have been fired from the same weapon. Identical comparisons were also made with other bullets found at Cloud's home, including spent bullets found on the carpet under the dining room table, beneath the couch, and under the house in a joist. In addition, the search produced blue air conditioner filter fibers that were seized from a work shed in the rear of Antone's house. Haskew had stated that these fibers were used to pack the silencer. Expert testimony indicated that the seized fibers compared favorably with fibers taken from the screen door at Cloud's house immediately following the murder. In support of Haskew's testimony, a neighbor testified that he had been standing in his carport and heard shots from the direction of Cloud's house. He looked up and saw a car with a driver in it. The engine was running and the passenger door was wide open. A few seconds later, a man ran from Cloud's house with a brown cardboard box in his hand, jumped in the car, and sped off. The record further reflects that cardboard fragments were found near the screen door of Cloud's house, and four bullet holes were in the door. Cloud's mother testified that a week prior to her son's death, a man she identified as Antone came to Cloud's home asking for him.

Antone testified in his own behalf and denied participation in this murder-for-hire scheme. Antone's counsel also presented testimony impeaching Haskew's reputation for truth and veracity. Haskew acknowledged during cross-examination that, with the advice of counsel, he had entered into a plea agreement with the state. Under the agreement, Haskew would receive a thirty-five-year sentence, and he expected to be eligible for parole in seven to eight years.

The jury returned a verdict of guilty and recommended that Antone receive the death penalty. The trial judge imposed the death sentence, finding aggravating circumstances: (1) Antone had previously been convicted of two armed robberies, felonies involving the use of threat of violence to another person; (2) this was a contract murder and therefore committed for pecuniary gain; (3) the victim was killed to disrupt and hinder the endorsement of laws; and (4) the murder was especially heinous, atrocious or cruel. The trial judge found no mitigating circumstances.

The First Round

On direct appeal, the Florida Supreme Court, after remanding Antone's case to the trial court for determination of whether the state had violated the rules of pretrial discovery, affirmed Antone's conviction and sentence in 1980. The U.S. Supreme Court denied review on October 14, 1980.

On January 6, 1982, Governor Bob Graham signed a death warrant requiring that Antone be put to death between the dates of January 29 and February 5, 1982. The prison scheduled the execution for February 2. Thomas McCoun was the attorney (in a two-person law firm) who would ultimately represent Antone through two rounds of state and federal postconviction litigation. Before the governor signed Antone's death warrant, McCoun had no knowledge of Antone's case.

On January 11, 1982, McCoun was contacted by Scharlette Holdman, director of the Florida Clearinghouse on Criminal Justice, who asked him to render pro bono assistance to Antone in the preparation of state and federal postconviction litigation. McCoun had been a member of the Florida bar and an attorney since 1977; he had served for three years as a state prosecutor. When he began representing

Antone, McCoun was in practice with one other attorney in a predominantly criminal trial practice. Although he had handled state court appeals both as a prosecutor and as a defense attorney, and had prosecuted and defended murder cases, he had never previously litigated a collateral attack under the state postconviction rule or the federal habeas corpus statute. Despite his lack of experience at the appellate level, McCoun recognized, as he explained later, that "the urgency of the situation and the finality of the punishment required that an attorney begin working on Antone's case," and therefore he agreed to represent Antone.

McCoun's first contact with the record in Antone's case was on January 12, 1982. On that day, McCoun met one of Antone's trial attorneys for the first time. McCoun learned at that meeting that this lawyer and a second attorney had jointly defended Antone at trial. One of the trial attorneys had represented Antone throughout the direct appeal pursuant to a court appointment and had also filed a certiorari petition for Antone in the U.S. Supreme Court.

Trial counsel informed McCoun that a witness with knowledge of and involvement in the case had contacted him. Based on this potential witness's testimony, trial counsel and his law partner were preparing a state postconviction motion and a petition for writ of *error coram nobis,* raising the single issue of newly discovered testimony. It was obvious to McCoun, however, that other legal issues, including ineffective assistance of trial counsel, had to be raised. It was equally apparent to McCoun that trial counsel could not argue that he himself was ineffective. At that point, McCoun informed trial counsel that McCoun would prepare a separate state postconviction motion raising any other legal claims that could be found in the record.

Between January 12 and January 19, 1982, McCoun reviewed the two-thousand-page record of Antone's case. He also reviewed the court file and researched numerous legal issues. He spent from twelve to fifteen hours each day on Antone's case, while his law practice was put on hold.

McCoun completed the state postconviction motion at 1:30 A.M. on January 20. The motion was filed later that day. Trial counsel had filed his state postconviction motion on January 15 and had begun conducting discovery. A hearing on both postconviction motions was set for January 21 at 3:00 P.M. McCoun spent the thirty-seven and a half hours remaining between his completion of the postconviction motion and the hearing attempting to locate witnesses to testify on the various legal issues raised; preparing additional motions, memoranda of law, and proposed orders; and continuing to research the issues raised.

During the time he had to prepare for the hearing, McCoun persuaded one attorney to testify on limited aspects of the issue of ineffective assistance of trial counsel and secured documents in support of these issues. He was, however, unable to find any attorneys who could, in the time remaining, review the record adequately to testify on other important dimensions of the issue. There was insufficient time for him to meet with trial counsel or to plan a strategy for the presentation of evidence at the hearing. During the period immediately prior to the hearing, Antone was in transport and thus unavailable to McCoun.

At the outset of the hearing, McCoun requested a continuance because he had had insufficient time to conduct discovery, contact witnesses, and prepare for the hearing. The motion was denied, and the hearing proceeded. McCoun called Antone and one other witness. He did not call either trial attorney, because he had lacked sufficient time to discuss with them the case or their participation in it. He had no knowledge of what their testimony would be, and thus was simply unprepared to present it. In addition, one of the trial attorneys informed the court that he would refuse to testify at the hearing because he was still acting as Antone's attorney.

Both state postconviction motions, as well as an application for stay of execution, were denied on January 21. McCoun immediately filed a notice of appeal to the Florida Supreme Court. He filed his appellate brief on January 26, 1982, the same day oral argument was heard in the Florida Supreme Court.

When he was preparing the state court pleading, McCoun was also preparing a petition for writ of habeas corpus for filing in the federal trial court, along with an application for stay of execution. On January 22, while the state postconviction appeal was still pending in the Florida Supreme Court, McCoun filed the petition for writ of habeas corpus in federal trial court. On January 28, the federal trial court held oral argument on the habeas petition. During the course of the argument, the Florida Supreme Court entered an order denying Antone's appeal. The federal trial court denied Antone's request for an evidentiary hearing, but allowed oral argument to continue on the legal issues presented.

On January 29, the federal trial court denied the habeas petition and the stay request. Because of the nearness of the execution date, the trial judge read his order orally into the record and ordered the transcript to be forwarded to the U.S. Court of Appeals for the Eleventh Circuit. McCoun immediately filed a notice of appeal as well as an application for stay of execution. These documents were completed at 1:00 A.M. on January 30. McCoun flew the pleadings and attachments to Atlanta for filing on Saturday, January 30, in the Eleventh Circuit.

On February 1, at 5:00 P.M., the Eleventh Circuit stayed Antone's execution and remanded the case to the trial court for more complete and reviewable findings of fact and conclusions of law. Several weeks later, the trial court filed a memorandum of decision in the Eleventh Circuit. The Eleventh Circuit heard Antone's case on an expedited appeal schedule. McCoun filed his principal brief on April 9, 1982.

Following oral argument, a panel of the Eleventh Circuit affirmed the judgment of the trial court on June 13, 1983. A petition for rehearing was filed on July 1 and denied on September 6. McCoun filed a petition for plenary review in the U.S. Supreme Court, which was denied on November 28, 1983.

The Final Round

The cycle then repeated itself. On January 4, 1984, the governor signed a second death warrant, requiring Antone's execution between noon on Friday, January 20, and noon on Friday, January 27, 1984. The prison scheduled the execution for 7:00 A.M. on January 24.

We scrambled to find Antone a lawyer. I wrote letters to every major law firm that had offered me a job, including New York's Cravath, Swaine & Moore:

December 6, 1983

David O. Brownwood, Esq.
Cravath, Swaine & Moore
New York, N.Y.

Dear David:

I wanted to let you know that I have accepted a job with the Capital Appeals Division of the West Palm Beach, Florida, Public Defender's Office. I also was wondering if the Cravath firm might be willing to take on a death penalty appeal or postconviction attack.

Involvement of the private bar in death cases, and particularly in Florida death cases, would bring a variety of benefits. The lawyers would gain "in the pit" experience in an intense and rapidly developing area of law; it would give them an invaluable perspective on the criminal justice system, where the battle for equal justice is being fought—and lost. It would also give the lawyers a visceral understanding of the plight of those who engage in crime. The casualties of Florida's death penalty crusade are the poor, uneducated, unemployed, minorities. Defendants with the intellectual and financial means to obtain adequate representation do not land on death row.

Lawyers are, of course, not the primary beneficiaries of their involvement in capital cases. The system gains forceful advocates for reform. Criminal practice gains added respectability by the participation of the leaders of the bar. Most importantly, criminal defendants, litigating for their lives, gain high-quality representation, as well as the assurance that they are not being relegated to the legal profession's underclass.

But the most compelling reason is the desperate need for your help. In Florida, the state's legal obligation to provide counsel for capital defendants ends with direct appeal and executive clemency. If the Governor denies clemency, then he can sign a death warrant, with the execution set to take place within three weeks. If the inmate is to stay alive, he must take his case to the federal courts, petitioning for a writ of habeas corpus. To do that successfully, he must have a lawyer. But he has no money to hire one. So friends on the outside begin frantically searching to find an attorney willing to take the case.

A good example of this is the case of Stephen Booker. Booker had pursued Florida, and then federal, postconviction avenues of relief. The United States Supreme Court denied certiorari on October 17, 1983, and at that point his lawyer ended his involvement in Booker's case. On October 25, the Governor signed Booker's warrant, calling for his execution on November 17. Because he had no lawyer, I read his trial transcript, and when I did

I found a number of substantial reasons why execution of Booker's sentence would offend the Constitution. At that point, I and others tried to find an attorney to prosecute the petition. We called over 150 lawyers before I prevailed upon a friend at Wilmer, Cutler and Pickering to assume responsibility for Booker's case. I wrote them a letter on my work up to that point, which I enclose as an example of the issues raised in these cases.

James Coleman, a partner, and Jeffrey Robinson and Marion Lindberg, associates, prepared the pleadings and argued the issues in several courts. A federal district judge agreed that the case raised substantial federal questions and granted an indefinite stay of execution. The Wilmer firm is now litigating the case as it should be litigated.

Booker was lucky, but too many others will not be. The United States Supreme Court denied certiorari in several Florida cases in recent weeks. Those inmates need lawyers. Others have just lost their appeals in the Florida Supreme Court. They need lawyers. Many clemencies are presently pending before the Governor. When those are denied (as they have been in 83 of 89 cases), those people will need lawyers.

In short, we need your help. I look forward to hearing from you.

Sincerely,
Michael Mello
Assistant Public Defender
West Palm Beach, Florida

I received a gracious response:

Cravath, Swaine & Moore
One Chase Manhattan Plaza
New York, N.Y.

December 29, 1983

Dear Mike:

Your letter asking the firm to help in the death penalty appeal cases is a compelling plea and we have taken it very seriously around here.

The firm has done a fair amount of similar work through the Legal Defense Fund, and as well has a number of other criminal appeals in process that it has taken on from both the Legal Defense Fund and the Legal Aid Society. My litigation partners have reluctantly concluded that our current pro bono workload is such that we ought not take on any additional cases other than through our regular "clients," namely the Legal Defense Fund and the Legal Aid Society. We have already committed to provide substantial help to those organizations and my partners feel we should remain in a position to meet that commitment. I appreciate your thinking of the firm and giving us this opportunity to participate in an important undertaking.

My best wishes to you for success in your work. If at some point you decide to take another look at the private sector I hope you will give me a call.

Sincerely,
David O. Brownwood

It was no good. We couldn't find Antone a new lawyer. Once again Antone had no lawyer other than McCoun, and so once again McCoun litigated the case pro bono.

It appeared initially that this time around the litigation battleground would be Antone's mental health. In *Among the Lowest of the Dead*, David Von Drehle provides this description:

> During an earlier stint in prison, Antone's head had been smashed in a case of mistaken identity. After that, things were never right between the ears of the amiable Antone. "They removed part of my brain due to an infection of cockroaches crawling in my brain," he explained. The spindly old man wandered the exercise yard sweetly giving his neighbors the creeps. He would buttonhole them to explain that he had discovered the secret to escaping gravity. Just push an invisible button and off you go. Flying!

After McCoun agreed to stay on as Antone's lawyer, he called the public defender office for help, and Craig Barnard and Dick Burr gave him me. The day after the warrant was signed, McCoun sent his Antone files to me via Greyhound bus. I picked up the four boxes of files at the bus station, drove to my office, and dug in. That was Thursday.

By Friday I had a dilemma. Antone's case had a constitutional issue—an issue that would, two years later, give rise to a unanimous U.S. Supreme Court win in Jim Hitchcock's case (see chapter 9)—that capital appeals lawyers had been raising in every death case. However, McCoun had not raised it in the first round of Antone's postconviction litigation. Because McCoun hadn't raised the issue before, the courts were likely to see raising it now as an abuse of the writ. The abuse-of-the-writ rule (which basically says that death row prisoners must raise *all* their claims in the first round of postconviction litigation; they are procedurally barred from raising any new claims in a second round of litigation) is a legal technicality that has sealed the fates of many death row prisoners.

The issue, which later became known as the *Hitchcock* issue, was really two issues. The first involved a portion of the standard instructions given to Florida juries at the time of Hitchcock's and Antone's trials. Capital juries were in essence told to ignore all mitigating evidence that could not be shoehorned into a statutory list of mitigating factors. In 1987, the U.S. Supreme Court would hold in the *Hitchcock* case that juries deciding life or death must be allowed to consider *all* mitigating evidence, not just the kinds of mitigating factors included in the statutory list. The second aspect of the *Hitchcock* issue concerned the chilling effect that the restrictive jury instruction had on defense lawyers; because juries were instructed to ignore nonstatutory mitigating evidence, defense attorneys did not investigate or present such evidence. McCoun had raised the first of these issues in Antone's earlier round of appeals, but he had missed the second.

I had to ask McCoun why he hadn't raised the second issue earlier. When I asked him about it over the phone on the night of Friday, January 4, there was a long silence on his end, and then he answered slowly: He'd simply missed it. In the crush and chaos of Antone's first round of appeals, he had just missed it.

Tom McCoun is a good man and an excellent lawyer. He was a hero for what he did for Antone in the first round of Antone's postconviction litigation. And the more I thought about it, the more convinced I became that the fault for his missing the issue earlier wasn't McCoun's. It was the fault of a legal system that forced even high-quality lawyers to litigate at the speed of light. It was unfair then to blame him—and his condemned client—for missing a subtle but important constitutional claim.

Thus my colleagues and I decided to put the capital appeals system itself on trial. It was the system's fault—not McCoun's fault, and certainly not his death row client's fault—that McCoun had missed the issue the first time around. McCoun had not abused the writ, the law itself had abused the writ. I spent the next week developing this argument.

We also had to make a hard decision about the internal research memo I'd written previously on executing the insane. Dick Burr argued against our giving the memo to McCoun, and he made two powerful points: (1) we needed to save the issue for *our* client, Alvin Ford, and (2) Ford was far more likely to win on the issue than Antone, because Ford was much crazier than Antone. If we gave the issue to Antone to lose now, it wouldn't be available for Ford later.

I offered a suggestion: Might we not accept McCoun's invitation to join him as cocounsel for Antone? That way, Antone would be *our* client, and we could really throw ourselves into the case. Craig Barnard reluctantly scotched this idea. Because ours was a state local public defender office, our jurisdiction was limited to Palm Beach County, and Antone's was not a Palm Beach County case. We could help McCoun behind the scenes, by sending him research and ghostwriting papers, but we could not appear formally as cocounsel.

We spent much of Tuesday, January 12, hashing over whether we ought to give McCoun my memo on executing the insane. In the end, we decided to do it—or, more precisely, we decided that we wouldn't be able to sleep at night if we didn't give McCoun the memo. We sent the memo to McCoun via overnight courier (this was in the days before fax machines, much less e-mail).

On Saturday, January 14, Dick, Craig, and I met for five hours on the Antone case. We decided that Dick would go to Tampa to help McCoun with the counsel-crisis-as-an-excuse-for-missing-the-*Hitchcock*-issue-the-first-time-around argument. I spent all day Sunday working on the execution competency claim. My diary for that Sunday shows that I was still struggling with our decision to give Antone the issue: "Antone's mind is going, and he's the oldest man on death row, but is he too crazy to be executed? Probably not, and it could kill the execution competency issue for Ford, who is *our* client, and who is really more nuts than Antone, to run the claim in a case like Antone's, where the facts of insanity are so weak."

On Monday, the execution competency issue in Antone's case became moot. Dick called from Tampa to tell us that he'd concluded that Antone was mentally competent enough to be executed. McCoun would not raise that issue. He would find some way to get the facts of Antone's deteriorating mental health before the courts, but he would not argue that Antone's mental illness made him incompetent to be executed. (Even profound mental illness is not necessarily enough to prevent a person's execution. To be found mentally incompetent to be killed, an individual must have a mental disability that prevents him or her from understanding what it means to be under a death sentence.)

McCoun and Scharlette Holdman thought they had another avenue for Antone. David Von Drehle describes their idea:

> [Holdman] racked her brain. A few hours before the scheduled execution, she came up with an idea. What about the Mafia? After all, they had gotten Antone into this mess; why couldn't they get him out of it? She decided to call the godfather. She would ask him to contact the governor and explain that Antone was just a pathetic pawn.
>
> Maybe Antone's delusions were contagious, or maybe Holdman was just being Holdman, never giving up, turning every stone, fighting to the end. Anyway, she asked Pat Doherty [a trial lawyer] to tell her the name of the man who ran Florida's mob. It seemed the sort of thing Doherty would know, and he did not disappoint: Santo Trafficante, he said. Holdman asked if he could get Trafficante on the phone, and Doherty, always game, offered to try.
>
> Some people believe that Santo Trafficante had a part in the crime of the century, the assassination of John F. Kennedy. In any case, it was certainly true that the don had racked up the better part of a century's worth of crimes. He was an old and powerful criminal, a man other thugs killed for and died for—not a man to trifle with. But Holdman had moxie to burn, and when Doherty pulled a few shady strings, found Trafficante's number, and rang him up, Holdman took the phone.
>
> "Uh, Mr. Antone is going to be killed," she said, in a quaver-

ing drawl. "I understand he used to, uh, work for you. And I was wondering, is there anything you can say or do to help him?"

There was a pause, and then Holdman heard a raspy whisper exactly like Marlon Brando's in *The Godfather*. "Tony was a good boy," Trafficante gasped. "Give him my regards."

The godfather idea was a dead end. Antone's life would be staked on the *Hitchcock* issue McCoun had missed the first time around. McCoun would use my research and drafting work on abuse of the writ and on the *Hitchcock* claim. McCoun would file in the state trial court in forty-eight hours, on Thursday. He would also lodge anticipatory filings in the federal trial court. (In Florida, the logistics of litigating cases under warrant—where cases can go from the state trial court in Miami to the Florida Supreme Court in Tallahassee to the federal trial court in Miami to the Eleventh Circuit in Atlanta to the U.S. Supreme Court in Washington, D.C., all in the space of a few days—have led to some unique procedural customs and practices. For instance, we "lodged" stay papers in courts well in advance of when the cases would reach those courts; later, if all the courts earlier along the assembly line denied a stay, we would place a phone call to "activate" the papers we had previously lodged.)

McCoun filed on Thursday, and three hours later, the state trial judge denied a stay. The Florida Supreme Court's briefs were then due by 5:00 P.M., and oral argument was set for 9:00 A.M on Friday.

We had some hope of a "Super Bowl stay." McCoun had asked the federal trial court to schedule a Saturday argument on his stay application. The Tampa court said no, however. It was Super Bowl weekend, and that year the Super Bowl was in Tampa. The hearing was set for Monday afternoon.

McCoun's oral argument in the Florida Supreme Court had given us hope that the case might not even reach federal court. The justices weren't hostile, and they seemed genuinely interested in the counsel crisis that had been the real reason McCoun had missed the *Hitchcock* issue in the first round of postconviction litigation.

According to newspaper reports, it took the Florida Supreme Court two and a half hours after the argument to deny the stay. Over Super Bowl weekend, however, we had no official word. That was understandable. What was puzzling was that the uncertainty continued into

Monday morning. By 10:00 A.M. on Monday—the day before Antone was scheduled to be killed—McCoun still had not seen the Florida Supreme Court's opinion, although the court had indeed ruled on Friday. When he did receive it, the future did not look bright for Antone. Procedural bar, abuse of the writ: McCoun should have raised it all in the first postconviction litigation.

More surreal bad news arrived just before McCoun was to present his argument. The federal court was refusing to accept any Antone papers without a filing fee. This was ridiculous—Antone, like virtually all death row prisoners, was a pauper, and paupers are not required to pay filing fees—but McCoun paid the fee out of his pocket, as he was paying all his other expenses in his pro bono representation of Antone, on this round as he had before.

The procedural barriers were high. McCoun had to explain to the federal court why the issues he was raising now had not been raised in the first round of postconviction litigation. He argued, as he had in state court, that he shouldn't be blamed for the flaws in his earlier filings because the pressure of the death warrant had simply denied him the time to do a good job.

The federal trial judge denied the stay at 4:10 P.M., McCoun's secretary told us; an hour later, McCoun himself gave us the dismal details. The argument lasted three hours, but it was a charade. The fix was in from the start. He sat down at the end of his argument, and the judge began reading his order without missing a beat. The only ray of light was that the federal trial court's order was very poorly written. Maybe the U.S. Court of Appeals for the Eleventh Circuit would grant a stay and send the case back down for the Tampa judge to try again.

The signals out of the Eleventh Circuit in Atlanta were mixed. The court's death clerk had told us that she was going home to change into jeans because, as she put it, "it's going to be a long night." A "long night" indeed. What did it mean that the Eleventh Circuit Court was in for a "long night"? Did it mean that the court needed time to write a solid opinion granting a stay, one that would hold up in the U.S. Supreme Court? Or did it mean that the appellate court needed time to explain why it was granting a stay and sending the case back down to the trial court? Or was the court writing a careful explanation of why legal technicalities prevented the federal courts from even considering Antone's constitutional claims?

How these matters would be decided—and whether Anthony Antone would die in a very few hours—depended in some measure on the legal issues we had raised. Much more important was who the judges were, and we wouldn't know that until they had ruled. It was, quite literally, a lottery. The judges were selected at random. If Antone got lucky, he'd get three judges who were willing to listen and consider our arguments. If he was unlucky, he was dead.

The lottery of judges. Trying to predict who Antone would draw was the sort of divination in which death row lawyers engage the night before an execution. In my diary that night I wrote, "We tried to guess which three judges we'd get for the Antone panel, but it was just reading tea leaves by scared people who don't have any *real* information to go on."

As it turned out, Antone was lucky, but not lucky enough. At 11:30 P.M., we lost unanimously on every issue. However, the court did give Antone a twenty-four-hour stay to give us an opportunity to seek a U.S. Supreme Court stay without needing to wake up the justices in the middle of the night. We went back to work.

Tuesday, January 24, was a disaster. The U.S. Supreme Court was screaming for our Antone papers, but all the D.C. airports were fogged in; our papers were in a holding pattern above the nation's capital, waiting for a break in the fog. By afternoon, it appeared that the airports would remain closed for the rest of the day, so we dictated summaries of the papers to David Kendall, a D.C. superlawyer and former capital appeals attorney. Perhaps out of sheer frustration—at the weather, at us, at Antone—the Court extended the stay for another twenty-four hours. Stay based on fog.

I spent Wednesday working on other cases and, as I recorded in my diary, "waiting for the ax to fall on Antone." The ax fell at 9:30 P.M., when the Supreme Court denied the stay. The vote was seven to two; Justices Brennan and Marshall dissented.

The opinion for the majority was unsigned, but I learned later that it was written by Justice Lewis Powell Jr. Powell summarily rejected Antone's claim that the "haste with which [his] first habeas corpus petition was prepared" was any excuse for missing issues on arguments the first time around: Although counsel Tom McCoun might have been "appointed when execution was imminent and therefore did not have time fully to familiarize himself with the case," this "contention is not new, has been rejected by the courts below, and is meritless." Justice Powell concluded: "Upon consideration of the extensive papers filed with the Court, we find that none of these challenges warrant further review. Indeed, the grounds relied upon by [Antone] all appear to be meritless. For these reasons, we . . . deny the application for a stay."

One justice in the majority wrote a concurring opinion explaining why he voted to deny the stay. He noted that all of the issues—including the *Hitchcock* claim—had been raised in Antone's first round of capital appeals. This was incorrect, of course. McCoun had not raised the *Hitchcock* issue earlier. The justice had missed the issue.

Sixteen months later, the U.S. Supreme Court ruled unanimously in favor of Jim Hitchcock. Anthony Antone was denied a stay of execution even though his death sentence was as constitutionally defective as Hitchcock's. Had Antone been alive at the time of the *Hitchcock* decision in 1987, he would have won a new sentencing trial. Anthony Antone was put to death by the state of Florida at 7:00 A.M. on Thursday, January 26, 1984.

The issue of executing the insane remained, however. The claim was raised and rejected in another case, that of Freddie Goode. Goode, a zealously unrepentant pedophile, was perhaps the most hated man on death row. My colleagues and I faced the same moral and ethical dilemma we'd faced in *Antone*: whether or not to give my execution competency memo to Goode's lawyers. We decided to give them the memo. An entry from my diary at that time reflects my divided loyalties and my ambivalence:

[Craig Barnard, Dick Burr, and I] met and discussed *Goode*: I played devil's advocate on possible problems with competency to be executed claims—discussed whether they'll have abuse-of-the-writ problems, whether it matters that Goode was found competent to stand trial (i.e., unlike *Alvin Ford*, it's not a matter of intervening insanity, i.e., insanity that came into being for the first time after the original trial): Goode's been crazy all along—not just since he was living on death row, as was the case with *Alvin Ford*. One reason *Ford* is so good as a test case on this issue was that his craziness clearly didn't begin until after he was on death row, i.e., it was intervening insanity—*Goode* is an especially bad test case since Dr. Barnard, who now says Goode is too nuts to die, was the same shrink, at the original 1977 trial, who said he was too nuts to stand trial—Dr. Barnard's views then, in 1977, just didn't carry the day, and it's doubtful they will now: bottom line is that *Ford* (who is our client) is a good test case vehicle for taking the execution competency issue to the Eleventh Circuit and U.S. Supreme Court, because Alvin is really very crazy (talking to spaceships crazy) and because his insanity was intervening, in that it began during (and was caused by) his time on death row. *Goode* (who isn't our client) is a terrible test case vehicle, since he's allegedly been crazy all along, and because his craziness is so offensive (his pedophilia press conference)—raising and losing the issue in *Goode,* in Eleventh Circuit and Supreme Court, could make it much harder for *Ford* to win on it later. But, still, we have to run the issue on *Goode*—we can't play god.

Goode's lawyers lost on procedural grounds, so the legal precedents set in his case did not torpedo the merits of the execution competency claim.

Freddie Goode had been dead less than three hours when Craig, Dick, and I met to survey the damage. I recorded in my diary:

We did postmortem on *Goode* litigation: how it will affect *Ford,* what the Florida Supreme Court decided and what they left open in *Goode,* and how to proceed from here. The way things played out in *Goode* could have damaged our ability to raise the issue in *Ford* much worse than we did. The issue is still clean in the U.S. Supreme Court, since no merits ruling, and I never thought we'd win the claim in the Eleventh Circuit—unlikely the circuit court will "overrule" [the old U.S. Supreme Court case] (they'll leave that to the U.S. Supreme Court), and our ways of distinguishing that case are also why *Ford* is distinguishable from *Goode,* since *Goode* was based on that old case. The old case *was* (1) a Due Process clause case, not an Eighth Amendment case, (2) the old case was decided in 1950, before the Court's modern Eighth Amendment jurisdiction—a jurisprudence grounded in an attempt to identify (by objective indicia and exercise of the Court's independent evaluation of the goals of punishment) the revolutionary standards of decency that mark the progress of a maturing society.

4

Executing the Insane: Alvin Ford

Alvin Ford made history as the man who forced the criminal justice authorities, lawyers, judges, politicians, and a host of others to seriously debate the question of what types of mental illness should exempt condemned prisoners from execution and how (and by whom) these life-and-death determinations should be made.

—Kent S. Miller and Michael L. Radelet,
Executing the Mentally Ill, 1993

Alvin Ford wasn't always crazy. When he murdered police officer Dimitri Walter Ilyankoff—who was attempting to prevent him from robbing a Red Lobster restaurant in Fort Lauderdale, Florida—Ford was sane as can be. Ford was African American. His victim was white.

When Ford was tried and sentenced to death for the murder, he was still sane. It was living on death row that drove him insane. It was waiting to be killed that drove him mad.

The Florida Supreme Court denied Ford's direct appeal in 1980. The U.S. Supreme Court declined to hear the case. Thereafter, no attorney represented Ford for approximately a year. Then Larry Wollin, a volunteer lawyer, agreed to prepare Ford's executive clemency proceeding and to represent him in collateral proceedings. Wollin had not actively practiced law for a number of years, having become a criminologist and faculty member at Florida State University in Tallahassee.

When Ford's death warrant was signed in November 1981, no postconviction proceeding litigation had been developed. A handful of issues had been identified, but that was all. Through consulting with other lawyers, Wollin developed and filed a postconviction pleading. Less than one week before Ford's scheduled execution, when state remedies had been exhausted and the district court proceedings had begun, only Wollin, the inexperienced postconviction lawyer, represented Ford. The issues raised in Ford's case were pretty complicated, and it took the courts years to sort them all out. Meanwhile, Alvin Ford was going unquietly insane.

The Madness of Alvin Ford

It began with mad letters to TV stations and courts. By 1984 it was clear that Ford was flamboyantly psychotic and delusional. This was not a problem for Florida—Governor Bob Graham signed Ford's death warrant anyway, and the state courts refused to intervene. So did the lower federal courts.

When our public defender office took on Ford's case in 1984, our claim was simple: the U.S. Constitution doesn't allow states to execute people who are insane. In the federal habeas corpus petition, our description of Alvin Ford's mental state at the time of his 1984 death warrant began:

> In the two and one half years which have passed since December, 1981, Alvin Ford has been on a roller-coaster ride which has led him into a world that none of us can know. He now lives in a world in which, as best we can tell, he thinks that he is on death row at Florida State Prison only because he chooses to be there. He lives in a world in which he thinks that the case of "Ford v. State" has ended capital punishment in Florida and, in particular, has deprived the State of Florida of the right to execute him. He is unable to tell us, in words that we can understand, anything more about the world that he now inhabits. He now mutters softly to himself, making gestures in which there seems to be a message, but a message that none of us can decipher.

We continued by saying that, as Ford's counsel during the period of his gradual decline into his debilitated state,

> we believe that Mr. Ford's condition is the product of illness and is genuine. We have seen Mr. Ford gradually lose touch with reality over the past two and one half years. We have seen his delusions

grow until they took over every aspect of his life. We have seen him gradually losing interest in his case, then becoming angry with us because of our failure to listen to and present information in the "FCC tapes," then becoming convinced that he had won his case and could not be executed. . . . we have seen him become utterly unable to communicate with us about any subject—concerning his case or anything else. Our experience has convinced us—beyond any doubt—that Mr. Ford is not only genuinely ill but is grossly incompetent. We believe he understands nothing about his current circumstances. We know that he can do nothing to assist us in representing him. Having said this, we do not make these representations lightly.

Further, Ford's condition as of May 1984 represented serious deterioration from his condition in November and December 1983, when Dr. Harold Kaufman found him to be suffering from paranoid schizophrenia, which in Dr. Kaufman's opinion made him even then incompetent to be executed, and when two of the three psychiatrists appointed by Governor Graham to evaluate Ford found him to be suffering from psychosis.

John O'Callaghan, who was also under death warrant in Florida and was housed in a cell next to Ford, recounted his observations of Ford since April 30, 1984, when he and Ford were placed on deathwatch. We listed these in the habeas petition as follows:

(a) Mr. Ford has repeatedly threatened to kill me and various guards. After he has made such threats, however, he will often ask me for a cigarette.

(b) Mr. Ford talks to himself in a high-pitched voice. He then frequently gets into arguments with this "other" person which become violent fights, with Mr. Ford punching, rolling around, and struggling. At the end of these fights Mr. Ford is panting.

(c) Mr. Ford frequently bangs his head against the wall and has fits, during which he is snorting and growling.

(d) When his mail is given to him, Mr. Ford throws it on to the walk without ever reading it.

(e) Mr. Ford sometimes walks around his cell as if he were a robot.

(f) Every now and then Mr. Ford draws marks on the walls of his cell and touches the marks with various parts of his body.

O'Callaghan further indicated that these behaviors were not isolated occurrences. They occurred over and over again during every hour that O'Callaghan was awake.

On May 23, 1984, Dr. Kaufman and a colleague spent two hours with Ford at Florida State Prison. Kaufman's observations about Ford during this attempted interview reflect symptoms of the same profound illness that produced the behaviors O'Callaghan had observed:

Mr. Ford was in the interviewing room handcuffed when we arrived. He appeared to have lost at least twenty (20) pounds since I had last examined him on November 3, 1983. He was neatly dressed and was wearing rubber shower sandals. He did not greet the four of us as we entered and sat down. He sat with his body immobile and his handcuffed hands in a prayerful position in front of his mouth. Occasionally he moved his hands, still in the praying mode, to each of us for no apparent reason. His lips were pursed intermittently, but his head moved little. His eyes were closed or fluttering most of the time, although he occasionally glanced at one or more of us. His hands and fingers appeared to be trembling. We took turns asking him questions, and little or no response was forthcoming. He began muttering to himself after about five minutes. These utterances were largely unintelligible. This is the overall picture of what took place for two hours.

Because of his lack of responsiveness to the group, each of us tried speaking with him alone with the others out of the room. His utterances increased in number, but they remained soft mumbles. To the extent that they could be understood they were largely incoherent statements about "God," "Hell," and a recitation of numbers. His hands remained in a praying position for the full two hours of the interview.

When I asked him whether he understood that the Governor of Florida had signed his death warrant and that he was to be executed on May 31, Mr. Ford gave no evidence of understanding what I asked him: his muttering continued and his hand remained in front of his face.

He occasionally motioned to be taken to the bathroom: it appeared that interaction with prison personnel was equally disorganized. The level of autism was much more profound than in November.

Based on Ford's behavior and thought processes, Kaufman concluded that Ford's schizophrenia had become far worse in the previous six months and that his incompetency to be executed was even clearer than it was when he evaluated Ford on November 3, 1983. He also stated:

> It is highly unlikely that he is malingering because he could not possibly know what the legal consequences of his behavior might be. Mr. Ford's condition, severe paranoid schizophrenia, has seriously worsened, so that he now has at best only minimal contact with the events of the external world. Accordingly, he has no understanding that he is soon to be executed, or what execution means, as a result of his psychosis. It is my opinion therefore that he is not competent to be executed under the provisions of Florida's statute.

The history of Ford's illness, including the previous evaluations of his condition by psychiatrists, confirmed that Ford suffered from the debilitating, incompetency-producing process of psychosis diagnosed by Dr. Kaufman. This history was extensive, and it showed a relentless progression through all the generally recognized symptoms of paranoid schizophrenia.

Prior to December 1981, Ford did not suffer from psychosis. No question concerning his competency had been raised before, during, or after his trial. Ford had been on death row for nearly seven years by December 1981. Up to that point, there had been no indication of serious mental illness. But gradually, from that time on, Ford began to lose touch with what the rest of us know as reality. This process began in an almost unnoticeable fashion: Ford began to believe that the personalities at a radio station in Jacksonville were talking directly to him over the radio. As it continued, relentlessly, he began to believe that he wrote the subjects for the radio station's opinion line.

He then began to believe that he had the power to see things in the world outside the prison that no one else, except those vested with the same powers of perception, could see. Through his powers of perception, Ford became convinced that he had found strong evidence implicating the Ku Klux Klan in the arson of a house in Jacksonville in which a black family was killed. Not long after that, Ford began to believe that the Ku Klux Klan had placed several of its members as guards in the prison. The task of these Klan members was to drive Ford to suicide, and they tried to do so by holding women hostage in the "pipe alley" behind Ford's cell, raping these women, putting dead bodies in the concrete enclosure under his bunk in his cell, and putting semen on his food. He also imagined other conspiracies against him. He claimed that he had written a book about Teddy Pendergrass, and that the work had been stolen from him and published under another title by another author. Even though the subject of the book he claimed he'd written was Paul Robeson, Ford said that the book was merely an encoded version of his work.

Longtime friends and others who had provided Ford support over the years suddenly became enemies in Ford's disordered mind. All were joined in a giant conspiracy with the Ku Klux Klan to drive him crazy or to make him commit suicide. During the time that these events were taking place in Ford's mental life, he was not always obsessed by these thoughts. He had interludes of clarity and of being in touch with reality. However, as time progressed, those interludes became fewer and much shorter.

By the summer of 1982, Ford seemed to be unable to regain contact with reality. By that time, he believed that the conspirators against him, most notably the members of the Ku Klux Klan, had begun taking hostages. At first Ford's mother, then other members of his family, then his lawyers, then radio and television personalities, and finally politicians and world leaders all became hostages in a Machiavellian scheme to drive Ford to insanity. For a period lasting months, Ford desperately wrote to everyone he could think of who he believed had the power to assist him and begged for help in ending the "the hostage crisis." He wrote repeatedly to President Reagan, the director of the FBI, the state attorney in Jacksonville and numerous assistant attorneys general in the state of Florida, and numerous judges.

In each letter to each of these people, Ford recounted the events leading up to the hostage crisis and begged for help. Over time, his pleas became more bizarre, less logical, and more nonsensical. At the same time, the events in Ford's fantasy world began to take on significance far beyond him. Thus, in April 1983, Ford wrote to an attorney in Miami, "This [hostage] crisis has to end, it is causing the racial unrest in your City, namely Liberty City."

By the summer of 1983, Ford's imagined world changed again. He seemed to gain new power within his world, and, as a result, he seemed to be in the process of resolving the hostage crisis himself. For example, on May 10, 1983, he wrote to Florida Attorney General Jim Smith:

> I have fired a number of officials at the institutional level and state level, with the final approval, from the Governor, and the President of the United States. Also your office. There will be a number of suits, criminal charges, all listed on the Federal Communication Commission. Also there will be testimony before a Presidential Subcommittee, on this hostage crisis.

And again, on July 27, 1983, in a letter in which Ford referred to himself as Pope John Paul III, he wrote:

> This investigation has been very successful, and to the exact point of my past letters. It's unfortunate so many, prison personnel will be cast in prison. Thankfully the CIA-FBI was in fact able to investigate UCI, the attorney general's office, all level of state and federal court. The Florida State Supreme Court, I have appointed new justices, I have appointed nine.

By November 1983, Ford's communications from his world became more fragmented. He was no longer focused on any particular subject, but would carry on about a multiplicity of subjects all in one uninterrupted breath. The best example of this behavior was captured by Dr. Kaufman during his evaluation of Ford on November 3, 1983. The following is part of what Ford said that day, as recorded by Kaufman:

> The guard stands outside my cell and reads my mind. Then he puts it on tape and sends it to the Reagans and CBS. . . . I know there is some sort of death penalty, but I'm free to go whenever I want because it would be illegal and the executioner would be executed. . . . CBS is trying to do a movie about my case. . . . I know the KKK and news reporters all disrupting me and CBS knows it. Just call CBS crime watch—there are all kinds of people in pipe alley (an area behind Mr. Ford's cell) bothering me—

Sinatra, Hugh Heffner, people from the dog show, Richard Burr, my sisters and brother trying to sign the death warrants so they don't keep bothering me. . . . I never see them, I only hear them especially at night. (Note that Mr. Ford denies *seeing* these people in his delusions. This suggests that he is honestly reporting what his mental processes are.) I won't be executed because of no crime . . . maybe because I'm a smart ass . . . my family's back there (in pipe alley) . . . you can't evaluate me. I did a study in the army . . . a lot of masturbation. . . . I lost a lot of money on the stock market. They're back there investigating my case. Then this guy motions with his finger like when I pulled the trigger. Come on back you'll see what they're up to—Reagan's back there too. Me and Gail bought the prison and I have to sell it back. State and federal prisons. We changed all the other countries and because we've got a pretty good group back there I'm completely harmless. That's how Jimmy Hoffa got it. My case is gonna save me.

In the same conversation, Kaufman asked Ford, "Are you going to be executed?" Ford replied, "I can't be executed because of the landmark case. I won. *Ford v. State* will prevent executions all over." Thereafter, Kaufman and Ford carried on the following colloquy:

KAUFMAN: Are you on death row?

FORD: Yes.

KAUFMAN: Does that mean that the State intends to execute you?

FORD: No.

KAUFMAN: Why not?

FORD: Because Ford v. State prevents it. They tried to get me with the FCC tape but when the KKK came in it was up to CBS and the Governor. These prisoners are rooming back there raping everybody. I told the Governor to sign the death warrants so they stop bothering me.

In December 1983, communication with Ford became virtually impossible. In two interviews conducted on December 15 and December 19, 1983, Ford spoke in a fragmented, codelike fashion. At times during these interviews, Ford appeared to be trying to respond to questions posed to him, but he seemed incapable of communicating by any of the conventional methods most people use to communicate. The following interchange occurred between Ford and Gail Rowland, a paralegal in his case, during the interview on December 15:

ROWLAND: Have you seen any newspapers or anything in awhile?

FORD: Yes one.

ROWLAND: Did you read about the Pope?

FORD: Looking one.

ROWLAND: And Bob Sullivan and the Pope . . .

FORD: Looking one.

ROWLAND: He made a nice statement. You saw it. I was very moved.

FORD: Hello one, need you one.

(pause)

Gail one, threaten one, kill one.

(pause)

Remember one, letter one? Say one, God one, blind one, klan one. Destiny one?

(pause)

Mine one. Stab one, say one crazy one.

(pause)

Need one, love one.

(pause)

But one, starve one, damn one.

(pause)

Damn one, say one.

ROWLAND: I see

FORD: Excuse one, need you one.

(pause)

Tell him one. Hello one.

ROWLAND: I see what you're saying and . . .

FORD: Review one, law one. Dead one.

Four psychiatrists evaluated Ford's competency during November and December 1983. Three of the four determined that Ford suffered from psychosis. One of these three, Dr. Kaufman, determined that Ford's psychosis was of such severity "that he cannot sufficiently appreciate or understand either the reasons 'why the death penalty was imposed upon him' or 'the purpose' of this punishment." The other two, Drs. Mhatre and Afield, who were appointed by Governor Graham to examine Ford, determined that Ford was competent despite their finding that he genuinely suffered from psychosis. Thus only the third psychiatrist appointed by Governor Graham, Dr. Ivory, found Ford to be suffering from no genuine illness.

We presented substantial reasons, however, why the opinions of the psychiatrists who disagreed with Dr. Kaufman's assessment of competency were wrong. In preparation for the hearing that we anticipated in the state trial court, we asked two forensic psychiatrists, Dr. George W. Barnard and Dr. Seymour L. Halleck, both widely recognized as highly competent experts within their field, to review the process by which the three state-appointed psychiatrists had found Ford competent. In the opinion of these experts, the evaluations conducted by the three appointed psychiatrists failed to measure up to minimum standards for forensic evaluation. The central reason for this opinion was that the appointed psychiatrists had failed to document the factual basis for their conclusions in the face of pervasive data supporting the contrary conclusion. Dr. Barnard observed:

> The materials which I reviewed give evidence of documenting symptoms in Ford which are consistent of the diagnosis of schizophrenia, paranoid type. These symptoms include delusions of persecution, delusions of grandeur, thought blocking, thought insertion, thought broadcasting, flat affect, loosening of associations and disturbance of speech with word gibberish. In the psychiatric interview conducted by the three examiners appointed by the Governor, Ford was uncooperative and he gave them few meaningful verbal responses so that they relied heavily on his nonverbal productions and their ability to read between the lines for what he might be meaning with his nonsensical replies to their questions. In my opinion, the three examiners give conclusionary opinions about Ford's competency to be executed without documenting in a satisfactory manner their evidence or facts upon which their inferences are based. As a result, in my opinion, the factfinder and, in this case, Governor Graham and/or the

Court is left with the dilemma of depending on conclusionary belief statements by the psychiatrists that Ford is competent to be executed without adequate documentation by the psychiatrists so that the factfinder must rely on the credentials of the psychiatrists rather than their data. In my opinion, this leaves the factfinder in a very unsatisfactory position when a man's life is at stake and in the absence of additional checks and balances is not in keeping with my understanding of due process.

Dr. Halleck similarly noted:

While Dr. Mhatre's and Dr. Afield's evaluations both did take into account the history and previous evaluation of Mr. Ford's condition, both, as did Dr. Ivory's, failed to account for the facts contained in this history which were central to the forensic task at hand: whether Mr. Ford's delusional processes which, among other things, had led him to believe that he had won his case and could no longer be executed, were relevant to the issue of his incompetence, in that he failed to understand why he was to be executed or, as Dr. Kaufman put it, failed to understand "the purpose" of his execution. Dr. Kaufman had previously concluded that Mr. Ford was incompetent precisely because of these delusional processes. Yet neither Dr. Ivory, Dr. Mhatre nor Dr. Afield dealt with this most crucial data in their reports.

None of these facts could save Ford's life, however, unless we could show that the U.S. Constitution forbids execution of the currently insane. So, in October 1983, while Dick Burr, Ford's lead attorney, put together the factual bases of Ford's descent into mental illness, I was given the job of fashioning a constitutional argument that would make these facts matter in court. I had a lot of material to work with. The Legal Defense Fund of the NAACP had researched the issue, as had lawyers in Atlanta. The Florida lawyers for Gary Alvord had raised a similar claim, and students at Yale Law School and Stanford Law School had published outstanding law review articles on the issue of executing the insane.

The Issue

On October 3, 1983, I was assigned the task of researching and writing a memo on why execution of the insane might offend the U.S.

Constitution. One obstacle to such an argument was clear at once: a U.S. Supreme Court decision from 1950 had held that the Due Process Clause of the Fourteenth Amendment did not prohibit execution of the insane. There was a way around the case, however, given that it pre-dated the Court's modern capital punishment jurisprudence, which was grounded in the Eighth Amendment's ban on "cruel and unusual" punishments rather than the Fourteenth Amendment's guarantee of "due process of law."

I was more encouraged by the fact that every capital punishment state in the United States exempted the currently insane from the ulti-mate penalty. This legislative consensus would allow us to argue that the nation as a whole had reached a consensus that executing the insane offended a constitutional provision grounded, as the Court had said, in "the evolving standards of decency that mark the progress of a matur-ing society." This legislative consensus was a double-edged sword for our argument, however. The same states whose laws formed the na-tional consensus against executing the insane all vested in governors—not the courts—the power to decide whether particular death row prisoners were too crazy to kill. Florida law was typical; the law pro-hibited execution of the insane, but it allowed the governor total dis-cretion in deciding who was or wasn't insane. We needed to argue that, while the national consensus recognized a constitutional right not to be executed while insane, the *courts* had a duty to ensure that the process of determining execution competency be fair and reliable.

The argument that the constitution forbids executing the currently insane appeared straightforward, but land mines abounded. For in-stance, the Eighth Amendment prohibits "cruel and unusual" punish-ments, but it might be argued that it is *less* cruel to execute a person who has descended into a world of delusions than it is to execute the lucid, because the sane can fully appreciate the horror of what is going to happen to them. Then there was the problem of what would be done with people who had been found too insane to be executed. Couldn't psychiatrists simply "treat" such people until they were sane enough to be executed? That might pervert medical ethics, but such a perversion probably would not offend the Constitution. After all, the claim in Ford's case was that the Constitution prohibits executing the *currently* insane.

The governor signed Alvin Ford's death warrant in May 1984. Dick

Burr told me at the time, "Your competency memo is the best thing I've ever seen on the subject, and we're going to file it verbatim" in Ford's case.

We filed the Ford papers in the state trial court at noon on May 21. The judge was on vacation, and we did it all by phone. At 4:00 P.M. our stay application was denied (another trial judge had signed the order for the vacationing judge). It took only four hours for us to lose a constitutional issue we had been developing for four months.

We did not expect to win Ford's case. Dick Burr decided that honor and duty required him to witness the Ford execution and to ask for clemency literally until the bitter end. Meanwhile, Ford himself was refusing to see anyone; according to Dick, Ford was "banging his head against the wall of his prison cell all day."

On Wednesday, May 23, while Dick spent the day with Ford at the prison, supervising psychiatric evaluations, the stay papers were filed in the Florida Supreme Court. The court set oral argument for 9:00 A.M. on Friday.

On Thursday we got more bad news. When Ford's case reached the federal trial court—and we had scant hope that we would win in the Florida Supreme Court, obviating the need to go into federal court—the case would come before the same judge who had blasted it through the last time around. The judge, "Stormin' Norman" Roettger, was hostile the last time Ford's case had called him into the office on a Saturday. We were on notice that the judge was less than happy about seeing the case again. Dick told me that the judge's law clerk had told Dick that the judge "gave you a hearing on Saturday last time, and I doubt he will do that again—I think he's done all he's going to do for Alvin Ford."

Before we could get to federal court, though, we had to go through the formality of losing in the Florida Supreme Court. The justices (five of the seven justices, anyway) heard oral argument at 9:00 A.M. sharp on Friday, May 25. I stayed in the office to work on the U.S. Supreme Court papers for Ford; Dick called to tell me that the argument went "real shitty," and that all five justices were hostile. The oral argument lasted an hour, and less than two hours after the argument ended, the court issued its opinion. We lost, of course. We filed in federal trial court that same afternoon.

That night I got a nice surprise, unrelated to Ford's case. A Florida death row prisoner won in the Eleventh Circuit federal court of appeals that day, and he won based on my old *Thomas* opinion for Judge Vance. The prisoner's lawyer told me that "*Thomas* is the best thing the Eleventh Circuit did last year." My diary entry for the day concluded: "I left the office after midnight, thinking about Joseph Thomas, Ivon Ray Stanley, Judge Vance . . . and me."

Saturday and Sunday were days of waiting and preparing—waiting for the federal trial judge and preparing to go to the Eleventh Circuit Court of Appeals and the U.S. Supreme Court when we lost. Dick Burr set our emotional tone. On Saturday, he was depressed and pessimistic, and so were the rest of us. On Sunday, he was upbeat: "Maybe *I'm* crazy, but I think we're going to win this thing." His spirits lifted ours, too. Throughout the weekend, we strategized, drafted legal papers, and waited.

On Monday we sent papers to be lodged in the Eleventh Circuit. I left the office at 4:30 P.M. At 9:00 P.M. Dick called me at home to tell me that the judge had set a hearing for 1:30 P.M. on Tuesday, and Dick wanted me to argue the merits of the landmark execution competency issue. The entry in my diary for that day shows how I was feeling:

> This will be the first time I will be arguing any issue, in any case, capital or non-capital, in federal court, and [Burr] wants me to argue one of the most important constitutional issues—and one of the longest shots, legally and factually complex constitutional claims—in a successive habeas corpus case filed by a Ft. Lauderdale cop-killer, in front of a judge whose nickname is "Stormin' Norman"; I think I will be learning to swim by being thrown into the deep end of the pool, but "what the hell," as Yossarian would say.

I got no sleep that night. I didn't even try. I read cases and wrote notes for my argument. I paced. I tried to play with my dog, but he was trying to sleep.

"Stormin' Norman" lived up to his nickname. Through his impressive handlebar mustache, the judge barraged me with questions about why he should rule that the Constitution forbids executing the insane. He clearly wanted to find a procedural reason to throw us out of court. As soon as we finished the argument, he ruled from the bench and did exactly that. Procedural bar, procedural bar, procedural bar.

Using a courthouse hallway pay phone, we called the Eleventh Circuit Court of Appeals in Atlanta to activate the papers we had lodged the previous day.

Dick and I arrived back in our office at 5:00 P.M. Thirty minutes later, we received a phone call from the Eleventh Circuit: oral argument would be held in Atlanta the next day. That was good news, and, on its face, there was more good news: the three appellate judges assigned to the Ford case were the same three who had recently stayed the execution of another of my clients. However, in that case, the U.S. Supreme Court, by a five-to-four vote, had dissolved the stay, and our client was killed. How would those same three judges respond to Ford's case? Would they stay the execution, as they had done previously? Or would the Supreme Court reversal of their earlier stay make them gun-shy?

On balance, we thought it unlikely that the Eleventh Circuit would stop Ford's execution. So, while Dick flew to Atlanta for the argument, Craig Barnard and I rewrote the papers for the U.S. Supreme Court. When I left the office at midnight, Craig—my boss—was typing up my work. After two hours at home, I decided that sleep was impossible, and so I headed back to the office. While Craig typed, I photocopied and organized the pages. By 6:00 A.M. the U.S. Supreme Court papers were ready. We handed them to one of our investigators, who then got on a plane to Washington, D.C., so the papers would be ready for filing if we lost in the Eleventh Circuit. The plane bearing our papers took off at 7:00 A.M. Alvin Ford was scheduled to be executed in exactly twenty-four hours.

By the time the papers were done, I was too keyed up to sleep and too exhausted—this had been my second consecutive all-nighter—to function very well. At 1:00 P.M. Dick Burr called from Atlanta. He said that it was hard to gauge how the argument had gone. The judges had asked about procedural bars, along with the merits of the execution competency claim. At 4:20 he called again. The Eleventh Circuit had stayed the execution—fourteen hours before Ford's date with death—but it was a split decision. Two judges voted to grant the stay, but the third had voted to deny it.

Now it was the prosecutors' turn to activate the papers they had previously lodged in the U.S. Supreme Court. We scrambled to throw together a reply to the state's motion to dissolve the Eleventh Circuit's stay. We had to write and file the reply blind, because we had not yet seen the Eleventh Circuit's opinion explaining the stay, the opinion we were trying to defend. We finally got the Eleventh Circuit's opinions at 7:30. It appeared that the majority opinion didn't need us to defend it; it seemed bulletproof. But the Supreme Court justices were an unpredictable lot.

Maybe it was my fatigue and fear, but the longer I looked at the Eleventh Circuit's stay opinion, the shakier it seemed. As the night wore on—this would be my third all-nighter in a row—Craig and I wrote papers like automatons. Our final papers were put on a plane to D.C. at 6:30 A.M.

By 7:00 A.M. on Friday, June 1, 1984—when Ford was to have been electrocuted—there were no more papers to write, nothing left to do. At 5:12 P.M. we got a call. The rumor among reporters was that the Supreme Court would lift the stay in *Ford* any minute. At 5:30 I went home to eat. At 7:00 P.M. I called the office: still no word. Finally, at 8:10, Craig called me: the Supreme Court had upheld the stay by a vote of six to three. The competency-to-be-executed issue was a real, live issue, and I had hopes that Alvin Ford would live long enough to litigate it, unlike Anthony Antone.

The Eleventh Circuit put Ford's case on an expedited briefing and oral argument schedule. Because we were swamped with warrant cases, we didn't have as much time as we would have liked to work on the briefs. We were in the midst of a death warrant in James Dupree Henry's case (which I discuss in chapter 6) when Dick Burr headed out to deliver the oral argument in *Ford*.

The Eleventh Circuit panel in *Ford* consisted of Judges Vance, Clark, and Stafford. Dick thought the argument went well. He told me that Judge Vance was "very friendly" and that Vance said he thought the Eighth Amendment to the Constitution created a right not to be executed while insane. Dick was optimistic, and I did nothing to dampen his enthusiasm.

It was a good sign that Judge Vance had spoken of an Eighth Amendment right, not a Fourteenth Amendment right, because that meant he knew how to get around the old Supreme Court precedent that had refused to find a Fourteenth Amendment prohibition against executing the mentally ill. That was some comfort. Still, I didn't share Dick's enthusiasm. I knew from hard experience that Judge Vance would be reluctant to predict that the Supreme Court would recognize a constitutional right not to be executed when insane. Judge Vance had in the past tried to divine where the Supreme Court would go in the future in death penalty cases. As I have described in chapter 2, he had tried to clear Alabama's death row, and his attempt brought him a stinging rebuke from the high court. I didn't think Judge Vance would take that gamble again, not in Alvin Ford's case.

A few months after Dick's argument in the Eleventh Circuit and before the court ruled in Ford's case, I phoned Judge Vance about a job reference. We didn't speak about Ford, of course, but Vance did say he'd been pleased to see my name on the Ford briefs and that he'd hoped I was going to argue it before him. He railed against Governor Graham and the Florida attorney general for, as he put it, always resorting to demagoguery in death cases; he'd cut his political teeth in George Wallace's Alabama, and he had no use for the demagoguery of politicians. I told him about a case I'd recently argued and lost in the Eleventh Circuit; I said I was up there arguing that "our" old *Thomas* case required a hearing in my case, but I still lost. That got a deep and very hard belly laugh from Judge Vance.

A few months after that chat, we lost Ford's case in the Eleventh Circuit. The vote was two to one. Judge Clark had written a nineteen-page dissent, and Judge Vance had written a seven-page opinion for the majority. Vance's opinion teed up the execution competency issue perfectly for U.S. Supreme Court review. He based his reasoning on the old due process case. This invited the Supreme Court to decide whether that old case remained good law or whether the evolving standards of decency that mark the progress of a maturing society required a different constitutional rule today.

In fact, the Supreme Court did decide to decide Ford's case, and then the Court held that the Constitution today forbids execution of the currently insane. It was a close thing, however. Initially, the Supreme Court justices decided that Ford's case wasn't worth their time. But then Justice Thurgood Marshall circulated to the other justices a draft opinion dissenting from the majority's refusal to hear Ford's case. Marshall's draft convinced enough of the other justices that Ford's case was worth their time. And, upon full consideration, a majority of the Supreme Court ruled in Ford's favor. The result was a landmark opinion saying that states can't execute crazy people.

Justice Marshall's opinion for the Court began by burying the old 1950 precedent that was based on the Due Process Clause of the Fourteenth Amendment. Ford's claim was based on the Eighth Amendment's ban on cruel and unusual punishments. The Court's jurisprudence of death had evolved substantially since 1950.

Marshall then reached back much further than 1950. He stated that the Eighth Amendment "embraces, at a minimum, those modes or acts of punishment that had been considered cruel and unusual at the time the Bill of Rights was adopted." Even in 1789, when the framers of the Bill of Rights wrote the Eighth Amendment, it was well-settled law that the government was forbidden to execute the insane.

"This ancestral legacy has not outlived its time," Marshall continued. "Today, no state in the union permits the execution of the insane." Marshall explained:

It is clear that the ancient and humane limitation upon the state's ability to execute its sentences has as firm a hold upon the jurisprudence of today as it had centuries ago in England. The various reasons put forth in support of the common-law restriction have no less logical, moral, and practical force than they did when first voiced. For today, no less than before, we may seriously question the retributive value of executing a person who has no comprehension of why he has been singled out and stripped of his fundamental right to life. Similarly, the natural abhorrence civilized societies feel at killing one who has no capacity to come to grips with his own conscience or deity is still vivid today. And the intuition that such an execution simply offends humanity is evidently shared across this Nation. Faced with such widespread evidence of a restriction upon sovereign power, this Court is compelled to conclude that the Eighth Amendment prohibits a State from carrying out a sentence of death upon a prisoner who is insane. Whether its aim be to protect the condemned from fear and pain without comfort of understanding, or to protect the dignity of society itself from the barbarity of exacting mindless vengeance, the restriction finds enforcement in the Eighth Amendment.

Marshall then turned to the specifics of Florida's statutory procedure for determining execution competency. He found Florida's procedure constitutionally inadequate. Because Florida's procedure failed,

Alvin Ford was entitled to an evidentiary hearing in the federal trial court, unless Florida were to adopt a procedure for determining execution competency that did pass constitutional muster. That was where things got dicey. For Marshall, only a full-blown minitrial would suffice. But on this point Marshall was not speaking for a majority of the Court.

The key opinion was a concurrence written by Justice Lewis Powell Jr. Powell would give the states a great deal of latitude in designing a state procedure for determining competency. Although Powell found Florida's procedure inadequate, he would require far less than Marshall's minitrial.

The Supreme Court did not hold that Alvin Ford was immune from execution because he was insane. Rather, the Court held that *if* Ford was in fact mentally ill in such a way that he was mentally incompetent to be executed, then and only then would Ford be out from under the death sentence. Before Ford could leave death row, we would have to prove, at a minitrial, that he was actually as ill as we claimed. Before that matter could be decided definitively, Alvin Ford died of "natural causes." He was still on death row at the time.

The Fallout

Alvin Ford's landmark victory in the U.S. Supreme Court established the principles that executing the currently insane offends the Constitution and that Florida's procedures for determining execution competency were constitutionally insufficient. Yet the Ford case opened up more questions than it answered.

Two such open questions were foremost in my mind when Ford's case was decided by the Supreme Court. First, if a prisoner was currently incompetent to be executed, could the state enlist psychiatrists to medicate him forcibly back to sufficient sanity that he could then be executed during a "lucid interval"? Second, could Florida execute an allegedly insane prisoner prior to the state's adoption of a constitutionally valid procedure for determining execution competency?

Both issues were presented in the Nollie Lee Martin case. Martin was convicted of killing twice. In North Carolina, he torched a house and three people died. In West Palm Beach, Florida, he robbed a convenience store, raped the clerk—an honors student on summer vacation— and then murdered her. The Florida crime made Martin infamous in

Palm Beach County. On my second day as a capital public defender, Craig Barnard assigned me to research the legal issues in Martin's case. I recorded in my diary for that day what Craig said to me: "When people talk about the death penalty, this is the case they use as an example; this is the Ted Bundy case of Palm Beach County. Lee Martin just wants to *live,* and he's happy to live in prison. He's spent his whole life in prison, and he gets along fine there. Every year, around Christmas, Lee asks me if he's going to make it for another year. So far, I've always been able to tell him yes. You keep it that way."

Martin's case brimmed with legal issues. He had twice confessed to the Florida police, but his *Miranda* rights had been violated. And he was mentally ill. As a child, he had suffered profound brain damage. CAT scans told the tale—parts of Martin's brain were literally damaged or missing.

When Governor Graham signed Martin's first death warrant, the case flew through the state courts and the federal trial court. The Eleventh Circuit Court of Appeals stayed the execution. After my oral argument, I was guardedly nonpessimistic that the judges had bought my *Miranda* arguments against Martin's confessions. They had, and they threw out Martin's first confession. It didn't matter, though, because they held that the second confession was allowable, and so the legal error in admitting the first confession into evidence was "harmless." Martin's murder conviction and death sentence would stand, despite the *Miranda* violation in his first confession.

Martin took the news hard, as I knew he would. I should have visited him right away, especially after I received a depressed-sounding letter from him. I wanted to visit him. I intended to visit him. I just didn't have the time, but that was no excuse. I should have made the time.

My neglect of Lee Martin ended with a phone call from his brother, Harry. The night before Harry called me, Lee had attempted suicide, slitting his writs and taking an overdose of pills. Harry had received the news from the prison chaplain. I phoned the prison chaplain and found out that Lee was in the Gainesville General Hospital, and he was in no immediate danger. In fact, he was cranky, which I took as a good sign. He was upset about the way he was being kept now: in a stripped cell with only a mattress, no shaving gear, cigarettes, or toothbrush, on twenty-four-hour suicide watch.

The precipitating event for the suicide attempt wasn't the court loss.

Lee had received a prison disciplinary report for possession of contraband. The contraband was a small plastic container of fruit cocktail.

A few months later, the governor signed a new death warrant on Martin. The only real issue he had left was mental competency to be executed. Dick Burr and I would serve as Martin's lawyers.

As I've said, Martin was mentally ill. However, the prison was treating him with antipsychotic drugs. So long as Martin was medicated, he could cope with life on death row. But he was also much less crazy, which undermined our claim that Martin was too ill to kill. An entry from my diary shows the ethical dilemma we faced:

Worked on *Ford*/competency to be executed issue in *Martin*. Reread cases and briefs. Called Dick Burr: he had a good meeting with Lee Martin yesterday; Lee says he's not at all like Ford, but Dick thinks his controls are slipping more each day without a stay of the warrant. Terrible moral dilemma: should I instruct the prison to stop medicating Lee's mental illness? That would cause his mental health to deteriorate even more, which improves his execution competency claim, and thus his chances of getting a stay. But that would come at a fearful price: Taking Lee off his meds would descend him into hell—lashed by demons, trying to keep Satan under the heel of his boot. So, do I send Lee into mental hell to try to keep his physical body alive for a bit longer? Or do I decrease his chances of a stay by having the prison pump him full of anti-psychotic drugs—so he'll be terrified, with a clear head, of sitting in the electric chair he fears so much? And it's my choice, not his: He's not mentally competent to decide whether or not to refuse medical/psychiatric treatment. Even with medication, he's very crazy, although probably not too crazy (or not crazy in the right way) to be executed under *Ford* test of execution competency. . . . Lee will stop trying to pretend that he's sane; concern that he may try to hurt himself this weekend: Burr and I talked about the ethics of appearing not to "be making him crazy," as opposed to simply removing impediments to make his craziness apparent and identifiable as such by a neutral observer: Craig feels we need to be very attentive to these ethical issues, and not cross the line.

After getting off the phone with Martin, I began thinking that it really *did* seem too good to be true. Governor Bob Graham was a master at the chess game of capital punishment politics. Might he be sandbagging me? Might he be baiting a trap? As soon as I withdrew Martin's court papers, did the governor plan to reinstate the warrant, ram through a bogus psychiatric exam, and kill Martin before we could respond properly in court? I didn't put it past Bob Graham. He played the politics of death with perfect pitch, and he was as ruthless a politician as twenty Caesars. He had built a political career on the electrocuted corpses of my clients. I couldn't trust him now.

I decided I didn't trust him now. When I called the U.S. Supreme Court, I told the death clerk that I was not withdrawing the stay papers in Martin's case. I wasn't pushing the justices to act on the papers, but I wanted to keep them in place in case Governor Graham changed his mind on short notice about the stay.

I returned to other cases during that weekend. Other of my office's clients had death warrants. There were briefs to be written.

By Monday I had all but forgotten Lee Martin's case (such was the nature of deathwork in those days). I was taken aback by the phone call at 7:30 P.M. on Monday from the U.S. Supreme Court. The justices had unanimously issued an indefinite stay of Martin's execution, notwithstanding the stay we already had from Governor Graham. I had to smile. It seemed the U.S. Supreme Court didn't trust Governor Graham any more than I did.

That stay kept Nollie Lee Martin alive for the next few years. In the end, he was killed in the electric chair that so terrified him. He was profoundly mentally ill until the moment he died, but he wasn't crazy in precisely the proper way to render him incompetent to be executed.

Martin's last round of litigation was based on an issue I had been arguing since my year as Judge Vance's death clerk: that Florida's "heinous, atrocious or cruel" aggravating circumstance was unconstitutionally vague. I had failed to convince Judge Vance. As a public defender, I argued the issue in every single one of my dozens of capital cases, and I failed to persuade any court.

With Martin facing imminent execution, the U.S. Supreme Court had agreed to decide the issue. Martin's lawyers asked for a stay until the Court had resolved the matter. The courts refused, and Martin was put to death. A few months later, the U.S. Supreme Court struck down the HAC aggravating circumstance as unconstitutional.

Nollie Lee Martin never should have been put to death. Ironically, one of my primary opponents in the case agreed with me—off the record, of course—on this score. After one spirited oral argument in Atlanta on the *Martin* case, the prosecutor and I went out for a drink. Two hours earlier, he and I had been arguing in court about why Martin should live or die. Now, however, we were out of court, having a civilized conversation, as lawyers on opposite sides often do. The prosecutor told me that he really didn't want to win the *Martin* case, and that he and his colleagues had talked seriously about pleading Martin to a life sentence. Nothing came of this conversation, of course. I lost the argument, and the prosecutor, his personal views notwithstanding, continued to press for Martin's execution.

ment caused by electrocution), and (2) now, with lethal injection, there is a more humane method of killing an otherwise healthy adult human being that isn't nearly as destructive of bodily integrity as electrocution, so (3) the Constitution requires states to use the lethal injection.

The draft was done—in handwritten form—around midnight. Between 1:30 and 2:30 A.M., I tried to find some documentary proof that electrocutions were not painless. At 2:30 A.M. we all proofread the papers. At 3:00 A.M., Dick and I were on the road from West Palm Beach to Jacksonville to hand deliver the papers to the court. That was the only way to get them there quickly in those days. As we traveled, Craig Barnard telephoned an attorney friend in Jacksonville, Bob Link. He woke Link from a sound sleep to ask him to file our lawsuit on Sullivan's behalf. Craig detailed our legal arguments for Link, which took a good portion of the night. By the time they got off the phone, it was almost dawn, and Dick and I were rolling into Jacksonville. We met Link at his law office at about 6:00 A.M., one hour before Sullivan was scheduled for electrocution. We handed the paperwork to him, and the three of us drove to the federal courthouse to file. When we filed the stay application, the clerk's office told us to sit and wait. We did—until around 6:45, when the clerk told us that the judge wanted us in open court—at once. We weren't there for long, though. Link argued for maybe three minutes before the judge denied the stay. The district judge then asked if we wanted to appeal to the Eleventh Circuit Court in Atlanta. Of course we did. Actually, we had already sent the stay papers to the Eleventh Circuit by plane, but the flight was delayed; the plane was circling the Atlanta airport when Bob Sullivan was put to death.

We didn't know where the plane was at the time, though. We filed the one-paragraph notice of appeal and set up a telephone conference call for the oral argument. The Eleventh Circuit had three judges in three different states standing by, and the execution was five minutes away. In a dash from the courtroom to the district judge's chambers on another floor of the building to make the conference call, somehow we had lost Dick. As 7:00 A.M. approached, with Link on the phone with the three (increasingly impatient) judges, it became clear to us all that Link would have to wing it without help from Dick. He did a great job outlining our legal argument.

At that point, we didn't even know if Sullivan was still alive. We couldn't get a call through to the death chamber at the prison, so we couldn't know if the execution had gone down as scheduled. The trial court clerk told us the case was in a "ghost status"—in the absence of a stay, we had to assume the execution had proceeded on schedule; the trial court called the prison and was told that Sullivan had "probably been executed." At about 7:02 the Eleventh Circuit panel denied the stay, and we decided it was over. By the time the Eleventh Circuit denied the stay, Sullivan was probably dead or dying.

I later heard that our last-minute lawsuit delayed Sullivan's execution by about five minutes. Maybe it did, but that didn't matter to me when, at about 7:10, Burr and I heard over the car radio that Sullivan was dead. A five-minute reprieve was less than worthless; most likely it only upset whatever equanimity and dignity Sullivan had been able to muster for his appointment with death.

The day after Sullivan's execution, I noted in my diary: "Went to Orlando with Jorandby, Dick Burr and Richard Greene to meet with Dr. Elisabeth Kübler-Ross, author of On Death and Dying; Susan Cary was there with Bob Sullivan before the killing, and she witnessed execution; and she said that Bob Sullivan was really ready to die—at peace and 'without malice.' I wish I could say the same about myself. This experience has left me with a hell of a lot of malice—trying not to think about how this will feel when it's one of *my* clients, someone I've come to know and fought for for years."

I sat in the electric chair once. Shortly after the creation of Florida's statewide capital appeals office (CCR), the office personnel took a tour of Florida's death row. Led by a soft-spoken correctional officer, we visited Q wing, where our clients lived in tiers of one-man cells connected by catwalks. Each nine-by-six foot steel and concrete cell had a black-and-white television set. Each prisoner was allowed two hours in the exercise yard each week and one shower per week. In July and August, temperatures in the death row cells hovered around a hundred degrees.

Our tour included the deathwatch cells and the execution chamber itself. We sat in the folding metal chairs where the witnesses sit, separated from the death squad and the chair by a clear Plexiglas partition. Then we toured the control room for the electrical mechanisms and, finally, gathered around the solid-oak, three-legged electric chair itself.

On impulse, I sat down in it, to the frown of our tour guide. It wasn't a wise idea. I had nightmares about the chair for months afterward.

Eleven days before Christmas in 1985, I recorded in my diary:

Tour of Florida State Prison, arranged by Larry Spaulding: I left for the prison in Starke at 6:30 a.m., in "nonsmoking" car with Larry, Lisa, and Sidney: the four and a half hour tour started at 9:15 a.m.—prison personnel Mathis and Reddish led us through the whole prison complex, from psych wings to Death Row cells (saw Bill Elledge there)—life there can't be described: tiny cells, only bars between them, two rows of bars to the catwalk where we stood—tour ended in death chamber, electric chair (I sat in chair), witness room: saw the switches—Mathis went through the whole "procedure" in an awful bureaucratic monotone ("then I help strap them in . . .")—I felt very weak and ill and dirty—then we went to Deathwatch cells, only 10 feet from chair; then we all went to Mike Radelet's house in Gainesville for meeting of the "family": Susan Cary talked about dealing with dying people, and Mike about research he wanted to do: deathwork politics flying around Radelet living room.

Even after the courts in Sullivan's case rejected our challenge to "Old Sparky," I continued to raise the claim in subsequent cases. In fact, I raised it in every single case. I kept raising it even after judges told me they were tired of seeing the same grisly arguments they had already rejected. I kept raising the issue because I wanted to remind the judges that the essential fact of capital punishment is *killing*. The legal challenge we raised could become technical and detached from the killing reality of capital punishment. I wanted the judges to know that when they ruled, men and women died.

So long as the electric chair functioned properly, legal challenges to it went nowhere. However, beginning in 1990, Florida's electric chair began to malfunction. The resulting botched executions breathed new life into the legal arguments against using the chair. In 1990, Jesse Tafero's head burst into flames during his execution. In 1995, Jerry White screamed in apparent pain during his execution. In 1997, Pedro Medina's face mask caught fire. In July 1999, blood poured from Allen Lee Davis's nose and mouth, covered his chest, and seeped through his shirt and the buckle holes of the chair's chest strap when the electric chair was activated.

The history of botched electrocutions is as old as the chair itself. The electric chair was the brainchild of Thomas Alva Edison. Prior to its first use—in 1890, at Auburn Prison in Auburn, New York, on a man named William Kemmler—Edison sent his electric chair around the country to show the dangerousness of his competitor's version of a device used to generate electricity. Dogs, cats, and an orangutan were strapped into Edison's chair and electrocuted, all to show the power of electricity.

The first electrocution of a man—Kemmler's in 1890—was botched, but even so, the device gained steadily in popularity as a relatively "humane" alternative to hanging. States without centralized death rows resurrected Edison's idea of the traveling chair. In Louisiana, for example, a portable electric chair was carried on the back of a flatbed truck from parish to parish, depending on who needed executing where. In the early 1930s, one occupant of Louisiana's portable electric chair was an African American man named Willie Francis. Perhaps the tarp covering the chair on its journeys had sprung a leak, or perhaps the ride over Louisiana's unpaved back roads had jostled loose one of the chair's electrical wiring connections. Whatever the reason, the chair didn't kill Willie Francis, although it shocked him and scared the hell out of him. After several unsuccessful attempts to electrocute Francis, the chair was declared broken, and Francis was taken back to jail.

After the portable chair was repaired, the Louisiana officials wanted to try it again on Francis, but his lawyers argued that that would constitute "double jeopardy" in violation of the U.S. Constitution. Four justices of the U.S. Supreme Court agreed, but that fell one vote shy of mattering for Francis. With Justice Felix Frankfurter casting the deciding vote, the Court decided that Louisiana could kill Francis in its now-repaired electric chair. Louisiana did exactly that.

Jesse Tafero's 1990 execution marked the beginning of the end for Florida's electric chair. The prison called Tafero's bungled execution a fluke, an accident caused by the execution squad's mistakenly substituting a synthetic sponge for the natural sponge they were supposed to dampen with a saline solution and place between the chair's cap and Tafero's shaved head, the better to conduct electricity. It would never happen again. Yet it did happen again.

On March 25, 1997, Pedro Medina was strapped into Florida's electric chair. As twenty-four hundred volts of electricity surged into his body, blue and orange flames leapt from the right side of his head, filling the execution chamber with smoke. According to Associated Press reporter Ron Ward, who witnessed the execution, "The smell of burnt flesh filled the witness room (separated from the death chamber by Plexiglas) and lingered." The *Washington Post* reported that, as witnesses gasped, a maintenance supervisor wearing electrical gloves patted out the flames while another official opened a window to disperse the smoke.

The state doctor in attendance said he thought the death had been instantaneous and painless. A report later released by the office of the governor said that the twenty-four hundred volts that killed Medina did so instantly, before the flames appeared, and that he had not suffered from the flames.

An investigation by the Department of Corrections found that the flames that engulfed Medina's head were caused by a corroded copper screen in the chair's headpiece. But the *New York Times* stated that a report prepared for Governor Chiles by two engineers and made public on April 11, 1997, had concluded that the accident occurred because one of the sponges placed under the headpiece was dry and caught fire. The report recommended that only one sponge should be used, and that should be dampened with a saline solution. In other words, Medina's botched electrocution had been caused by human error—much as human error regarding sponges had caused flames and smoke to rise from the head of Jesse Tafero seven years earlier.

Two years later it happened again. In July 1999, Allen Lee Davis, a three-hundred-pound triple murderer known as Tiny, was killed in Florida's electric chair. As the switch was thrown, Davis's body reared back against the chair's restraints, giving witnesses a grotesque glimpse under the black hood designed to hide the face of the condemned. His face was grossly contorted, the flesh seeming to knot, and colored a vivid purple. Blood poured from Davis's nose, ran down the wide leather strap that covered his mouth, and soaked his white shirt. After the power was turned off, Davis was still alive. Witnesses said his chest rose and fell about ten times before he went still.

In the summer of 1999, the Florida Supreme Court declared a moratorium on executions while the court undertook to determine whether the electric chair was unconstitutionally "cruel and unusual" punishment. On September 24, 1999, a divided court rejected a constitutional challenge to the electric chair. According to the majority, the trial court's findings of fact "were supported by competent, substantial evidence. The trial court's findings included: (1) the electric chair functioned as intended during the execution of Allen Lee Davis; (2) the execution protocol was not deviated from during the electrocution of Davis; (3) Davis did not suffer any conscious pain; (4) the nose bleed suffered by Davis began before the electrical current was administered; and (5) any pain associated with affixing the restraining straps was necessary to ensure that the integrity of the execution process is maintained." Justice Shaw dissented:

> Execution by electrocution—with its attendant smoke and flames and blood and screams—is a spectacle whose time has passed. The fiery deaths of Jesse Tafero and Pedro Medina and the recent bloody execution of Allen Lee Davis are acts more befitting a violent murderer than a civilized state. The color photos of Davis [which are appended to the dissenting opinion] depict a man who—for all appearances—was brutally tortured to death by the citizens of Florida. Violence begets violence, and each of these deaths was a barbaric spectacle played by the State of Florida on the world stage. Each botched execution cast the entire criminal justice system of this state—including the courts—in ignominy.

As he said he would in his dissent, Justice Shaw put photos of Allen Lee Davis's electrocuted corpse on the court's Internet Web site. So many people visited the site to view the ghastly photographs that the site crashed.

The U.S. Supreme Court decided to decide the question of Florida's use of the electric chair. Briefs were filed and oral argument was scheduled for February 28, 2000. Then, on January 6, a special session of the Florida State Legislature convened by Governor Jeb Bush voted overwhelmingly (unanimously in the Senate and 102 to 5 in the House) to replace the electric chair with lethal injection. The legislature also passed a bill that "reformed" the capital appeals process to speed up executions. Governor Bush's top policy aide on capital punishment was quoted as saying: "I hope that we become more like Texas. Bring in the witnesses, put them on a gurney, and let's rock and roll." The aide later apologized for the remark. Governor Bush signed both bills into law on January 14, 2000.

The electric chair. When I was working full-time as a Florida death-worker, in the 1980s, it seemed that every year someone or other in the state legislature would raise the possibility of introducing a bill to change Florida's method of execution from the electric chair to the more "humane" method of lethal injection. I never knew whether to support such technological innovations. On the one hand, I was acutely aware that some of my clients would face Florida's execution method of choice. Ought I not therefore work for the most painless, dignified, and humane method?

Why, you might ask, did Florida not simply long ago replace its three-legged solid oak electric chair, built in 1923 by prison inmates, with lethal injection? It's not that simple. Floridians—and Florida politicians—*like* the electric chair as a visible symbol of their tough-ness on crime. The chair has a "mystique." During the special legisla-tive session convened for the purpose of considering replacement of the chair with lethal injection, people could be seen wearing T-shirts proclaiming "Needles Are for Sissies."

Opponents of capital punishment have our own reasons for being squeamish about the shift to the sanitized, pseudomedical execution method of legal injection. Executions by lethal injection can be, and frequently are, botched. This is so in part because the Hippocratic oath precludes doctors and other highly trained medical personnel from par-ticipating in executions (and for this reason, Florida's medical lobby opposes lethal injection as a method of execution). In fact, no mecha-nism of execution is foolproof, because it is not easy to devise a way of killing an otherwise healthy human being that is quick, painless, and not horrible for the state-selected witnesses to watch. Nothing about capital punishment is as easy or simple as it may first appear, even the choice of execution method.

Aside from the issue of the manner of execution, Bob Sullivan's case presented me with an excruciating ethical dilemma. In 1983, my public defender office had received, through informal channels, a prepublica-tion copy of a crucial statistical study conducted by Samuel Gross and Robert Mauro of the influence of victims' race on sentencing patterns in capital cases. We knew that two of our clients, James Adams and

James Dupree Henry, would get death warrants soon, and, because they were African Americans, we intended to use Gross and Mauro's study in their cases. But Bob Sullivan got a death warrant first. Sullivan wasn't my office's client; he was represented by a large New York law firm. Sullivan's lawyers didn't have Gross and Mauro's statistical study.

Thus the ethical dilemma: Should we give the study to Sullivan's lawyers? There were arguments against doing so. Sullivan wasn't our client, and Adams and Henry were; if Sullivan's lawyers litigated the study and lost, that would hurt Henry when his warrant was signed. Also, because Adams and Henry were African American and Sullivan was white, Adams's and Henry's cases were better vehicles for raising the study (although the study focused on the races of victims, we agreed that it would be more useful for African Americans to raise claims concerning racial discrimination).

Notwithstanding these reasons, I argued that we should give the study to Sullivan's lawyers. We couldn't play God. It was only luck that we, and not Sullivan's lawyers, had the study. And how would we feel if the roles were reversed, and they sat on a study that might save our clients' lives?

In the end, my argument carried the day. We gave the study to Sullivan's lawyers. They litigated it, and it won their client a forty-eight-hour stay in the Eleventh Circuit. Then Bob Sullivan was executed, and a precedent was set: the study alone was insufficient to justify a stay.

The U.S. Supreme Court justices divided bitterly over the discrimination issue in Sullivan's case. The Court's majority opinion, which was unsigned, noted that Sullivan was white and that, "although some of the statistics are relatively new, many of the studies were conducted years ago and were available to [Sullivan] long before he filed his most recent state and federal habeas petitions." The court found "no bases for disagreeing" with the courts that had previously "considered this data and determined in written opinions that it is insufficient to show that the Florida system is constitutionally discriminatory."

The majority opinion explained further: "This case has been in litigation for a full decade, with repetitive and careful reviews by both state and federal courts, and by this Court. There must come an end to the process of consideration and reconsideration." To eliminate any doubt that the justices blamed defense lawyers for gaming the system, Chief Justice Burger wrote a concurring opinion, which said in its entirety:

In joining in the opinion of the Court, I emphasize that this case has been in the courts for ten years and is here for the fourth time. This alone demonstrates the speciousness of the suggestion that there has been a "rush to judgment." The argument so often advanced by the dissenters that capital punishment is cruel and unusual punishment is dwarfed by the cruelty of ten years on death row inflicted upon guilty defendants by lawyers seeking to turn the administration of justice into the sporting contest that Roscoe Pound denounced three-quarters of a century ago.

Justices Brennan and Marshall dissented. Justice Brennan wrote:

Even if I accepted the prevailing view that the death penalty may constitutionally be imposed under certain circumstances, I would grant the application because *Sullivan* has raised a substantial claim concerning the constitutionality of his death sentence. In particular, *Sullivan* alleges that application of the Florida death penalty statute violates the Equal Protection Clause because it discriminates against capital defendants solely on the basis of their race and the race of their victims. For support, *Sullivan* has proffered numerous scholarly studies, several of which are yet to be published, that provide statistical evidence to substantiate his claim. Although the Court has avoided ruling on similar claims in the past, and continues to avoid the issue by its decision tonight, the claim is clearly deserving of further consideration. I see no reason to depart from that sensible approach in this case. In fact, the Court has had only twenty-four hours to examine the voluminous stay application and exhibits that have been filed on Sullivan's behalf. The haste with which the Court has proceeded in this case means not only that Sullivan's claim has not received the thoughtful consideration to which it is entitled, but also that the Court has once again rushed to judgment, apparently eager to reach a fatal conclusion.

The Eleventh Circuit and the Supreme Court employed procedural technicalities to avoid even considering the merits of Gross and Mauro's statistical study. That was bad for Sullivan but good for my ability to use the study in my own cases. Indeed, a friend of mine who was clerking in the U.S. Supreme Court at the time told me that had the justices considered the merits of the statistical issue, they would have slaughtered the issue in Sullivan's case. Their ruling against Sullivan on procedural grounds meant that Sullivan would die but the statistical issue wouldn't die with him. That was the theory, at any rate.

A few months after Sullivan was executed, our clients Adams and Henry got death warrants. We litigated the study, along with case-specific evidence of racism, but to no avail. The Sullivan case was cited as precedent against our clients' claims of racial discrimination.

6

Racism:
James Adams and
James Dupree Henry

A nigger male.

> —The rape victim referring to James Adams at his 1962 trial

Racism has been the Gettysburg of capital punishment issues in the modern era. The claim that current systems of capital punishment are as racist as the old systems were has been seen as the last chance to knock out capital punishment itself in a single stroke.

I believe that capital punishment is at its core a civil rights issue. As a product of the American South, and as a capital public defender in a southern state, I have always understood the death penalty to be intimately related to matters of race. Historically, capital punishment has been largely reserved for African American men accused of raping white women or of killing white men or women. (In 1977, the U.S. Supreme Court struck down the states' use of the death penalty as punishment for rape.)

Today, the racial aspects of death as a punishment are more complex. African Americans are still sentenced to death in numbers disproportional to their representation in the population at large. Approximately 50 percent of the prisoners on death row today are African American, even though African Americans make up only about 12 percent of the U.S. population. Further, killers of white victims are far more likely to be sentenced to death than are killers of African American victims; this systematic undervaluing of African American life has formed the basis of recent challenges to the racism embedded within capital punishment as a legal system.

Numerous statistical studies of the administration of capital punishment in Florida, Georgia, and elsewhere have found that matters of race warp this institution as they warp other legal and social institutions in America. The leading Florida study on the subject, conducted by Samuel Gross and Robert Mauro, found that between 1976 and 1980, killers of white victims in Florida were eight times more likely to be sentenced to death than were killers of African American victims. African Americans who killed white victims were the most likely to receive death sentences.

As I've described in chapter 5, Bob Sullivan's lawyers introduced Gross and Mauro's study in their argument in the Eleventh Circuit. The study was enough to win Sullivan a temporary stay, but that was all. The *Sullivan* case—and the legal precedent it established—demonstrated that the study alone was not enough to win a real stay. We knew that, to help our clients, we would need to show more. We would need to prove, in addition to the generalized discrimination demonstrated by the statistical study, that intentional racial discrimination had occurred in the individual case. We would continue to use Gross and Mauro's study to show context, but to win a stay after *Sullivan,* we would need evidence of case-specific discrimination.

James Adams

In James Adams's case, we thought we had the sort of case-specific evidence of racism we would need. To begin with, it helped that Adams was African American. Florida had not executed an African American for twenty years. Adams would be the first since 1964.

In 1962, Adams had been convicted of raping a white woman in Tennessee. In the early 1960s, wrongful and racist convictions of African American men for raping southern white women were fairly common. The rape victim, testifying at the trial, referred to Adams as a "nigger." Further, Adams was found guilty by an all-white jury; African American men, and all women, regardless of race, were systematically excluded from the jury in Adams's trial. He was sentenced to life imprisonment.

Adams was housed in a low-security facility. One day, he got access to a truck and simply drove away. He ended up in Florida, where, in 1976, about a year after his escape, he was arrested on a charge of capital murder. The evidence against him was relatively weak. A shaky eyewitness identified Adams as the driver of a car the witness had seen leaving the crime scene. He was found guilty and sentenced to death, mainly because of his 1962 Tennessee rape conviction. The racist rape conviction thus formed the basis of Adams's death sentence in the Florida murder case. The taint of race bias in this case was indirect— we would have had a stronger race claim if the discrimination had occurred directly in the murder case—but we thought it should be sufficient for a stay of Adams's death warrant.

Racism wasn't our star claim when Adams got a death warrant on April 12, 1984. Our star claim was innocence. Our investigator, Leon Wright, had uncovered strong evidence that the eyewitness misidentified Adams. More important, a piece of physical evidence that was not disclosed before Adams's trial tended to exculpate him. The murder victim had been found clutching a piece of human hair. Lab tests had led a forensics expert to conclude that, although the hair belonged to an African American, it could not have come from James Adams.

In capital appellate litigation, lawyers tend to get the attention, the credit, and the glory. However, it is the gumshoe investigators, people like Leon Wright, who unearth the evidence that the lawyers take into court. Facts, not law, typically win stays of execution. Wright had a passionate belief in Adams's innocence, a belief he maintained long after the Adams case was over.

Innocence would be our lead claim. Race discrimination would be our fallback. We filed the stay papers in the state trial court in Fort Pierce on April 24. The judge in Fort Pierce set an evidentiary hearing for the next day on all issues. Dick Burr would present evidence on and argue the innocence issue. I would argue race.

Dick and I got on the road to Fort Pierce early. I argued first, because the prosecutor had moved to strike our race claim. I lost in short order. If we were going to get a stay, it would have to be on the basis of innocence.

The evidentiary hearing on the innocence claim was a nightmare, a slow-motion train wreck. The prosecutors blew our factual case apart; we were right and they were wrong on the facts, but we couldn't *prove* it. There just wasn't time. The judge ruled against us and made killer fact-findings that gutted the innocence claim's usefulness later in federal court. The worst precedent against us on the innocence issue was the *Stanley* opinion I had drafted for Judge Vance.

At the end of the hearing, James Adams was more upbeat than his lawyers. In my diary for that day, I wrote, "Met with James Adams for an hour and went over his chances; he's in reasonably good spirits and has faith." Thus did our condemned client cheer us up after we had lost his case.

Adams's life now depended on the race bias claim concerning the 1962 rape conviction. The race claim took center stage in the Florida Supreme Court, and for a while it seemed that the justices were interested in it. At the oral argument, they asked more questions about the 1962 conviction than they asked about how the *Sullivan* precedent had damaged our race claim. They finally ruled against us, though, unanimously finding that all of our claims were procedurally barred; we had raised them too late. The court explained that, as to the Tennessee rape conviction, "this issue could have been raised in the first appeal to this court and, consequently, it will not support a collateral attack." And regarding the statistical study, the court ruled that "this same issue has been raised and disposed of by this court in *Sullivan.*" Such legal technicalities would also virtually foreclose any meaningful federal review of Adams's arguments.

We had one thing going for us in federal court. After Bob Sullivan's lawyers had unsuccessfully raised the Florida statistical study, the Eleventh Circuit had taken up the case of Warren McCleskey. McCleskey, a Georgia death row prisoner, was staking his life on a statistical study of capital sentencing in Georgia. The Georgia study was far more comprehensive than our Florida study, but we still hoped that McCleskey's case might increase our chances of a stay in Adams's case.

On Thursday, May 3, the federal trial judge scheduled oral argument for the next morning. I worked until 1:30 A.M. preparing and was back in the office by 6:00 A.M. The argument before Federal District Judge Gonzales took an hour, thirty minutes on each side. Dick argued very well, and Judge Gonzales seemed bothered by the Tennessee racism issue, which we took to be a good sign. The prosecutor argued procedural default and the merits of our argument.

In the end, Judge Gonzales found against us on every possible ground. We went back to the office and worked on our papers for the Eleventh Circuit until midnight. On Saturday, May 5, I started writing the petition argument for review of the case by the full (en banc) Eleventh Circuit. Dick Burr and Craig Barnard finished the papers for the

Eleventh Circuit on Sunday and put them on a 7:00 A.M. flight to Atlanta.

On Monday, May 7, I completed the en banc petition and put it on a 2:30 P.M. plane to Mobile, Alabama, where the judges of the Eleventh Circuit were attending a judicial conference. At lunch that afternoon, we discussed which of us would go to the prison to witness Adams's execution, if it came to that.

At 7:00 Monday evening, the Eleventh Circuit clerk told us not to expect any action from the court that night. I suggested asking for en banc consideration then, at the outset, before the panel even ruled, because time was running out. At 8:00, the Eleventh Circuit clerk called to tell us that oral argument had been set for the next day, Tuesday, at 11:00 A.M. in Mobile. Dick was to argue, and he asked me if I wanted to go, but he had already made his flight plans and it turned out to be too late for me to get a flight.

Our petition to the U.S. Supreme Court went out on a 3:00 A.M. plane on Tuesday. At 2:30 P.M., Dick called to tell us that the Eleventh Circuit oral argument had gone very well. He had argued for an hour and a half before Judges Henderson, Anderson, and Clark on the Gross and Mauro statistical study issue only. At 3:22, we heard that the judges had granted a stay of execution. The vote was two to one, with Henderson dissenting. Judge Anderson said that the fact that Warren McCleskey's case was pending in the Eleventh Circuit required a stay, distinguishing *Sullivan* on two grounds: (1) Sullivan was white and Adams is black, and (2) the Eleventh Circuit didn't take up *McCleskey* until after *Sullivan* was decided. Judge Henderson dissented, based on *Sullivan*: "In *Sullivan,* this court found the same Gross and Mauro study at issue here was insufficient to sustain a claim of discriminatory intent. The U.S. Supreme Court affirmed in *Sullivan.* We are bound by that decision."

The state immediately asked the U.S. Supreme Court to dissolve the Eleventh Circuit stay, and we heard that the justices were planning to meet at 4:00 to decide on the stay application. We decided to file a short paper in opposition to the prosecutor's application to dissolve the stay. Richard Greene and Dick Jorandby left for Florida State Prison in Starke.

By noon on Wednesday, May 9, we still had no word from the

Supreme Court. When we got our copies of the state's papers request-
ing that the Court dissolve the Eleventh Circuit panel stay, Dick dictated our reply over the phone to me from Mobile, and I in turn dictated
the response to someone at the Wilmer, Cutler & Pickering law firm's
message center; someone there would type it up and file it for us.

That afternoon, we lodged the en banc papers in the Eleventh Circuit; we were told that they would be circulated informally to all of the
Eleventh Circuit judges. A little later, we heard from a clerk at the U.S.
Supreme Court that a decision on the stay was still pending, and that it
might be as late as 8:00 or 9:00 P.M. before any decision was delivered.
Dick told us that the clerk for the Eleventh Circuit had told him that he
doubted the U.S. Supreme Court would dissolve the Eleventh Circuit
panel's stay. Did he have inside information? Was his opinion based on
wishful thinking or an educated guess? Whatever his reason, we saw
this as a small ray of hope.

Late in the afternoon, a rumor began in the Tallahassee press corps
that the stay was to be lifted, and about 8:30 P.M. we got word that the
U.S. Supreme Court had dissolved the Eleventh Circuit panel stay; the
vote was five to four. The five justices in the majority said nothing, but
Justice Marshall, bless his heart, wrote a blistering dissent:

> Yesterday, May 8, 1984, a majority of a panel of the Court of Ap-
> peals for the Eleventh Circuit stayed the impending execution of
> James Adams. The Court of Appeals concluded that Adams' peti-
> tion for federal habeas corpus relief presents the same issues that
> are currently pending before the Court of Appeals in *McCleskey v.
> Zant* (to be argued in June, 1984), and that "the en banc cases
> [now] pending in the Eleventh Circuit require a stay in this case."
> Adams, like McCleskey, maintains that the death penalty is ad-
> ministered on the basis of impermissible factors, including race
> and geography. The panel, after full briefing and oral argument,
> and with the benefit of a record and complete filing of appen-
> dices, were satisfied that Adams, an indigent Negro, had raised
> this issue in state and federal court, but has never been afforded
> an evidentiary hearing or appointment of experts. The Court of
> Appeals was also satisfied that evidence on which Adams relies in
> his second petition for habeas corpus only became available to
> him after his first federal habeas proceedings.

After having had less than a day to consider the judgment of the Court of Appeals, this Court now vacates that judgment, thereby opening the way to Adams' execution. The haste and confusion surrounding this decision is degrading to our role as judges. We have simply not had sufficient time with which to consider responsibly the issues posed by this case. Indeed, the Court is in such a rush to put an end to this litigation that it has denied my motion to defer its action for 24 hours in order for me to write a more elaborate dissent than that which is now possible given the pressing time restraints within which I have been forced to work. The Court's jurisprudence is increasingly being marked by an indecent desire to rush to judgment in capital cases.

This case, however, is especially egregious. In lifting the stay imposed by the Court of Appeals, the Court has resorted to an exercise of power that is unusual and that should only be resorted to on the rare occasion in which a lower court has flagrantly abused its discretion. Repeatedly, the Justices of this Court have recognized that the power of a single Justice or of the court as a whole to vacate a stay entered by a lower court should be reserved for exceptional circumstances. Here, however, caution has been thrown to the winds with an impetuousness and arrogance that is truly astonishing. What appears to have been forgotten here is that we are not dealing with mere legal semantics; we are dealing with a man's life. Because the Court has utterly failed to attend to this case with the careful deliberation that it deserves and has thus committed an error with respect to process as well as result, I respectfully dissent.

I called Florida State Prison to tell James Adams that the stay had been dissolved. At 11:00 P.M. the clerk for the Eleventh Circuit called to tell us that none of the circuit's judges in active service had asked for an en banc poll.

I made plans to go to Florida State Prison with Craig Barnard and Dick Burr. Once there, we went to the area where demonstrators gather across from the prison, where we were joined by Richard Greene and Dick Jorandby. The five of us formed a circle and gave our own testimonials. At 7:10 A.M., we saw the white flags of the Associated Press and United Press International at a window of the prison, signaling that an execution had occurred.

Dick Jorandby and Richard Greene were witnesses; they told us that James was calm and at peace, gentle as ever, at the end. Mostly, they said, he was concerned about how *we* would take it, and about our keeping up the fight. We spent the rest of the day in Gainesville and attended a memorial service that night.

As devastating as losing the Adams case had been, we could not afford to dwell on it. Another of our clients, Alvin Ford, was in the middle of a death warrant, and he had at least one landmark constitutional claim: execution of the insane. And a third client of ours, James Dupree Henry, would get a warrant at any time.

There is one last thing I want to say about the killing of James Adams. Dick Jorandby, the head of our public defender office, was our designated witness. The experience annihilated him. For weeks afterward, his eyes had the look of a man who had seen the end of the world.

James Dupree Henry

James Dupree Henry had only a single issue left: race discrimination. Now we had to get around the precedents of Bob Sullivan's and James Adams's cases.

Henry's was the case that broke Craig Barnard's heart. Craig had represented Henry forever, and they had become friends. Craig won Henry's case in the federal court of appeals, and the U.S. Supreme Court reversed and remanded for reconsideration. He won again in the court of appeals, and again the Supreme Court reversed and remanded for reconsideration. By the third round, the appellate court had gotten the message; it upheld Henry's conviction and death sentence.

James Dupree Henry was convicted in 1974 of killing Z. L. Riley, an eighty-one-year-old civil rights leader in Orlando. Riley, who was Henry's next-door neighbor, was one of the most prominent African American citizens in central Florida. Within three months and two days of Riley's murder, Henry had been arrested, tried, convicted, and sentenced to death.

Henry had broken into Riley's home with the intention of robbery. He had beaten, cut, bound, and gagged Riley and then stolen sixty-four dollars and some credit cards. Riley died as the result of strangling on the gag Henry had placed in his mouth. Henry claimed that he never meant for Riley to die. Henry was sentenced to death under the felony murder rule, which says that even an accidental death can count as capital murder if it occurs while the defendant is in the course of committing certain specified felonies, including burglary and robbery.

James Dupree Henry did not intend to kill Riley; he only intended to steal from him. In fact, Riley's death was a fluke; he strangled on the gag. Still, because Riley died in the course of Henry's burglary and robbery, Henry was culpable for capital murder.

In fact, Henry's death sentence was about much more than Riley's death. Two days after Riley's death, a white police officer, Ronald Ferguson, went to Henry's home to take him into custody. Henry jumped Ferguson, took his gun, and shot him twice. The wounds were not life threatening, but this assault on a police officer would play a large role in Henry's case.

Henry was offered a plea bargain of life imprisonment in exchange for a plea of guilty to first-degree murder, but he refused. He was subsequently convicted on this charge, and the jury voted seven to five to recommend that the punishment be set at death, and the judge followed the jury's recommendation.

The Florida Supreme Court affirmed Henry's conviction and sentence, and Governor Bob Graham signed Henry's first death warrant in November 1979. A federal district court stayed the execution pending resolution of Henry's petition for a writ of habeas corpus. In this petition, Henry alleged that the court imposed the Florida death penalty in an arbitrary manner because of geography, poverty, and other (unspecified) factors. The federal trial court held an evidentiary hearing on this claim and received evidence that the death penalty was applied with disproportionate frequency in Orange County (Orlando) and that it was applied disproportionately to indigent defendants. The court ultimately rejected this claim, but concluded that Henry's death sentence was unconstitutional based on a jury instruction that permitted the jury to consider nonstatutory aggravating circumstances.

The Eleventh Circuit Court of Appeals, after initially affirming and then reaffirming the ordering of resentencing for Henry, eventually reversed. The court, in rejecting Henry's assertion that the penalty was imposed unconstitutionally due to geography and poverty, stressed that "Henry alleges no racial, sexual or other inherently suspicious discrimination."

Florida's Governor Graham signed a second death warrant on August 21, 1984. Henry then sought a stay of execution from the state trial court, alleging that "the decision to sentence the defendant to death was motivated by racial discrimination." As in James Adams's case, the basis of this contention consisted of two components. First, Henry proffered statistical evidence tending to show that racial factors play a role in the selection of who is sentenced to death in Florida. Henry also introduced case-specific "qualitative" evidence of the historical legacy of racism in Florida. Although such background evidence is relevant to drawing an inference of purposeful discrimination, by the time of Henry's execution it seemed clear—because of the Sullivan and Adams cases—that the Florida data, standing alone, were legally insufficient to state a ground for relief under the Eighth or Fourteenth Amendment, despite the fact that these data never had been the subject of an evidentiary hearing and fact-finding.

The focal point of Henry's claim was the case-specific portion of his proof: his attempt to show "the specific sequence of events leading up to the challenged decision." Henry argued that the jury and judge in his case were far more troubled by Henry's assault against Officer Ferguson (the white police officer) than they were about the murder of Z. L. Riley (the black citizen). The best evidence available of the concerns of the community from which the jurors were drawn indicated much more concern about Officer Ferguson's welfare than about Riley's. This portion of Henry's claim rested in large part on an analysis Michael Radelet had carried out on the *Orlando Sentinel*'s coverage of the case.

Oral argument on Henry's race claims occurred in the state trial court on Tuesday, September 11, 1984. Dick Burr and I were to do the argument, and we caught an early afternoon plane to Orlando. We decided that we would divide the argument: I would do the initial argument, then the prosecutor would answer, and Dick would do the rebuttal.

The oral arguments went beautifully. I was adequate; the prosecutor was dreadful; Dick was magnificent; the judge stole the show. The judge took careful notes and asked few questions, but those he did ask made it clear that the court knew the record and the law cold. As Dick and I flew home, we discussed our strategy for the Florida Supreme Court.

I arrived back in my office at 10:00 the following morning. There had been no word from the judge. I started working on the federal papers. At 11:00, the judge's office called and told us to expect a decision in forty-five minutes. Hours went by. The ruling finally came at 3:45. We'd won. It was a stay, and the prosecutor was taking an immediate appeal to the Florida Supreme Court. Briefs would be due in the court by noon the next day. We would have to write the briefs before we could see the trial judge's order explaining his reasons for granting the stay.

At 5:00 P.M., the trial judge's law clerk called to read the opinion to us. Craig Barnard put the call on his speaker phone, and he, Dick, and I took notes while the clerk read it to us. We then divided up the night's work. Craig would finish our Florida Supreme Court brief, and I would write the federal papers. Dick had to prepare for oral argument the following day in Alvin Ford's case. I went home at 1:00 A.M.—I don't know when, or if, Craig and Dick went home.

On Friday, September 14, we decided that someone would fly the papers to the Florida Supreme Court, and that Craig would do the oral argument in that court on Monday. I would drive to Orlando with Richard Greene, and we would file Henry's papers in the federal trial court in Orlando if the Florida Supreme Court dissolved the state trial court's stay.

Saturday and Sunday were marathons of work on the federal papers in Henry's case. The procedural barriers to receiving federal review of the racism claim—particularly the *Sullivan* and *Adams* precedents—were nothing less than monumental. We argued over whether we should even take the claim into federal court, and in the end we decided the long shot was worth it. In the back of our minds that weekend was the hope that the stay we had would hold up in the Florida Supreme Court.

Oral arguments in the Florida Supreme Court would start at 8:00 A.M. sharp on Monday, so Craig had flown to Tallahassee Sunday night. That's when the bad luck began. When he landed in Tallahassee, he discovered that his luggage—in which he had packed the clothes he planned to wear for the oral argument the following morning—had landed in Jacksonville. He could hardly appear before Florida's highest court in the blue jeans he had worn on the plane, and no flight from Jacksonville could possibly get his luggage to him in time for the 8:00 A.M. argument. So a friend picked the bags up at the Jacksonville airport, put them in a cab, prepaid the $250 round-trip fare, and sent them on their journey across north Florida. The bags reached Craig with two hours to spare.

The wayward luggage was a portent of things to come. When Craig called us at 10:00 A.M., after the argument, his voice had a hard edge of despair. The justices didn't care about the racism claim; they shoved the *Sullivan* precedent down our throats. All they asked about was whether they had jurisdiction to dissolve the trial court's stay.

With the stay looking more fragile than ever, Richard Greene and I flew to federal court in Orlando. When our plane landed, I called the office. No word yet from the Florida Supreme Court. We headed over to the federal courthouse, where we checked in. Still no word. We ate lunch in the courthouse cafeteria and divided up the argument.

At 1:00 P.M., a rumor swept the building that we'd lost in the Florida Supreme Court. By 1:30 it was official. We had lost on procedural grounds—that is, on the basis of the *Sullivan* precedent. The vote was six to one; the stay was dissolved. James Dupree Henry was scheduled to die in thirty-eight hours. Richard and I had work to do.

When we arrived at the clerk's office to file Henry's stay papers, the prosecutors were already there. We filed our papers and they filed theirs. We served our papers on them, they served theirs on us.

Richard and I then walked over to the local public defender's office, where we prepared the oral arguments we hoped to deliver before the federal trial judge, G. Kendall Sharp. At 3:30 P.M., Judge Sharp's clerk phoned to say we should be back in court at 5:00. That was a good sign, we thought; it indicated that we would get a chance to orally argue our case. However, at 5:00, we were told to come back at 9:00 A.M.

That evening, Richard and I ate dinner at the local Howard Johnson's. As we stood up to leave the restaurant, we saw Judge Sharp's law clerk enter. We froze; maybe there had been a decision, and the law clerk was looking for us. The law clerk saw us staring at him, and he gave us a curt nod and averted his eyes. He wasn't there to find us; he was there simply for dinner. But that moment when our eyes met seemed endless. I told myself later that night that our encounter with the clerk meant nothing. I continued to work on the argument I had convinced myself I would have the opportunity to give before Judge Sharp the next day.

In the morning, after we'd had breakfast, Richard and I called the court. There was no word on when we should show up to argue. At

9:30 A.M. we got the news: there would be no argument. There would be a ruling and an opinion, and we would get both of them before noon.

We went to the federal courthouse and camped out in the coffee shop there, checking in with Judge Sharp's clerk's office every half hour. The judge beat his own deadline by two minutes. We got his ruling and opinion at 11:58 A.M. We had lost.

I called Craig Barnard back at our office and read the opinion to him. He told me that the Eleventh Circuit had scheduled oral arguments for 6:30 the next morning, and that the clerk had let slip a bombshell: Judge Vance would be one of the three appellate judges who would hear Henry's case. Craig asked me how I would feel about arguing the racism issue before an Eleventh Circuit panel that included Judge Vance. I jumped at the chance, because I knew that racism was the one constitutional claim that Vance understood in his bones. It was decided that Richard and I should drive back to West Palm Beach, and that Dick Burr and I would then fly to Atlanta for the Eleventh Circuit argument.

As we drove home, my mind reeled. The Eleventh Circuit had scheduled oral arguments at 6:30 in the morning, thirty minutes before Henry's scheduled execution. And I was to argue our racism claim before Judge Vance, a veteran of Alabama's race wars of the 1960s. I had always hoped to have a chance to argue before Judge Vance, but I never thought I would have to do it with only twelve hours' notice. And to argue *this* case, and *this* issue, was almost overwhelming.

By the time Richard and I got back to West Palm Beach, however, the landscape had changed entirely. Judge Vance would not be on our panel. The Eleventh Circuit had issued a twenty-four-hour stay, and the argument had been moved back from 6:30 to 8:30 A.M. Dick wanted to do the argument alone, and I agreed. That night, I drove home rather than to the airport.

The oral argument went very well. It was unusually long, two and a half hours, and Dick thought the judges had bought what he was selling. The Eleventh Circuit's clerk said it would be a "long time" before the court would rule. Hopefully not too long, though—Henry was still scheduled to be killed at 7:00 A.M. the next day. At 4:00 in the afternoon, Craig walked into my office, his face ashen. "We lost *Henry* in the Eleventh Circuit. It was unanimous."

Technically, we still had the U.S. Supreme Court to try, but we knew that the *Adams* and *Sullivan* precedents were the death knell for James Dupree Henry. We filed the papers, but as soon as we did we knew our jobs as lawyers for Henry were over. The official word from the Supreme Court just confirmed what we already knew. The race discrimination study had bought Henry twenty-four extra hours of life, but that was all. He would die as scheduled.

That night, Craig and I weren't thinking or acting like lawyers. Craig was a man about to lose an old friend; he'd represented Dupree—that's what he called Henry—for more than a decade. Craig had won Dupree's case twice, only to have the U.S. Supreme Court snatch the victories away from him. Craig couldn't even say good-bye to his friend. He'd tried all day to reach Henry by phone, but the lines at the prison were messed up.

No, that night Craig and I weren't lawyers. He was a grieving man, and I was trying to be his friend. I mostly listened while Craig talked about the twisting road he and his friend had traveled. We sat in Craig's office until it was close to midnight. At one point we decided to go to the prison—maybe one of us should witness the execution. Instead, we got a pizza. Then we went home.

Z. L. Riley's two closest relatives, his two nieces, appealed to the governor to spare the life of their uncle's killer, as did the Orlando branch of the NAACP, in which Riley had been active. Their pleas echoed those of Riley's own son, William, who had written to the governor in 1979 to ask that Henry's life be spared. William Riley passed away before Governor Graham signed Henry's second death warrant in 1984. Other civil rights leaders, including Coretta Scott King, the Reverend Joseph Lowery, and the Reverend Jesse Jackson, as well as the Congressional Black Caucus, also appealed to Governor Graham for a stay of execution and investigation of racial and class bias in the application of the death penalty in Florida. Their appeals—like those of Henry's lawyers—fell on deaf ears, and James Dupree Henry was executed on September 20, 1984.

My diary entry for that day notes that, according to newspaper accounts, "Henry fought and screamed his innocence to the end and had in the end had to be 'stuffed into the chair'; I'm not sure why, because that's a horrible way to spend your last few moments of life, but deep down I'm glad that Henry fought."

Three days after the execution, the Reverend Joseph Lowery, president of the Southern Christian Leadership Conference, presided over a burial service, and Henry was laid to rest in Quincy, Florida. Scharlette Holdman attended the funeral. She later told me that it was very moving; sixty-five people were there, and everyone, even the reporters, were crying.

Warren McCleskey

As I mentioned above, the fact that Warren McCleskey's case was pending in the Eleventh Circuit had won James Adams a brief stay of execution. There were actually several such cases in the Eleventh Circuit, and they all involved the most in-depth statistical study ever conducted on racial patterns in capital sentencing. The lead case was Warren McCleskey's.

McCleskey's was a watershed case by any measure. The legal and political stakes were astronomically high. It was the last case, for the foreseeable future, with the potential of reaching all condemned prisoners, or at least of reaching large groups of them. Had McCleskey's constitutional claim prevailed in its broadest aspects, capital punishment in Georgia (and, I believe, in most other states by implication) would have ground to a halt immediately. The moral stakes were higher yet. In claiming that constitutionally unacceptable racial factors permeated the system of capital sentencing that put him on death row, McCleskey demanded that the courts confront the nation's efforts to purge a racist past.

Warren McCleskey, who was African American, was convicted and condemned in Georgia. He claimed, first in state court and then in federal district court, that Georgia's capital statute allowed factors of race to affect the administration of capital sentencing. As proof, he offered the results of a statistical study conducted by Professor David Baldus and his colleagues, the most sophisticated study of sentencing patterns ever undertaken. The federal trial court rejected McCleskey's claim, holding that the database for Baldus's study was flawed and that in any event the study was insufficient as a matter of law to carry McCleskey's constitutional challenges to the statute. The court held that McCleskey had "failed to demonstrate that racial considerations caused him to receive the death penalty."

The Eleventh Circuit, using the extraordinary procedural device of taking the case to the en banc court in the first instance, affirmed. The majority opinion held that the same standards of proof govern racial discrimination challenged under the Equal Protection Clause of the Fourteenth Amendment and the Cruel and Unusual Punishment Clause of the Eighth Amendment. Intentional discrimination must be shown under either constitutional provision.

The majority opinion recognized that "due process and cruel and unusual punishment cases do not normally focus on the intent of the governmental actor." The court ultimately concluded, however, that when "racial discrimination is claimed . . . on the basis of the decisions made within that process, then purpose, intent and motive are a natural component of the proof that discrimination actually occurred." To prevail under either constitutional theory, a prisoner must offer proof of a "disparate impact [that] is so great that it compels a conclusion that the system is unprincipled, irrational, arbitrary and capricious such that purposeful discrimination . . . can be presumed to permeate the system."

Applying this analytic framework to the Baldus study, the majority opinion reaffirmed previous Eleventh Circuit holdings that statistical evidence of racially disproportionate impact "may be so strong that the results permit no other inference." Yet no evidentiary hearing would be required on statistical studies of capital sentencing discrimination, regardless of their quality, unless they "reflect a disparity so great as to inevitably lead to a conclusion that the disparity results from intent or motivation." The court reasoned that "it is a legal question as to how much [racial] disparity is required before a federal court will accept it as evidence of the constitutional flaws in the system."

Judge Vance concurred, although his vote was not needed to form a majority rejecting McCleskey's constitutional claim. Vance noted, however, that he was "troubled by [the majority opinion's] assertion that there is 'little difference in the proof that might be required to prevail' under either eighth amendment or fourteenth amendment equal protection claims of the kind presented [by McCleskey]." Vance wrote that the Eighth Amendment inquiry should center on "the general results of capital sentencing systems," and that the constitutional provision "condemns those governed by such unpredictable factors as chance, caprice or whim. An equal protection inquiry is very different. It centers not on systemic irrationality, but rather [on] the independent evil of intentional, invidious discrimination against given individuals."

Vance was able to join in the majority opinion, however, because he believed that in McCleskey's case the difference between the constitutional tests would not influence the result. He agreed with the majority that the statistics presented in *McCleskey* were "insufficient to establish intentional discrimination in the capital sentence imposed in his case." As to the Eighth Amendment claim, he doubted that "a claim of arbitrariness or caprice is even presented, since [McCleskey's] case is entirely devoted to proving that the death penalty is being applied in an altogether explicable—albeit impermissible—fashion."

Judge Vance's opinion closed with this telling sentence: "Claims such as that of petitioner are now presented with such regularity that we may reasonably hope for guidance from the Supreme Court by the time my expressed concerns are outcome determinative in a given case." Perhaps I am projecting, but I detect in Judge Vance's statement a hope that the Supreme Court would do what Vance felt disempowered to do as an intermediate federal court judge.

The U.S. Supreme Court granted review affirmed by a razor-thin margin in a vote of five to four. The opinion for the majority was written by Justice Lewis Powell, the courtly Virginian whose record on matters of race as chair of the Richmond School Board during the crucial period from 1952 to 1961 was mixed even according to his admirers. I will not discuss the *McCleskey* majority and dissenting opinions in detail here; it is enough to note that, in essence, Justice Powell's opinion held that the touchstone of McCleskey's constitutional claims must be intentional discrimination "against him personally." Purporting to assume as valid the Baldus data showing that a death sentence is four times more likely when the victim is white than when he or she is black, the majority reasoned that discrepancies are inevitable. This given, however, did "not include the assumption that the study shows that racial considerations actually enter into any sentencing decisions in Georgia." Because "discretion is essential to the criminal justice process," the Court "would demand exceptionally clear proof before . . . [it] would infer that the discretion has been abused." The Court found that the Baldus study did not "demonstrate a constitutionally significant risk of racial bias affecting the Georgia capital sentencing process."

Justice Powell noted that statistical disparities ordinarily must be "stark" to be accepted as the sole proof of discriminatory intent. Apparently the Baldus study's showing of a 300 to 400 percent disparity based on race of victim was not sufficiently stark, even when that disparity could not credibly be explained away in a nonracist way.

Justice Powell also offered a rationale that Justice Scalia had suggested (I thought at the time tongue in cheek) during oral argument. Accepting McCleskey's claim of racial discrimination, Powell wrote, would mean that ugly people might be the next group to whine about discrimination. Criminal defendants and their crafty lawyers would not be satisfied with raising proportionality claims based on race. They would, Powell prophesied, assert claims that discrepancies in sentencing also existed based upon sex, membership in other minority groups, or, indeed, "any arbitrary variable, such as the defendant's facial characteristics, or the physical attractiveness of the defendant or the victim." Having thus caricatured McCleskey's claim, the Court solemnly stated the obvious: "The Constitution does not require that a State eliminate any demonstrable disparity that correlates with a potentially irrelevant factor in order to operate a criminal justice system that includes capital punishment."

Justice Brennan wrote an eloquent dissent, one that will resonate down the years, "We cannot pretend that in three decades we have completely escaped the grip of an historical legacy spanning centuries," Brennan observed. McCleskey's evidence "confronts us with the subtle and persistent influence of the past. His message is a disturbing one to a society that has formally repudiated racism. . . . Nonetheless, we ignore him at our peril, for we remain imprisoned by the past as long as we deny its influence in the present."

Perhaps most important, Justice Brennan's dissent refocused the case on Warren McCleskey, an African American person condemned to die in the Georgia electric chair. By restoring a face and a name to the statistical abstractions favored by the majority, Brennan reminded us that at its core the case was not about numbers, even though it was full of numbers, data, and statistical jargon. There was something numbing about the use of all of this ciphering to resolve an ultimate question of morality. Brennan captured well the human dimension lurking behind the statistics in McCleskey's case:

> At some point in this case, Warren McCleskey doubtless asked his lawyer whether a jury was likely to sentence him to die. A candid reply to this question would have been disturbing. First,

counsel would have to tell McCleskey that few of the details of the crime or of McCleskey's past criminal conduct were more important than the fact that his victim was white. Furthermore, counsel would feel bound to tell McCleskey that defendants charged with killing white victims in Georgia are 4.3 times as likely to be sentenced to death as defendants charged with killing blacks. In addition, frankness would compel the disclosure that it was more likely than not that the race of McCleskey's victim would determine whether he received a death sentence: 6 of every 11 defendants convicted of killing a white person would not have received the death penalty if their victims had been black, while, among defendants with aggravating and mitigating factors comparable to McCleskey's, 20 of every 34 would not have been sentenced to die if their victims had been black. Finally, the assessment would not be complete without the information that cases involving black defendants and white victims are more likely to result in a death sentence than cases featuring any other racial combination of defendant and victim. The story could be told in a variety of ways, but McCleskey could not fail to grasp its essential narrative line: there was a significant chance that race would play a prominent role in determining if he lived or died.

Justice Brennan also warned: "It is tempting to pretend that minorities on death row share a fate in no way connected to our own, that our treatment of them sounds no echoes beyond the chambers in which they die. Such an illusion is ultimately corrosive, for the reverberations of injustice are not so easily confined." To the contrary, "the way in which we choose those who will die reveals the depth of moral commitment among the living."

Near the end of his life, after he had retired from the U.S. Supreme Court, Justice Powell changed his mind about his decisive vote and opinion for the Court in *McCleskey*. Powell has been praised for his change of heart, but I can't join in the applause. I believe that there must be a special place in hell for people who do evil things when in power and then regret them later, when they're no longer in power and impotent to repair their earlier actions. Lewis Powell should be in that special place for all eternity. Powell's epiphany notwithstanding, his *McCleskey* opinion remains the law of the land.

Ivon Ray Stanley

The Baldus statistical study of the relationship between race and sentencing in Georgia was not enough to remove anyone from death row. While the *McCleskey* case was pending in the courts, however, many Georgia prisoners won stays of execution. Others fell through the cracks; Ivon Ray Stanley was one of those. In chapter 2, I explained how I drafted the opinion for Judge Vance upholding the death sentence for Stanley, a mentally retarded African American man. That opinion was a brooding presence in my life from the day it was issued, February 10, 1983. On that day, my role in Stanley's case ended. His life went on, for a while at least.

Fifteen months after the opinion in *Stanley* was issued, Ivon Ray Stanley was executed. To the end, his lawyers argued that the Baldus study and the *McCleskey* case—then pending in the Eleventh Circuit—required a stay in *Stanley*. The Eleventh Circuit and the U.S. Supreme Court disagreed.

Stanley was executed only minutes after the Supreme Court ruled. He refused to make a last statement or hear a final prayer. He was twenty-eight years old when he was put to death on July 12, 1984. He was the first African American to be executed in Georgia since 1963 and the twenty-first person executed in the United States since executions resumed in 1976.

The Associated Press gave this account of the execution:

Stanley was ushered into the execution chamber at the Georgia Diagnostic and Classification Center here at 12:07 A.M., a half-hour after the Supreme Court refusal to stay the execution.

He walked unassisted and without hesitation to the electric chair and watched closely as guards strapped him in. He looked once at Warden Ralph Kemp and once toward the audience of 11 witnesses separated from him by a windowed partition.

He never spoke.

Asked by Kemp if he had a final statement, he shook his head. Asked if he wished to have a prayer said, Stanley again shook his head.

While prison officials waited for the 12:15 A.M. execution time, Stanley clenched and relaxed his fists and his breathing grew noticeably heavier. A mask covered his face.

Then three hidden volunteers pressed buttons that sent more than 2,000 volts of electricity through Stanley. His body arced violently upward, straining against the straps, and his fists clenched.

His body relaxed when the current was shut off two minutes later, and six minutes after that three physicians declared him dead.

I learned of the execution the following morning. During the elevator ride up to my law office, another attorney in my office mentioned that "Stanley was executed last night." He didn't need to explain who Stanley was, and he knew it. Everyone in the office knew that I had drafted Judge Vance's opinion upholding Stanley's death sentence.

When my colleague gave me the news, I just nodded. He was looking for my reaction, and I was determined not to show him one. He got off the elevator at his floor, and then I got off at mine. I went into my office, shut the door, and cried. Then I stopped crying, wiped my face, opened my door, and went back to work. We had a client scheduled to be executed the next morning (and he was). I went back to work. But something had cracked in my heart.

7

Executing Juveniles: Paul Magill

The legislators who passed our current death penalty laws did not intend to force grotesque issues to the center stage of constitutional adjudication. The death penalty was supposed to be about getting even with Charles Manson and Ted Bundy, not executing teenagers and the retarded, or wrestling condemned schizophrenics to the gurney for forced doses of Haldol. But here we are.

—David Bruck, "Does the Death Penalty Matter?"
speech delivered at Harvard Law School, 1990

Of all my clients, Paul Magill is perhaps the one I found both the most understandable and the most incomprehensible. He was a really nice guy who could hold up his end of a complex conversation about the nuances of Greek philosophy. And he had been found guilty of committing a murder when he was seventeen years old.

Magill, a white, middle-class high school student with decent grades, a member of his school's band, decided on impulse one day to rob a convenience store. He didn't intend to kill anyone, but crimes like robbery can get out of hand rapidly. The robbery led to the kidnapping, rape, and murder of Karen Young, the store's clerk. I don't know why Magill went so far; neither does he. He has always maintained that he has no memory of his crimes, and I believe him. He'll spend the rest of his life trying to understand what he did, torn with remorse for the killing he committed as a high school student.

The Trial

Magill's case presented a constitutional issue that, when he first raised it, had never been decided by the U.S. Supreme Court or the federal courts of appeal: whether the U.S. Constitution forbids the execution of people who were minors—juveniles—at the time they committed capital murder.

The events leading up to Magill's arrest were recounted at his trial. Danny Hall, who was the same age as Magill, testified that at approximately 8:00 P.M. on December 23, 1976, he had ridden his bicycle to the Jiffy Food Store located on Highway 27, south of Belleview, Florida. He was halfway through the door of the convenience store when Magill, who was already inside, turned to face him, pointed a gun at him, and told him to leave. Hall then left the store and rode his bike to the top of a nearby hill, from which he watched Magill take the clerk, Karen Young, from the store.

Hall saw Magill and Young get into a Ford Mustang which then proceeded toward Belleview. Several other customers who had been approaching the store at the time testified that they had seen a young man and woman in a Mustang just prior to the time they entered the store and found it to be unattended. These customers were greeted by Danny Hall, who had run back to the store to call the police.

Officer John Harrison of the Belleview Police Department received a radio call at approximately 8:17 P.M. alerting him to the robbery and abduction and advising him of the description of the vehicle. Harrison ultimately encountered the car described in the radio call and attempted to pull the driver over. The driver, however, increased his speed and headed back toward the Jiffy Food Store. After a brief chase, Officer Harrison forced the Mustang off the road, approximately two-tenths of a mile north of the store. The driver of the vehicle, later identified as Magill, got out of the car and attempted to run, but he was stopped by Officer Harrison.

Deputy Eddie Wright Jr. of the Marion County Sheriff's Department was at the convenience store and saw Officer Harrison stop the vehicle and pat down Magill. Deputy Wright proceeded to the area and advised Magill of his *Miranda* rights. After Wright told Magill that his car matched the description of a car involved in a robbery and asked him why he had run from a police vehicle, Magill started to sob and said that he had robbed, raped, and killed the convenience store clerk. Wright placed Magill in his vehicle and called for an ambulance. He asked Magill to take him to where the woman was, in hopes that she might not be dead, although Magill said that he was sure she was dead. Following Magill's directions, Deputy Wright drove to a secluded wooded spot near Jaybird Point at Smith Lake, where he found the body of Karen Sue Young.

Later that evening, Magill gave a tape-recorded statement to Captain Gerard King of the Marion County Sheriff's Department. Magill stated that he had robbed Karen Young of an undetermined amount of money and that he had intercourse with her. Magill told King that he shot the victim three times with a .44 caliber pistol when he realized she could identify him. He then tried to drag her body into the bushes and he put the gun in the trunk of his car.

A search of the vehicle conducted with Magill's consent produced a .44 caliber pistol that was later identified by a firearms expert as the weapon that had discharged five spent .44 caliber cartridge cases found at the scene of the crime.

Magill was charged with the crimes of first-degree murder, sexual battery, and armed robbery. Although he was seventeen years old at the time of the offense, and therefore a juvenile under federal law, he was tried as an adult. A plea of not guilty was entered. Magill's jury trial commenced in Marion County, Florida, on March 21, 1977.

The state called the witnesses who had been at the scene of the kidnaping, the police officers, and various technical witnesses. Together, these witnesses established the facts relating to the offenses. Magill took the stand on his own behalf and, after relating a history of psychological problems, told the jury that he had committed the offenses impulsively. He said that, at the time, he did not feel that he had any control over his actions, and that it was "totally against [his] thinking to harm a person like that."

The jury found Magill guilty as charged of the offenses of murder in the first degree, involuntary sexual battery, and armed robbery. The state produced no evidence of aggravating circumstances in the penalty phase proceedings, which began shortly after the verdicts were announced. Magill testified on his own behalf during this portion of the trial and called other witnesses in an attempt to establish the existence of certain mitigating factors.

Magill was asked by defense counsel how he felt about having committed the offenses in question, but the prosecutor's objection to the question was sustained. Defense counsel then asked Magill if he had any statement he wished to make to the jury concerning the offenses, but the prosecutor's objection to that question was likewise sustained. The trial judge explained to the jury that he was "sustaining the objections because [the questions] fall without purview of these factors set forth by the legislature, which you should consider in mitigation."

The jury returned an advisory verdict recommending the imposition of the death penalty, which was ultimately accepted by the trial court at sentencing. The court found four aggravating circumstances: (1) that Magill had committed "three felonies"; (2) that the capital felony of murder was committed while Magill was "engaged in the commission of, or flight after committing, the crimes of robbery and rape"; (3) that the capital felony was "especially heinous, atrocious or cruel"; and (4) that the capital felony was committed in "connection with the crime of robbery which was perpetrated for pecuniary gain." The trial judge found "no mitigating circumstances which outweigh the . . . aggravating circumstances."

The Florida Supreme Court affirmed Magill's conviction, rejecting his argument that the trial judge had committed constitutional error in rejecting a particular juror. Counsel for Magill (a different attorney handled the appeal) argued that the mitigating factors should have served as a constitutional bar to the imposition of the death penalty. Chief among these mitigating factors was Magill's age. Magill's attorney considered this so important that she took the position that "youthful age alone may be such a significant mitigating circumstance that death could not be considered the appropriate sentence." The Florida Supreme Court did not accept this proposition. The court also rejected Magill's contention that the trial judge erred in restricting his penalty phase testimony to evidence relating to the statutory mitigating circumstances.

The Florida Supreme Court did, however, vacate Magill's sentence. The court held that the trial judge erred in failing to "list the mitigating circumstances which he may or may not have considered." The case was remanded to the trial judge for a new sentencing hearing.

On January 26, 1981, following the new sentencing hearing before the court, the trial judge entered a new judgment and written findings of fact. He concluded that the same aggravating circumstances were applicable and found the existence of three mitigating circumstances: (1) that Magill was seventeen years of age at the time of the offense, (2) that he had no significant prior criminal record, and (3) that a member of his family had passed away on December 28, 1975, almost precisely one year prior to the crime. The ultimate conclusion of the trial judge was that there were "insufficient mitigating circumstances to outweigh the aggravating circumstances." Accordingly, the trial judge resentenced Magill to death. The Florida Supreme Court affirmed.

The state courts denied all relief. So did the federal trial court. I came into the case when it was on appeal to the Eleventh Circuit Court of Appeals. By that time I had left the West Palm Beach Public Defender's Office and was working at CCR in Tallahassee.

Killing Kids

As a capital public defender, I had come to dread holidays. Judges don't like death getting in the way of their holiday plans. Once, a Florida Supreme Court justice demanded that I file stay papers before they were ready so that the case would not interfere with his Thanksgiving. I got the papers in and he voted to deny the stay. I hoped he enjoyed his turkey.

The Paul Magill case walked into my office eight days before Christmas in 1985. Magill was being represented in the Eleventh Circuit Court of Appeals by two excellent trial lawyers. Their main brief was due in less than a week—on the day before Christmas eve—and it had not yet been written. The lawyers asked CCR to help them with the brief, and CCR assigned me to the case.

I first met with Magill's lawyers on the morning of December 17. We hit it off. The lawyers had identified several strong issues in Magill's case, in addition to the landmark issue of executing people who had been juveniles at the time they committed capital murder. Although these attorneys were first-rate trial lawyers, brief writing was not their forte. They asked me to research and draft the portion of the brief dealing with the juvenile issue.

Although I knew nothing about the issue at that time, I had a head start. I had obtained a manuscript draft of a comprehensive soon-to-be-published law review article by Professor Victor Streib, the nation's leading expert on juveniles on death row. The article was a gold mine of information, and it led me to many other materials. By midnight I was convinced the issue was a winner.

I began with the commonsense assumption that the U.S. Constitution must set some minimum age below which a juvenile's crimes can never constitutionally be punished by death. Surely the law must forbid the execution of six-year-olds. The problem presented by the Magill case resided in the issue of where the line is drawn. I argued that our society has drawn that line at age eighteen. Throughout the American legal system, age eighteen is the recognized dividing line between adult responsibilities and childhood. In most states and for most purposes, minority status—defined as younger than age eighteen—confers a host of legal disabilities. Minors are treated differently because minors are different from adults. The diverse legal disabilities are based on the commonsense and empirically supported notion that minors lack the maturity, judgment, impulse control, and experience of adults.

In Florida, a minor is defined as a person under age eighteen unless otherwise provided by statute. A person under age eighteen cannot vote in any Florida statewide primary or general election, or in any municipal primary or election; cannot serve as a petit juror or grand juror; cannot buy or possess alcoholic beverages; cannot play bingo or assist in the conducting of bingo; cannot enter a billiard room where alcohol is sold unless accompanied by parent; cannot obtain a driver's license without parental consent; cannot obtain a license to carry a pistol or revolver or to sell firearms; cannot consent to most forms of medical treatment; cannot refuse medical treatment; cannot donate any part of his or her body as a gift to take effect upon death; cannot serve as a notary public, court reporter, court clerk, district attorney, judge, county administrator, or state adjutant general; cannot hold public office; cannot be licensed or employed as a peace officer, state trooper, narcotics agent, firefighter, pharmacist, dietician, nursing home administrator, dispensing optician, polygraph examiner, private detective or assistant employed by a private detective, or real estate salesperson or broker; cannot be an incorporator of a bank or trust company; cannot be a director of a business corporation; cannot be an incorporator of a business corporation or partnership; cannot be a director of a nonprofit corporation; and cannot be an incorporator of a nonprofit corporation.

Florida is not unique in this regard. Minority status universally confers a host of statutory disabilities. Eighteen years is the line selected by Congress and the states in their enactment and ratification of the Twenty-sixth Amendment to the Constitution, which governs voting age. Following extensive hearings, both state and federal legislatures agreed to give constitutional significance to age eighteen as the time when young people should first be permitted to participate in the most basic civic responsibility of adults in a democracy. Eighteen also is the minimum age at which a citizen may be drafted into the armed services, as well as the minimum age at which a person may enlist without parental consent.

In most states and for most purposes, a minor is considered to be a person younger than eighteen years. Some examples:

- All states set the age of majority at eighteen or older. Forty-three states set eighteen as the age of majority, two states set it at twenty-one, three set it at nineteen, and two do not set a uniform age of majority.

- In no state may anyone below the age of eighteen serve on a jury. Forty-four states require jurors to be eighteen or older, three require jurors to be at least nineteen, and three require jurors to be at least twenty-one.

- No state has lowered its voting age below eighteen.

- All but three states require that individuals other than emancipated minors be eighteen years old to marry without parental consent. In one jurisdiction, the minimum age is nineteen, and in one other it is sixteen. In still another, females may marry at age fifteen without parental consent.

- Thirty-six states establish eighteen as the age of consent for most forms of nonemergency medical treatment; one state puts the age at seventeen, one puts it at sixteen, one sets it at fifteen, and one puts it at fourteen. Two permit treatment if the minor is able to understand the decision, and eight states have no legislation in this area.

- Thirty-three states require a person to be eighteen to receive a driver's license without parental consent; four states set the age at seventeen, and thirteen set it at sixteen.

- Of the thirty-nine states that permit gambling, thirty-one set the minimum age at eighteen, four set it at twenty-one, one sets it at nineteen, one at seventeen, and two at sixteen.

- Many localities have juvenile curfew ordinances. The most common upper age limit is eighteen.

A simple recounting of such statistics, however, would not be enough to show that American culture has set age eighteen as the line dividing childhood and adulthood. I still needed to show *why* that line had been chosen, and I still had to demonstrate that setting the age limit for execution eligibility at eighteen would not undermine the effectiveness of capital punishment.

I argued that exemption of minors would not detract from the penological justifications for the death penalty. Jury behavior demonstrates that execution of minors would not materially advance the interest in retribution. Juries, the representatives of the community whose outrage is being expressed by death sentences, seldom vote to condemn minors.

Further, exclusion of minors from the death penalty would not abate the deterrent force of the penalty for other minors. Adolescents are less likely to make the kind of cost-benefit analyses that attach weight to the possibility of execution. Exemption of minors from execution also would not dilute deterrence for adults, because adults would most likely not identify with condemned minors. And juvenile executions are so rare that preclusion of such executions would have little impact on the deterrence force of the death penalty for the population at large.

On December 18, I met for four hours with one of Magill's lawyers. I think my excitement over the juvenile issue—which we called the "killing kids" claim—might have overwhelmed him. He asked me to come into the case as cocounsel and to orally argue the killing kids issue in the Eleventh Circuit. Because I already had a full caseload, my superiors at CCR were reluctant to cut me loose to work on Magill's case. We agreed that I could do it, as long as my other work didn't suffer. Magill's lawyer—not the CCR support staff—would handle the word processing of the brief.

I worked all that night on the Magill brief. I wrote then as I write now: with a pen on yellow legal pads. All day on December 19, I wrote and handed the pages to Magill's lawyer, who typed what I had written into his word processor. It was slow going. By the end of the day, my handwriting was far ahead of his typing. When I left the office to go home at 1:00 A.M., he was still typing away.

I overslept on Friday, December 20, and didn't reach my office until 9:30 A.M. The bleary-eyed lawyer was still there, typing away, his mouth a slit of angry determination. Around noon, I suggested that he call the Eleventh Circuit and ask for an extension of time for filing the brief. He made the call, but the court's death clerked talked him out of the extra time. The brief would remain due on Monday.

At 2:00 P.M. that Friday, Chris Cox, a CCR investigator, offered to take over the word processing from the Magill lawyer. By 5:00 she had finished and handed the disk to the lawyer to print out the brief. Chris then left to join much of the CCR staff for a pre-Christmas party.

I was sitting in my office when I heard the lawyer's strangled curse. Somehow, the computer had crashed, and the entire 138-page brief was lost. He would have to reconstruct and retype the whole thing. At 8:30 P.M. I declared an emergency. I phoned CCR's senior secretary, Eloise Williams, and then I called the CCR party. Some of the troops were full of holiday spirits, but by 3:30 A.M. the brief had been reconstructed, retyped, and edited. I finished proofreading it at 5:30 A.M.

The lawyer and I then went over to his office to make the multiple copies of the brief we needed to send to the court. That's when I learned that his photocopying machine was slow as a glacier. It could make only one copy at a time, and it had no automatic feed, so we had to feed each page by hand. To make matters worse, the cheap paper the lawyer had on hand kept jamming the machine.

By 6:30 A.M., I'd reached the end of my tether. In the course of feeding the copier, page by page, I'd discovered that the brief still contained numerous typos and other errors. This was a brief in a landmark case. There was no escaping the conclusion that the brief needed one more round of edits and that CCR would have to make them. We would then have to make the needed copies on CCR's much more efficient photocopier. I must have sounded ragged when I called Mark Olive to break the news that I was reneging on our Magill deal and that CCR would have to fix the mess I'd made. Mark was gracious, and he agreed. CCR would take over the brief.

I edited all day, burning through draft after draft. I began proofing at 8:00 P.M., and then Mark took over and finished the job. I went to rest on the couch in Mark's office, fell asleep, and stayed asleep until noon the next day. I awoke to find, next to the couch, fifteen beautiful bound copies of the brief in Paul Magill's case. The briefs were put on a noon plane to Atlanta.

Paul Magill's case was one of the first to present a federal circuit court of appeals with the claim that it was unconstitutional to execute a person who had been a juvenile at the time he committed a capital crime. I briefed that issue to the Eleventh Circuit, along with several narrower, case-specific issues.

At the oral argument in *Magill*, Judge Frank Johnson was clearly interested in the juvenile execution issue. But because there was also an extremely conservative judge on the *Magill* panel—and because I wanted a unanimous win in *Magill*—I kept trying to shift the argument back to the narrower, case-specific issues in the case. Somewhat frustrated with my efforts to evade the issue that would have made *Magill* a landmark case—and a case likely to go to the Supreme Court, where I feared reversal—Judge Johnson explained to me why the court should resolve the juvenile issue first: if Paul Magill won on that issue, he would be per se ineligible for the death penalty (no resentencing, no chance of another death sentence); if he won on a narrow, case-specific ground, he'd only get a resentencing, and thus might be sentenced again to death.

Judge Johnson was right, of course. But I answered that I wanted the court to resolve the case-specific issues first, even though that would give my client less relief than if he won on the juvenile issue. I think I saw a hint of a smile on the face of the conservative judge when I said this.

A few days after the oral argument, I wrote to Paul Magill's mother:

April 14, 1986

Dear Mrs. Magill:

As I believe [my cocounsel] has discussed with you, I am working with him on Paul's case. I apologize for not contacting you or Paul earlier, but since last October my office has been kept fairly busy with active death warrants. I am delighted to be working on Paul's case and hope to meet you and Paul soon.

Enclosed are copies of the briefs we filed in the Eleventh Circuit Court of Appeals. Although we raise five issues, the court at oral argument was most interested in two: the age claim and the claim based on the sentencing judge's limitation on his consideration of mitigating circumstances. The questions asked by the three judges on the panel suggested that they were really struggling with the case. That, to me, is the best sign at an oral argument: we seem to have gotten their attention. That only means that we have a *chance* of convincing them, that they are open to what we are arguing. But that's more than we have in a lot of cases.

I don't know if [my cocounsel] told you about who our three judges are, but the lineup is hopeful. Peter Fay of Miami presided. Judge Fay was reared in Fort Lauderdale, did his undergraduate work at Rollins College and received his law degree from the University of Florida. He had a thriving civil litigation practice before President Nixon appointed him to the federal trial court bench in 1970. President Ford elevated Fay to the Court of Appeals in 1976. Judge Fay generally votes with the state in capital cases. When he votes our way, he tends to opt for narrow grounds that would not affect many other cases. Still, even the "liberals" on the court have great respect for his legal mind. Because his fellow judges hold him in such high esteem, Judge Fay is a very powerful judge on the Eleventh Circuit.

The balance to Judge Peter Fay is Judge Frank Johnson, one of the true legends on the federal bench. Judge Johnson is perhaps best known for his invalidation of racial segregation in Alabama's transportation facilities, voter registration processes, schools and colleges, administrative agencies, system of jury selection, jails and prisons, and political parties. In fact, most of Alabama's major racial crises, including the Montgomery Bus Boycott, were resolved in his courtroom.

Johnson is considered a "liberal" in criminal justice matters, but the label doesn't really fit. Johnson is a tough guy and a tough judge. His feeling is that trials must be scrupulously fair but that once they are the punishment should be harsh. He is something of a loner on the court: His 24 years as a District Judge, at the center of Alabama's most vitrolic race cases since reconstruction, have made him fiercely independent. Johnson is also an intellectually brilliant judge; his opinions often tend toward the scholarly doctrinal analysis usually associated with legal academies.

Tom Clark, the third judge on Paul's panel, is the newest addition to the Eleventh Circuit; President Carter appointed him in 1979. Clark went to Washington and Lee undergraduate (right down the road from where I went to law school, at the University of Virginia) and got his law degree from the University of Georgia. He was in private practice in Tampa, between 1957 and 1979, with the firm of Carlton, Fields, etc.

Judge Clark almost always votes in favor of the inmate in capital cases. For this reason, I think he is not the most credible judge on the court; the assumption seems to be that Clark will almost automatically vote for the defense if given a credible reason to do so.

The oral argument in Paul's case was dominated by Judges Johnson and Fay. Johnson was interested in the age issue; Fay was interested in the limitation-on-mitigating issue. I was in a dilemma. A victory on the age issue would be the most we could win, because then Paul would be per se ineligible for the death penalty; victory on the limitation-on-mitigating issue means a resentencing, with the possibility that Paul would again be sentenced to death. My fear is that if the panel of the Eleventh Circuit rules on age, the full Eleventh Circuit or the U.S. Supreme Court would reverse. A nice, narrow opinion on the limitation-on-mitigating claim would have a much better chance of holding up later on down the road.

So the dialectic of the argument was that Johnson kept trying to pin me down to say that the age issue must be decided *before* the limitation-on-mitigating issue, and Fay kept trying to see if ruling our way on the limitation-on-mitigating issue would allow the court to avoid deciding the age issue. Johnson finally asked, in effect, "Why should we put your client through a resentencing if he's per se ineligible for the death penalty?" I wanted to say: "Because if you go off on age and decide he is per se ineligible for the death penalty, then you'll be reversed and the other issue might get lost in the shuffle." Johnson also asked the Assistant Attorney General how the state could execute one who was too young to drink, vote or sit on his own jury.

Oral arguments can be very deceptive, and I certainly don't want to get your hopes up. But all three of the judges clearly were very troubled by the obvious problems in Paul's case. They clearly had done a lot of homework before the argument and their questions were right on target.

I hope this is helpful to you. I also hope to meet you and Paul in the near future. If you have any questions, please don't hesitate to call or write.

Sincerely,
Michael A. Mello
Assistant Capital Collateral Representative

The Eleventh Circuit decided *Magill* on a case-specific claim not really featured at the oral argument (ineffective assistance of trial counsel), ordering a resentencing. The opinion was unanimous. The full court denied the state's rehearing motion. The U.S. Supreme Court denied the prosecutor's petition to review and reverse the Eleventh Circuit.

Paul Magill's resentencing took place in the spring of 1988. Magill's trial attorney asked me to be there, and I was. Mrs. Magill insisted that I stay at her home, the house in which her son had grown up. The night before a jury would begin hearing evidence on whether her youngest son would die for his crimes, Mary Lou Magill cooked me a meal of meatloaf and mashed potatoes. "Comfort food," she explained, "and food for good luck." I slept that night in Paul's old bedroom, which remained unchanged since his arrest for capital murder at age seventeen, twelve years before.

The resentencing trial lasted three days. While it was going on, Mrs. Magill knitted a maroon and white afghan. After the jury voted for life, she gave me the afghan. It was my fee, the best fee I've ever received as a lawyer.

Meanwhile, the U.S. Supreme Court had taken up the juvenile execution issue. Wayne Thompson was fifteen years old when he committed the crime that caused him to be sentenced to death. The Supreme Court, by a vote of five to four, threw out his death sentence and suggested that the Constitution does indeed set *some* minimum age for execution eligibility. However, the Court did not exactly set that age at fifteen; Justice O'Connor's swing vote was based on the specifics of the state statute at issue in that case.

The same day the Court decided Thompson's case, it granted review in two other juvenile cases. Heath Wilkins had been sixteen years old at the time he committed his crime; José High had been age seventeen. I was invited to write the brief for *High*. After the brief had been filed, and after it was decided that I would do the Supreme Court oral argument, the state filed a motion claiming that José High was in fact older than age seventeen at the time of the crime—an argument not easily disproved, because where José was born in Texas, no accurate records had been kept on the births of Hispanics.

I visited José in prison to sort out the factual problem the state had introduced into the case. But the Court sidetracked the *High* case, granting review in Kevin Stanford's case to decide the juvenile issue. In 1989, the court held in *Stanford* that executing juveniles (sixteen- and seventeen-year-olds) does not violate the U.S. Constitution—exactly the outcome I had feared in Paul Magill's case. The Eleventh Circuit ruled our way on the juvenile claim.

To this day, I wonder if I made the right call during the *Magill* oral argument. Things ended well, but they could easily have gone the other way. Paul Magill and I were lucky.

As of this writing, Magill has been in prison for twenty-six years. I am still in touch with him, and with his mother. I hope that he will be paroled soon. He has served his hard time, most of it on death row. He has grown up in prison, and he no longer poses any threat to society. He committed his crimes as a teenager. He is quite literally a different person now.

8

The Poet:
Stephen Todd Booker

Stephen Todd Booker is a remarkable poet. The emotional strength in his poems is to be marveled at, especially since [they were] written on death row, in the shadow of the electric chair. . . . almost every poem in this book has a herculean calm, a mighty lifeblood which may defeat the angel of death.

—Menke Katz, on the back cover of Stephen Booker's book of poetry, *Waves and License*, 1983

When I was a Florida capital public defender, my colleagues and I were always looking for creative constitutional issues. One such issue, which never made it into a court filing, posited that, because people change on death row, in any given case the government may not be executing the same person who was sentenced to death years previously. Had I ever raised this constitutional claim, it would have been in the case of Stephen Todd Booker. When the state of Florida executes Booker, it will be killing a man who is vastly different from the person sentenced to death in 1978.

This is a chapter about time and change. Condemned people—and their lawyers, like me—are often accused of delaying cases in the courts. The stories I have told up to now provide a general sketch of the appeals process in death penalty cases. In this chapter I flesh out the capital appeals process in a bit more detail by focusing on the case of Stephen Todd Booker.

The Capital Appeals Assembly Line

In Florida, the litigation stages from imposition of death sentence to execution can be diagramed as shown in Exhibit 8.1. As the exhibit illustrates, the capital appeals assembly line can be divided into three clusters of stages: the trial and direct appeal stage (column A in the exhibit), the state postconviction stage (column B), and the federal habeas corpus stage (column C).

At the beginning of the first cluster of steps, there is a traditional trial to determine guilt or innocence (Step 1). This is followed by a penalty phase, which constitutes, in essence, a separate trial on the issue of sentencing (Step 1). Following conviction of a capital offense and imposition of the death penalty, the condemned person in Florida has a right to a direct (plenary) appeal to the Florida Supreme Court (Step 2). On direct appeal, the inmate argues that legal errors at trial require a retrial or resentencing. Only legal issues appearing within the trial record can be raised on direct appeal.

If the Florida Supreme Court rules against the prisoner on direct appeal, he or she may attempt to convince the U.S. Supreme Court that

A	B	C
Step 1 Trial and sentence in Florida state trial court	Step 4 State postconviction motion in state trial court (Rule 3.850 motion)	Step 7 Federal habeas corpus petition in federal district court
Step 2 Affirmance of conviction and sentence on direct/plenary appeal to Florida Supreme Court	Step 5 Appeal to Florida Supreme Court of state postconviction motion (Rule 3.850 motion); filing of original proceedings	Step 8 Appeal to Eleventh Circuit Court of Appeals Step 9 Request for plenary review (cert) in U.S. Supreme Court
Step 3 Request for plenary review (cert) in U.S. Supreme Court	Step 6 Request for plenary review (cert) in U.S. Supreme Court	Step 10 Executive clemency

Exhibit 8.1. Stages of litigation in Florida from death sentence to execution.

his or her case is worthy of the Court's consideration by filing a certiorari (cert) petition (Step 3) and then, if unsuccessful, may seek postconviction relief in state court (Step 4).

The prisoner then moves into the steps shown in column B of the exhibit, the state postconviction cluster of steps. Filing a state postconviction motion (Step 4)—in Florida called a Rule 3.850 motion—provides a procedural mechanism for raising claims that were not or could not have been raised at trial or on the direct appeal. These Rule 3.850 motions typically raise claims that are outside of the trial record (record-based claims must be raised earlier, on direct appeal). The quintessential Rule 3.850 motion claim is a claim of ineffective assistance of trial counsel—an argument that trial counsel should have conducted a more thorough pretrial factual investigation into the defendant's background and life history. Because presentation of evidence that trial counsel did *not* investigate (and therefore present at trial) requires postconviction counsel to go *outside* the trial record, such extra-record-based claims are properly presented in a Rule 3.850 motion.

Such a motion must be initiated in the state trial court and, if denied, appealed to the Florida Supreme Court (Step 5). State postconviction litigation may also be initiated in the state appellate court (Step 5). Following Florida Supreme Court affirmance of the trial court's denial of the Rule 3.850 motion and denial of any litigation initiated directly in the Florida Supreme Court, the prisoner may seek cert in the U.S. Supreme Court (Step 6).

Following exhaustion of state postconviction litigation and denial of cert in the U.S. Supreme Court, the Florida inmate moves into the steps show in Column C of the exhibit and is entitled to petition the federal district court for a writ of habeas corpus mandating retrial or resentencing (Step 7). Think of a federal habeas corpus petition as a combination of all direct appeal (column A) issues and state postconviction (column B) issues (or, Step 7 = column A trial-record-based issues plus column B outside-the-trial-record issues). If the habeas petition is denied in federal district court, the prisoner then appeals to the Eleventh Circuit Court of Appeals (Step 8). Then, if the inmate loses in the appellate court, he or she may seek cert in the U.S. Supreme Court (Step 9). At any time following direct appeal, a condemned prisoner may file an application for executive clemency or pardon (Step 10). In Florida, a grant of clemency requires the votes of the governor and a majority of the executive cabinet.

At any point beyond the plenary direct appeal, an execution date may be set by the governor. In most states—Louisiana and Texas, for example—execution dates are set by the state courts. In other states, such as Florida and New Hampshire, execution dates are set by the governor. Once a date is set, the condemned inmate must obtain a stay of execution in order to remain alive to pursue postconviction remedies in state and federal courts.

The stories in this volume involve many cases that were litigated "under death warrant." Such litigation is fairly rough-and-tumble, with the defense lawyers flying from court to court in search of a stay as the case moves down the assembly line of the capital appeals process: from state trial court to Florida Supreme Court, to the U.S. Supreme Court, to federal trial court, to the Eleventh Circuit, to the U.S. Supreme Court, sometimes in a matter of days. The Ted Bundy case, for example, was decided by three different courts in one day. The Stephen Todd Booker case provides an excellent illustration of how the various steps in this assembly line work.

The Problem

Stephen Todd Booker is an accomplished and published poet. He is also a convicted killer. Booker was tried, convicted, and sentenced to die for the rape and murder of ninety-four-year old Lorine Demoss Harman in Gainesville, Florida. It was a brutal crime, and Booker confessed. Booker is African American. His victim was white.

The most important issue in Booker's capital trial was not his guilt or innocence, but his sentence. During the penalty phase of the trial, Booker himself testified about his personal history and background. A psychologist also testified, describing Booker's childhood of poverty and abuse.

Booker's sentencers had before them at least ten items of significant evidence that, separately or in some combination, reasonably could have led to a life sentence rather than a sentence of death. However, none of these factors was listed in the capital statute as mitigating, and therefore none was given independent mitigating weight by the sentencers. All were matters that the Florida courts have recognized, in the years since *Lockett v. Ohio* was decided in 1978, as nonstatutory factors reasonably justifying a life sentence:

- *Psychiatric institutionalization:* Booker had been hospitalized nine times for mental problems, beginning at age thirteen. In Florida this is mitigating. On one case, the Florida Supreme Court ruled that hospitalization for mental problems weighed as mitigating evidence; in another case, the defendant's testimony about time in "mental institutions" was sufficient to require penalty-phase inquiry into whether "the mental condition of the defendant was less than insanity but more than the emotions of an average man"; in another case, a defendant's institutionalization as a youth and psychological reports of schizoid personality were properly weighed in mitigation.

- *Paranoid schizophrenia:* There were indications, during one of Booker's psychiatric commitments, that Booker suffered from paranoid schizophrenia. In Florida this is mitigating. The Florida Supreme Court has held that paranoid schizophrenia could reasonably form the basis of a jury's life recommendation, thus rendering a jury override improper; that history of paranoid schizophrenia and other disorders could require setting aside a death sentence; that schizophrenia, paranoid type, is a mental illness requiring setting aside a death sentence, on proportionality grounds, notwithstanding a jury's recommendation of death; and that the fact that a defendant was a "borderline personality with paranoid and schizoid features" was properly considered in mitigation.

- *Hallucinations:* Booker had suffered visual and auditory hallucinations since age six or seven. In Florida this is mitigating. The Florida Supreme Court has held that the nonstatutory mitigating circumstances of personality change after a defendant's returning from combat in Vietnam, as well as the defendant's belief that God spoke to him, should have been considered in mitigation, vacating a death sentence; that trial judges cannot improperly ignore as a mitigating factor mental illness and hallucinations; and that such disregard would require a reversal of a death sentence.

- *History of drug and alcohol problems:* Booker had a history of alcoholism and drug abuse, and there was evidence that he was under the influence of both at the time of the crime. In Florida this is mitigating. The Florida Supreme Court has concluded that "a history of drug and alcohol problems" properly should be considered by the jury in mitigation of the sentence of death; that one defendant "proffered evidence that he suffered from alcoholism and was under the influence of alcohol on the night of the murder. . . . The jurors should have been allowed to consider these factors in mitigation." In another case, a judge's override of the jury's life recommendation was ruled improper due in part to the defendant's "drinking problems" and history of alcoholism, notwithstanding the defendant's testimony that he was "cold sober" on the night of crime. The Florida Supreme Court has also "held improper a jury override where, among other mitigating factors, there was some 'inconclusive evidence that defendant had taken drugs on the night of the murder,' along with 'stronger' evidence of a drug abuse problem"; that "history of drug abuse" is a factor rendering a jury override improper; that alcoholism and organic brain syndrome justified a jury instruction on statutory mitigating factor of substantial mental impairment; and that history of drug abuse and intoxication and drug dependency are reasonable bases for a jury's recommendations of life imprisonment.

- *Split personality:* Soon after Booker's arrest, he acted, as the Florida Supreme Court put it, in a "bizarre manner" and evidenced a split personality. Booker became glassy-eyed, chanted, clenched his teeth until they cracked, laughed uncontrollably, and suddenly cried. The arresting detective testified that in his opinion Booker was sincere, and not faking, during these events. In Florida this is mitigating. In various cases, the Florida Supreme Court has decided that a personality disorder may be given mitigating weight; that potentially mitigating evidence of schizoid personality was properly admitted and weighed at trial; that a defendant's refusal to wear civilian clothes at trial, insistence that he was black when he was actually Caucasian, and insistence on testifying at sentencing only to assert the Fifth Amendment privilege were properly weighed in mitigation; and that a defendant's abnormal appearance and behavior on the night of the shooting of which he had been convicted was a matter properly weighed by the jury in deciding whether or not the defendant deserved to die.

- *Organic brain damage:* There was evidence that Booker suffered from organic brain syndrome, secondary to drug use. In Florida this is mitigating. In various cases, the Florida Supreme Court has concluded that a new sentencing hearing was required if examinations by court-appointed psychiatrists ignored clear indications of organic brain damage; that evidence of brain damage was one factor requiring an evidentiary hearing on mental competency to stand trial; that alcoholism and organic brain damage justified a jury instruction on statutory mitigating factors of substantial mental impairment; and that a trial judge adequately considered the potentially mitigating effects of organic brain disorder and other factors.

- *Deprived and turbulent childhood:* Booker had a turbulent childhood, with little structure, stability, or supervision and with no male role model. Left to his own devices, Booker quit school in the eighth grade and became involved in alcohol and drugs. In Florida this is mitigating. In one case, the Florida Supreme Court has ruled that "the jury could have concluded that appellant's psychological disturbance was influenced in part by his difficult childhood; childhood trauma has been recognized as a mitigating factor"; that the jury's life recommendation could reasonably have been based on the fact that the defendant "grew up without a father and was reared by his mother and another woman"; that shock effects produced by childhood traumas may have mitigating weight; that history of childhood abuse and difficulty of childhood are considered as mitigating circumstances; that suggesting that "deprived upbringing without a father" was proper consideration in mitigation; and that it was erroneous for a trial court to exclude the testimony of a defendant's mother concerning the defendant's background and upbringing at the sentencing phase of a capital trial.

- *Cooperation with police:* There was evidence that Booker cooperated with the police. The police received an anonymous telephone tip that the crime had occurred, and defense counsel argued in closing argument that Booker made that call. The police described Mr. Booker as "cooperative." He voluntarily gave fingerprints and hair samples. In Florida this is mitigating. The Florida Supreme Court has held that "defendant's cooperation with law enforcement officers can be grounds for reducing or suspending a sentence"; that "cooperation can be grounds for reducing or suspending a sentence"; and that a death sentence was not appropriate where there was one valid aggravating circumstance and several nonstatutory mitigating circumstances, including a voluntary confession.

- *Remorse:* Booker asked to be sentenced to death, but that request could reasonably have been viewed by the jury and judge as evidence of the sort of remorse that shows openness to rehabilitation. Defense counsel so argued. In Florida this is mitigating. The Florida Supreme Court has held that "any convincing evidence of remorse may properly be considered in mitigation"; that remorse, among several nonstatutory mitigating circumstances, might make a death sentence inappropriate; that remorse, considered by the Florida Supreme Court in its search of record for possible nonstatutory mitigating factors, could justify a life sentence; and that "the state of mind of a murderer during or immediately after commission of the crime may be legitimately examined for remorse."

- *Honorable discharge from the military:* Booker enlisted in the army during the Vietnam War, and he was honorably discharged. In Florida this is mitigating. The Florida Supreme Court has concluded that the fact that a defendant was a wounded and an honorably discharged Vietnam veteran, among mitigating factors properly considered, would have justified a life sentence; and that the trial court properly found the defendant's honorable service in Vietnam to be mitigating.

This was the evidence *presented* to the jury at the penalty phase of Booker's trial by his court-appointed public defender. The problem was that Booker's jury was instructed by the judge not to *consider* any mitigating evidence that did not fit within the narrowly circumscribed list of mitigating factors enumerated in Florida's capital statute. Little of Booker's evidence fit within the statutory list. Thus, in effect, Booker's sentencing jury was instructed to ignore virtually all of the mitigating evidence presented by Booker's defense counsel.

This mitigating evidence seems to me substantial. Whether or not it is sufficient to outweigh the heinous nature of the murder Booker committed is beside the point. The rule of *Lockett* does not command that a capital sentencer be persuaded that nonstatutory mitigating circumstances require a sentence of less than death. It does require, however, that capital sentencers must be permitted to consider, and to give independent mitigating weight to, all the relevant evidence that the person on trial for his or her life wishes the sentencer to consider. *Lockett* requires that the capital sentencer listen to the capital defendant's case for life imprisonment rather than execution.

Depriving a capital defendant of the right to have the sentencing jury consider evidence in mitigation is the equivalent of denying the defendant the right to defend him- or herself at the sentencing stage of the trial. And in Stephen Todd Booker's case, that is what happened. The advisory sentencing proceedings in Booker's case took place on June 19, 1978, and on that date the jury—by a vote of nine to three—recommended death. The U.S. Supreme Court decided *Lockett* on July 3, 1978.

As I discuss in more detail in chapter 9, no principle of modern capital punishment jurisprudence is more basic and less ambiguous than the one involved in Sandra Lockett's case. As the Supreme Court put it in *Lockett*, "The eighth and fourteenth amendments require that the sentencer . . . not be precluded from considering, *as a mitigating factor*, any aspect of a defendant's character or record and any circumstances of the offense that defendant proffers as a basis for a sentence of less than death."

However, prior to *Lockett* in 1978, when Booker was tried, all the relevant actors—attorney, judge, and jury—assumed that the only mitigating evidence that could be considered before a death sentence was imposed was evidence relevant to the seven factors listed in Florida's 1972 capital statute. Thus, although substantial nonstatutory evidence favoring a sentence less than death was available, none was affirmatively presented by counsel or considered by either jury or judge. At every stage of the sentencing process—prehearing investigation and presentation of evidence by defense counsel, deliberation and recommendation of sentence by the jury, and consideration and imposition of sentence by the judge—Booker, on trial for his life, was deprived of a sentencing trial of the scope and depth constitutionally required by *Lockett v. Ohio*.

At every stage of Booker's trial—from the beginning of jury selection to the jury instructions issued by the judge at the penalty phase—the jurors were told unequivocally that in recommending a sentence for Booker they could consider only the mitigating factors set out in Florida's capital statute. That message was hammered home by the judge, the prosecutor, and, at various stages of the proceedings, the defense counsel himself. As a consequence, although substantial nonstatutory mitigating evidence was introduced at Booker's trial, the jury and judge considered that evidence only as relevant to the statutory factors.

At the very beginning of the jury-selection process, the trial judge instructed the prospective jurors that at the penalty phase the "jury makes a recommendation of what sentence the judge should pass, *based on factors the law has written down*, aggravating circumstances and *mitigating circumstances*" (emphasis added).

Following the jury's finding of guilt of first degree murder, the judge instructed the jury that "at the conclusion of the taking of the evidence and after argument of counsel, you will be instructed on *the factors* in aggravation and *mitigation you may consider*" (emphasis added). This instruction clearly defined the limits of the jury's understanding of the evidence it would hear at the penalty phase and was reinforced by the final jury instructions.

The prosecutor's penalty-phase evidence consisted of certified copies of Booker's prior convictions. The defense's penalty-phase evidence consisted of Booker's testimony, together with the evidence adduced at the guilt/innocence phase—particularly the testimony of a psychiatrist and a police detective. That evidence involved almost exclusively matters not included on the statutory list of mitigating circumstances.

The prosecutor's closing argument to the jury stressed that "there is a list" of aggravating and mitigating circumstances. In his closing argument, defense counsel conceded that only the statutory mitigating factors counted. As a consequence, he tried to fit all of the evidence into the statutory factors.

With the foregoing as context, the judge in Booker's case gave the jury Florida's standard jury instruction on mitigating circumstances. This consisted of the statutory list of factors, prefaced by the words, "The mitigating circumstances which you may consider, if established by the evidence, are these." The jury recommended death, the judge agreed, and Booker was sentenced to die in Florida's electric chair.

Marking Time

Booker took a direct appeal of his conviction and sentence to the Florida Supreme Court (Step 2 in Exhibit 8.1). On this appeal, Booker's lawyer was limited to issues within the trial record, and he argued that Booker's death sentence violated the requirements of *Lockett*. In rejecting this argument and affirming Booker's conviction and death sentence, the Florida Supreme Court noted: "In light of *Lockett,* the defendant says that Florida's death penalty statute is too narrowly defined in the range of mitigating circumstances which the sentencing authority may consider. This argument was rejected by this Court in [a prior decision in another case]." The Florida Supreme Court's rejection of Booker's arguments was unanimous.

In 1982, Governor Bob Graham signed Booker's death warrant. Booker's execution was scheduled for twenty-eight days hence. At that point, Booker had no lawyer. The Gainesville public defender who had represented Booker at his trial and on his direct appeal to the Florida Supreme Court was willing to continue to represent Booker and to attempt to win a stay of his pending execution, but there was a problem. The legal issue most likely to win Booker a stay of execution was a claim based on ineffective assistance of trial counsel (Step 4 in Exhibit 8.1). If Booker's trial and direct-appeal lawyer were to continue to represent Booker at the postconviction stage of the legal proceedings, that would mean the attorney would be arguing to the courts that he himself had rendered ineffective assistance during Booker's capital trial.

What Booker needed—and needed fairly desperately, given the four-week countdown to his execution—was a new postconviction lawyer, an attorney who could conduct an independent investigation and present to the postconviction courts the argument, if credible, that trial counsel rendered ineffective assistance during Booker's trial. But there were no other lawyers. In 1982, Florida law did not provide legal aid to death row prisoners in the postconviction stages of capital appellate litigation. A desperate scramble ensued, inside and outside of Florida, to try to locate a law firm that would be willing to undertake Booker's representation pro bono.

That attempt failed. With less than two weeks remaining before Booker's scheduled electrocution, it had become clear that Booker had only two choices: he could attempt to represent himself in the postconviction process, which almost certainly would have resulted in his execution as scheduled, or he could agree to accept his trial lawyer's offer, to let the trial lawyer represent him in the postconviction system. If he took the latter course, Booker would also have to waive, then, there, and forever, any legal challenge to the effectiveness of the lawyer's representation of Booker at the capital trial. The trial attorney told Booker that he had read the trial transcripts and that he didn't think he had been ineffective during Booker's trial. Given this Hobson's choice, Booker reluctantly agreed—the trial lawyer could represent him.

Over the next two weeks, Booker's trial attorney investigated and filed legal papers asking the courts, state and federal, to stay Booker's execution. The attorney filed a state postconviction motion (a Rule 3.850 motion) and an application for stay of execution in the state trial court (Step 4 in Exhibit 8.1) and, when that was denied, he appealed to the Florida Supreme Court (Step 5). When the Florida Supreme Court denied both the Rule 3.850 appeal and the stay application, Booker's counsel filed a habeas corpus petition and stay application in the federal district court (Step 7). When the federal district court denied habeas and denied a stay (Step 7), the *Booker* case moved on to the Eleventh Circuit (Step 8), from which Booker's lawyer finally obtained a stay. In all of these courts, Booker's counsel raised a number of constitutional issues, including the *Lockett* issue.

During part of the time that Booker's case was pending before the Eleventh Circuit Court of Appeals, I was clerking for Judge Robert Vance in Birmingham, Alabama. In the end, Judge Vance voted against

Booker. Although Vance did not write a separate opinion in the case, as Judge Vance's death clerk, I read the trial transcript of the Booker case. I found it odd that Booker had not raised a claim of ineffective assistance of trial counsel, as such claims are routinely raised in death penalty cases. Also, it didn't seem to me that Booker's trial lawyer had put on much of a case for a life sentence at the penalty phase of Booker's capital trial.

When my clerkship for Judge Vance had concluded, in the summer of 1983, and I left Birmingham for deathwork in Florida, I took Stephen Booker's case with me in my mind. I had not been working long as an assistant public defender in the capital appeals division of the West Palm Beach Public Defender's Office when Governor Graham signed Booker's second death warrant. My bosses, Richard Jorandby and his chief assistant, Craig Barnard, had been the principal architects of the *Lockett* constitutional challenge to capital punishment as a legal system in Florida. Now, in October 1983, as during Booker's first death warrant in 1982, the West Palm Beach Public Defender's Office could not represent Booker. Our jurisdiction was limited to raising legal issues contained within those capital cases tried within our limited geographic area, and that did not extend to Gainesville, where Booker had been tried and condemned in 1978.

I wanted to help Booker somehow, but I also had the ethical complication of having worked on the Booker case during my clerkship for Judge Vance. I called Vance for advice and he told me that the Eleventh Circuit had no formal rules covering the matter and that I should use my own judgment and common sense. I asked him whether I could help Booker find a lawyer and then help that lawyer, so long as I didn't represent Booker directly. He said it was up to me.

I rationalized that I hadn't actually drafted an opinion for Judge Vance in *Booker*; I had just read the papers and discussed the case with the judge. Now, I wouldn't actually be serving as Booker's lawyer; I'd just be finding him an attorney, and then I'd be helping that attorney.

I didn't have much time to think this through. Now, as in 1982, Booker had an active, twenty-eight-day death warrant and no attorney. But because the Booker case had bothered me since my days in Birmingham, I did everything I could think of to find Booker a lawyer other than the trial/appeal/postconviction lawyer who had represented him at trial and during his first death warrant. I called dozens of my old law school classmates who were working at large law firms throughout the United States and asked them to take on Booker's case as a pro bono project. They all expressed sympathy, but they all declined. I also called several of my old law school professors and made the same plea. They also declined.

With the clock ticking, I called Jeffrey D. Robinson. Jeff and I had met and become friends during the summer of 1982, the summer after I graduated and the summer before Jeff began his third year of law school at Yale. In the years since then, Jeff had become my best and closest friend; when I called him about Booker's case, however, I fully expected him to decline. But he didn't. He took my request to James Coleman, a partner at the Washington, D.C., law firm of Wilmer, Cutler & Pickering, where Jeff had worked since his graduation from Yale Law School. Wilmer, Cutler & Pickering, was perhaps the best law firm in a city full of and known for its law firms. Jeff, Jim Coleman, and another Wilmer associate, Marion Lindberg, persuaded the firm to take the case.

Jeff asked me to write him a letter summarizing my thoughts on the Booker case. I wrote:

November 1, 1983

Marion Lindberg
Jeffrey Robinson
Wilmer, Cutler & Pickering
Washington, D.C. 20006

Dear Jeff and Marion,

I was delighted to learn that you would be able to take on Stephen Booker's case and look forward to working with you. Though Booker has already been through one round of federal habeas, he has a number of strong issues which should not be procedurally barred. Initially, I should say that several of these issues have been or are being developed by my office and LDF in other cases. I will send to you what we have now and will supplement that as we go along. In any event, I think that Booker has a number of good possibilities.

Ineffective assistance, of trial and appellate counsel. The basic difficulty at the guilt phase was that counsel didn't put on much of a defense. The defense, which appeared to be insanity, primarily consisted of a 5-page examination of one witness, a psychiatrist who did not testify that Booker was insane at the time of the crime. The doctor testified that he was unable to reach a conclusion as to whether Booker was insane. This witness was shredded on cross-examination. He said there was nothing to suggest that Booker was insane at the time of the offense, and that Booker's bizarre behavior to the contrary was a self-serving device. The state's rebuttal consisted of one psychiatrist who reinforced what Booker's doctor had said on cross. Counsel did not cross-examine the state's doctor.

The superficiality of the defense's case suggests to me that little or no preparation was done. One item is especially tantalizing: a report from Walter Reed Hospital suggested that Booker was suffering from an organic brain syndrome. Nothing indicates that that lead was ever pursued. You might also think about Richard Rattner or Dorothy Lewis, who have special expertise in this area.

The other questionable aspect of the guilt phase defense involved Booker's confession. At the time of the confession, Booker was behaving strangely and seemed to be acting out a "split personality." He was describing himself in the third person as Steve and calling himself Aniel, which he described as a demon. This confession was not challenged as involuntary and in fact its substance was adduced during cross-examination of the detective by Booker's attorney. He also mentioned it in his opening statement. The difficulty with our challenging this now is that counsel's decision to forgo attacking the confession would probably be deemed strategic. Also, Booker's bizarre behavior at the time of confession is the only indication that the confession might have been coerced. Still this conduct was bizarre, and maybe a psychiatrist would find his actions suggest that the state, while mentioning the confession in closing, didn't dwell on it.

The more fertile ground is penalty phase ineffectiveness, or a variant on it. Counsel, at the time of trial and advisory jury proceeding, was under the impression that he could not present non-statutory mitigating evidence. He argued in his reply brief in the 11th Cir. (which I didn't get from LDF) that he didn't object to jury instructions, which limited consideration of non-statutory mitigations, because the instructions were consistent with Florida law at the time. This may allow us to raise the *"Cooper/Lockett"* issue.

Cooper/Lockett attempts to impale Florida on the horns of a dilemma. In *Cooper v. State,* the court said that mitigating circumstances were limited to the statutory list. Two years later, in *Lockett v. Ohio,* the United States Supreme Court said that mitigating circumstances cannot be limited to the statutory list. The advisory jury stage (but *not* the judge sentencing stage) of Booker's case occurred after *Cooper* but before *Lockett.* Counsel's belief about his limitations was based on *Cooper.* If counsel's belief was unreasonable, then he was ineffective in failing to present non-statutory mitigating evidence. On the other hand, if counsel's belief was reasonable, we cannot argue ineffectiveness, but we *can* argue that *Cooper* was a straight violation of *Lockett.* We argued this in *Hitchcock v. State* (Fla. 1983) and so far have lost in the Florida Supreme Court and in federal district court.

The ineffectiveness issue is especially good in this case. Trial/appellate counsel has indicated that he will be cooperative in maintaining that he did not think he could introduce non-statutory mitigating evidence. Also, there should be no successive petition/abuse of the writ problem here: because appellate and original habeas counsel were one and the same person, ineffective assistance obviously could not credibly have been raised then. Finally, ineffective assistance is a "hot issue": there have been a plethora of cases on it and *Strickland v. Washington* is presently pending beneath the Big Tent.

The difficulty with this issue is the chronology. The jury proceeding was in June 1978, before *Lockett* came out. Then *Lockett* came out in July. Also in July, counsel submitted a memo on *Lockett,* but not on the part of *Lockett* that matters now. He argued that *Lockett* rendered Florida's death penalty unconstitutional. He did not argue that *Lockett* invalidated the previous jury proceeding, from which non-statutory mitigating circumstances were not allowed; the memo suggests that counsel was not aware of or didn't understand this portion of *Lockett.* In any event, the actual judge sentencing was then held in October. It is not clear what counsel thought at that time, though it appears that non-statutory mitigations were not offered then, either.

A further difficulty is that Booker might have been recalcitrant about providing counsel with leads on mitigating evidence. Booker, against counsel's advice, told the advisory jury that he wanted to die; Scharlette also tells me that counsel filed a motion in which he said that his client was not cooperating with his defense efforts. There should be a way around this. Booker couldn't have knowingly and intelligently waived his right to present non-statutory mitigating evidence if counsel, because he was unaware, never told him he could do so.

Counsel's closing arguments were curious. It didn't sound as though even he believed the insanity claim, but he also argued that the crime was "depraved," "bizarre" and "ritualistic" and that the only way around it was insanity. He argued that there were some mitigating circumstances present, but then there will be some in every case. He said that he couldn't deny that some of the aggravating circumstances were present.

Finally, counsel did not object to the inflammatory prosecutorial misconduct, discussed below.

Prosecutorial Misconduct. The eleventh circuit is presently deciding the proper standard for granting the habeas writ on the basis of misconduct by a state prosecutor in a capital case.

Three aspects of the state's argument here were improper. First, the prosecutor made an appeal to the jury to use the death penalty in the war against crime. Second, the prosecutor repeatedly offered his own opinion, thus placing in issue his own credibility and the credibility of his office. Both practices have been condemned by the Eleventh Circuit. Finally, the prosecutor quoted from U.S. Supreme Court opinions. The Georgia Supreme Court has held this improper because it shifts responsibility for the death decision from the jury to the appellate courts and suggests that the higher courts would favor a death sentence in that case.

The major difficulty with this is that counsel apparently raised this issue in his federal habeas petition. I don't have the petition here, but in any event it seems that he abandoned it on appeal. We may be able to get around this by arguing change in the law.

Counsel didn't object to this misconduct, so there might also be a procedural default problem. But we have argued that Florida doesn't apply procedural default to the penalty phase of capital cases, and that's where most of the misconduct occurred here. I sent a draft of our argument on this to LDF, and Steve should send it to you.

Proportionality Review. Nothing on the face of the Florida Supreme Court's opinion suggests that it compared Booker's case to others to determine comparative excessiveness. Florida does purport to conduct proportionality review. But given that there is at least a Florida-created right to proportionality review and probably an Eighth Amendment right as well, an argument can be made that due process requires that such review be evident on the face of the opinion. The Florida Supreme Court rejected this argument, but it's not dead yet, I hope. I have drafted the argument for Ford's case, and enclosed is a handwritten copy.

The Heinous, Atrocious, and Cruel (HAC) Aggravating Circumstance. Booker's death sentence was in part based on a finding that the crime was "especially heinous, atrocious or cruel." I have drafted in Ford's case an argument that this circumstance is unconstitutionally vague on its face and as applied. I enclose a handwritten draft of this.

Competency to Be Executed. Booker's trial transcript suggests that this may be worth raising, even though now he appears sane. This also is an issue in *Ford* and I enclose a copy of my draft.

Electrocution as Cruel and Unusual Punishment. Counsel raised this issue before the Florida Supreme Court, but the argument was pretty halfhearted. That may not be fatal, since at the time the lethal injection trend really hadn't gotten under way; thus at that time it was a futile argument. If we can get around that, there *is* a colorable argument here that the recent move toward lethal injections indicates that electrocution is cruel and unusual.

In sum, there is still a bit to argue about in *Booker.* We must find what mitigating evidence could have been presented, since I think that *Cooper/Lockett* is our best shot. Scharlette tells me that she is developing some most helpful evidence in this regard.

If there's anything I can do to help you or her, please don't be shy about calling.

Sincerely,
Michael Mello
Assistant Public Defender

I also sent along to Jeff something I had received in the mail: Booker's recently published book of poetry, *Waves and License*. Booker's poetry was striking in its power and in its silence about the fact that its author was writing the poems while on death row. The "about the author" note at the end of the book contains the only reference to Booker's status as a condemned prisoner. His interest in poetry began in 1978, after he had been sentenced to death. I thought that Jeff and his colleagues might like to read their new client's poetry.

So now, with an imminent execution date, Stephen Todd Booker finally had a lawyer other than his original trial attorney. Hell, he had a whole law firm—one of the best in the world. And the firm treated Booker's case as it would treat the case of any client. Jeff, Jim, and Marion conducted a massive factual investigation into the claim that Booker had been forced to abandon in 1982, during his first death warrant—the argument that the trial lawyer had rendered ineffective assistance of counsel during Booker's capital trial in 1978. This investigation unearthed massive amounts of additional mitigating evidence that Booker's trial lawyer could have found had he bothered to look, either during the trial in 1978 or during the first death warrant in 1982.

Booker's new lawyers filed a motion for postconviction relief (a Rule 3.850 motion) in the state trial court in Gainesville (Step 4 in Exhibit 8.1). The principal claim was ineffective assistance of trial counsel, the claim Booker had waived under duress during the first death warrant. The trial judge, John Crews, the same judge who had presided over Booker's original trial in 1978 and who had rejected the trial lawyer's first motion for state postconviction relief and stay of execution in 1982, ruled that it was too late for Booker to raise the argument that the trial attorney had rendered ineffective assistance of trial counsel. Deriding the choice with which Booker was confronted during the first death warrant in 1982, Judge Crews concluded that Booker and his trial/postconviction attorney had abandoned any claim that trial counsel rendered ineffective assistance by not raising the claim in the first state postconviction proceeding in 1982.

Then, for reasons that are murky to me to this day, Judge Crews ordered an evidentiary hearing on the selfsame claim of ineffective assistance of trial counsel that he had found abandoned by Booker and trial/postconviction counsel in 1982. Booker's new lawyers brought in a Miami criminal defense attorney to represent Booker at the evidentiary hearing. At the hearing, the trial/postconviction lawyer testified that he did, in fact, conduct a particular investigation, and he also solicited certain expert opinions from a psychiatrist who had examined Booker. Notwithstanding vigorous cross-examination by Booker's Miami attorney, the trial/postconviction attorney stuck to his story under oath. Following the hearing, Judge Crews denied Booker a retrial or resentencing. Judge Crews also denied a stay of execution.

The next venue was the Florida Supreme Court. Booker's Wilmer, Cutler & Pickering lawyers threw together an appellate brief. The court heard oral arguments and then rejected those arguments and refused to issue a stay of execution.

The lawyers moved on to federal district (trial) court, where, to my great surprise, Judge Maurice Paul stayed Booker's execution. Judge Paul said that he needed time to study Booker's argument that his 1982 waiver of the claim of ineffective assistance of trial counsel was more of a Hobson's choice than a knowing and intelligent waiver of a known right or privilege. If he found that Booker's waiver was coerced, it would be invalid. After considering the issue, however, Judge Paul ultimately agreed with the Florida courts that Booker's 1982 waiver was knowing and voluntary. Booker's new lawyers appealed that ruling to the U.S. Court of Appeals for the Eleventh Circuit, and in 1985 the Eleventh Circuit affirmed Judge Paul.

Although Governor Graham knew perfectly well that Booker's lawyers intended to appeal the Eleventh Circuit's decision to the U.S. Supreme Court, the governor decided to sign Booker's death warrant anyway—before Booker's lawyers had an opportunity to file a petition in the U.S. Supreme Court asking the Court to grant Booker's case plenary review. The governor's signing of the new death warrant at this point, when Booker's case was between courts—between the Eleventh Circuit Court of Appeals and the U.S. Supreme Court—was an obvious ploy designed to rush the federal courts to judgment, denying Booker a meaningful opportunity to ask the U.S. Supreme Court to review the lower federal courts' decisions in his case.

Governor Graham's transparent attempt to manipulate the dockets of both the Eleventh Circuit and the U.S. Supreme Court offended the sensibilities of the Eleventh Circuit judges, who, like many jurists, did not appreciate being manipulated by politicians. So, even after they had decided that Judge Paul's decision in Booker's case was correct, the Eleventh Circuit judges decided that Booker should have an opportunity to seek U.S. Supreme Court review of the Eleventh Circuit's determination, and to seek that review without the intense time pressures of an active death warrant and a scheduled execution date. Thus the Eleventh Circuit issued a stay of execution pending Booker's filing and disposition of a petition asking the U.S. Supreme Court to hear his case.

At the time, I thought that was the end of it. In the mid-1980s, the U.S. Supreme Court almost never vacated a lower federal court's decision to grant a stay of execution in a death penalty case. So when the Florida prosecutors asked the U.S. Supreme Court to dissolve the stay that the Eleventh Circuit had issued, I told my friend Jeff not to worry. That, as it turned out, was not good advice.

To my appalled amazement, the U.S. Supreme Court dissolved the Eleventh Circuit stay. Of the justices voting to dissolve the stay, only Justice Lewis Powell Jr. wrote an opinion explaining why. He stressed that lower court stays in capital cases were "not automatic" and would be reviewed by the Supreme Court. In one respect, Powell's opinion was atypical: he trashed the lower court rather than Booker's lawyers. Perhaps this was because Booker was represented by a powerhouse law firm rather than by a state public defender.

The Court's unusual action in dissolving the Eleventh Circuit's stay sent an unmistakable message to the federal judiciary with jurisdiction over Florida: Stay the hell out of the state of Florida's attempts to execute Stephen Todd Booker in one week. That message had come from Justice Powell himself.

It's over, I thought—Stephen Todd Booker is a dead man. Not only was he scheduled to be executed in one week, but the nation's highest court had dissolved a lower federal court's stay of his execution. Thus, not only did Booker not have a stay, or any apparent legal issues with which to get a stay, but the U.S. Supreme Court had sent a strong message that the federal courts were to let this execution proceed as scheduled.

Then lightning struck. Booker's new lawyers discovered that his trial/first postconviction counsel had lied when he testified at the evidentiary hearing before Judge Crews in 1983. If anything might persuade Crews to stay Booker's third death warrant, this would be it. Judges really hate it when lawyers lie under oath in their courtrooms. Still, it was a long shot. This was a third death warrant. At that time, no Florida inmate had ever survived a second death warrant, much less a third.

But sometimes long shots pay off. Judge Crews stayed the execution and ordered an evidentiary hearing to determine whether or not the trial attorney had committed a "fraud on the court" during his testimony in the 1983 evidentiary hearing on ineffective assistance of trial counsel. Following that evidentiary hearing, which occurred in 1986, Judge Crews concluded that the trial lawyer had not lied during his 1983 testimony and therefore that he had not committed a fraud on the court. Booker's lawyers appealed that decision to the Florida Supreme Court.

Still Alive

In January 1987, I left full-time deathwork in Florida and accepted a job as an associate at Wilmer, Cutler & Pickering. That is where I was working in May 1987, when a unanimous U.S. Supreme Court decided James Hitchcock's case and found that the *Lockett* issue in Stephen Todd Booker's case, raised by the trial lawyer at trial and in the first state postconviction motion filed during the first death warrant in 1983, had, in fact, been right all along. Booker had been right all along. The trial lawyer had been right all along. Jim Hitchcock had been right all along. And those Florida death row prisoners who were still alive to raise the *Lockett* claim again, after *Hitchcock* was decided in 1987, would almost certainly win new sentencing trials based on *Hitchcock*.

The U.S. Supreme Court issued its unanimous *Hitchcock* decision on April 22, 1987, at 10:00 A.M. As soon as I heard the news, I dispatched a courier from our law offices on M Street, just up from Georgetown, to the Supreme Court's building. I was reading the Court's opinion by 10:30. I was, of course, delighted for Jim Hitchcock and Steve Booker and all of my other clients and former clients lucky enough to still be alive when Hitchcock's case was decided, but I couldn't help thinking about Anthony Antone, James Adams, James Dupree Henry, Bob Sullivan, and all the others who had already been executed.

Steve Booker was still alive. Ninety-six days after the Supreme Court's decision in *Hitchcock*, Jim Coleman and I filed a petition for a new trial for Booker based on the *Hitchcock* decision. We filed it directly in the Florida Supreme Court because, by that time, we had worn out our welcome in Judge Crews's courtroom. The Florida Supreme Court scheduled oral argument, which I did later, in Tallahassee, in 1987.

In early 1988, a five-judge majority of the Florida Supreme Court ruled that, although *Hitchcock* error had occurred in Booker's case, that error was harmless beyond a reasonable doubt. Two justices dissented, vigorously, but the bottom line was that we had lost. Coleman and I filed a petition seeking U.S. Supreme Court review of the Florida Supreme Court's judgment, which was denied by a vote of seven to two. In June 1988, Jim Coleman, Jeff Robinson, and I filed a petition for writ of habeas corpus, right back in Federal District Judge Maurice Paul's courtroom.

In mid-June 1988, I moved to Vermont to begin a full-time teaching job at Vermont Law School. At the time, I was in a relationship with a former legal services attorney who was convinced, not without substantial justification, that my devotion to deathwork interfered with my ability to be a full partner in our personal relationship.

In August 1988, I persuaded my significant other that my work for the summer was done, and that we should take some time off and go to the coast of Maine to relax. We left for Ogunquit, Maine, on August 8, and during the three-hour drive from Vermont I reiterated that I had not given the phone number of the Colonial Motel, where we would be staying in Ogunquit, to anyone other than my secretary. This was almost true. I had, in fact, also given the Colonial's number to Jeff Robinson, but both Jeff and my secretary knew not to disturb us absent a genuine emergency.

Thus, imagine my surprise—and my companion's horror—when, as soon as we identified ourselves at the motel check-in desk, I was handed a message asking me to call Jeff Robinson as soon as possible. My companion was furious. I was petrified. She didn't know Jeff, but I did, and there was only one possible reason Jeff would have called: the governor of Florida must have signed a fourth death warrant on Stephen Todd Booker. Only one Florida death row prisoner, Willie Jasper Darden, had survived a fourth warrant, and he had been executed on his sixth warrant.

I didn't call Jeff right away. First, my companion and I took a long walk on the beach. By the end of it, I was still anxious and she was still furious. I called Jeff from a parking-lot pay phone; sure enough, the governor had signed Booker's death warrant. But he and Jim Coleman had everything under control, Jeff said. To our already filed and pending habeas corpus petitions, they would add a short application for stay of execution based upon the same grounds set out in the habeas petition.

In a single stroke, and in a single order, Judge Maurice Paul issued an opinion staying Booker's execution and ordering a resentencing trial, with a new jury, based solely upon the *Hitchcock* decision. Booker had been scheduled to be executed at 7:00 A.M. on September 20, 1988. Judge Paul issued his stay of execution and resentencing order on September 17.

For the next ten years, the state of Florida filed petition after petition, appeal after appeal, attempting to invalidate Judge Paul's order that Booker must receive a new (and fair) sentencing trial. All of these petitions and appeals by the state were rejected by court after court, but the state of Florida kept on trying. Finally, after the state had exhausted all of its appeals, Booker had his resentencing trial. At that trial, in March 1998, Booker was represented by the local public defender.

The defense first introduced into evidence an affidavit from Booker's deceased grandmother, Florence Edmund, a longtime resident of Brooklyn, New York. Edmund stated that Booker was born on September 1, 1953, and grew up without knowing his father. The affidavit recounted how Booker lived at different times with Edmund or with his mother, and how his behavior, which had generally been good, took a turn for the worse when he was about twelve years old. According to his grandmother, Booker was shot while in a fight, and during his hospital stay he roomed with a person who used drugs; Edmund suspected that Booker began using drugs after that. Edmund's affidavit further recounted that Booker's mother died as the result of a stroke just before Booker's seventeenth birthday, and Booker joined the army shortly thereafter. After his discharge from the army, Booker initially lived with Edmund, but he then unexpectedly moved to Florida. The last time that Edmund heard from Booker was through a letter he sent to her from jail in Fort Myers, Florida, and the first time that Edmund heard that Booker had been convicted of first-degree murder and sentenced to death was October 29, 1983.

The defense next introduced an affidavit from Patricia R. Singletary, a former employee of the New York City public school system. In the affidavit, Singletary summarized Booker's erratic educational history: Booker transferred in and out of eleven different schools between kindergarten and the sixth grade. Generally, the educational records described Booker as intelligent, doing particularly well in artistic endeavors, but the records also contained several references to disciplinary problems, including aggression. Absenteeism became an increasing problem as Booker grew older, and he officially left school in February 1970, at the age of sixteen.

As Booker's first in-person witness, the defense presented Dr. George Barnard, a psychiatrist, who testified as an expert in both psychiatry and forensic psychiatry. Dr. Barnard's first contact with Booker came in December 1977, when he evaluated Booker pursuant to court order. After that and several other subsequent evaluations in early 1978, Dr. Barnard testified for the state during the guilt phase of the trial that Booker was both sane at the time of the murder and competent to stand trial. Dr. Barnard's next contact with Booker occurred in 1985, when defense counsel asked Barnard to review Booker's case to determine whether any mitigating circumstances existed. After reviewing Booker's case, Barnard determined that (1) Booker was under the influence of extreme mental or emotional disturbance at the time of the crime, and (2) at the time of the crime, Booker's ability to understand the criminality of his conduct or to conform his conduct to the requirements of the law was substantially impaired.

In 1997, Booker's counsel again requested that Dr. Barnard evaluate Booker, and Barnard spent seven and a half hours with Booker to make that evaluation. In addition, Barnard reviewed various materials that had been gathered regarding Booker's case since the time of the initial trial. Dr. Barnard then summarized for the jury various events in Booker's life as well as Booker's mental health history.

Dr. Barnard testified that Booker started using alcohol and drugs at age thirteen or fourteen. When he was sixteen, a family court ordered

Booker to undergo a psychiatric examination at Kings County Hospital in New York City because he had been threatening his mother and drinking alcohol. Booker was discharged after being in the hospital for slightly over three weeks, with the recommendation that he receive some outpatient psychotherapy or counseling. To Dr. Barnard's knowledge, Booker never received any such therapy.

Barnard further testified regarding three instances of sexual abuse Booker endured as a child, abuse perpetrated by two different babysitters and by an aunt. In addition, Barnard stated that while Booker was in the army, he would regularly become intoxicated and engage in fights, and that he had been hospitalized in Okinawa on one occasion for five to seven days after suffering various injuries. Booker experienced blackouts during this period, and army medical personnel thought that he suffered from schizophrenia; he was treated with two antipsychotic drugs. Booker was then medically evacuated from Okinawa to Walter Reed Army Medical Center in Washington, D.C., where he was admitted to the psychiatric unit and continued to be treated with sizable dosages of Thorazine. Booker remained at Walter Reed for fifty-five days. He continued to serve in the army for a short time after he was discharged from the hospital, and he received an honorable discharge from the army in 1974.

Within a year of being discharged from the army, Booker was taken away in an ambulance after he was found wielding a knife and threatening several people in a New York street. He was again admitted to Kings County Hospital, and then he was transferred to another hospital where he was evaluated overnight and released. He had been diagnosed at Kings County as having a paranoid reaction, but at the second hospital the diagnosis was intoxication. Several days prior to this incident, at least one member of Booker's family had communicated to a nurse at one of the hospitals that Booker had engaged in bizarre behavior a few days earlier.

Dr. Barnard further testified that Booker was incarcerated in Florida during the early 1970s, and Booker's medical records for that period of incarceration showed that he (1) was seen by a psychiatrist because he thought that the water was tainted, causing a skin rash and possible impotence; and (2) was given the antiseizure medication Dilantin. Booker had told Barnard that during that period of time he was having hallucinations of the devil sitting on his chest or pushing against his chest with a fist. Finally, Dr. Barnard testified that while Booker was in Gainesville in 1977, he was admitted to Bridge House and to another facility for treatment of alcohol abuse and problems with substances such as marijuana, LSD, heroin, hashish, and glue.

Based on all of his preceding testimony, Dr. Barnard concluded at the close of direct examination by the defense that Booker was suffering from depression, alcohol and drug addiction, an "altered state of consciousness," and an antisocial personality disorder at the time of the crime. Further, consistent with his conclusion in 1985, Dr. Barnard opined that (1) Booker was under extreme mental or emotional disturbance at the time of the crime, and (2) Booker's ability to appreciate the criminality of his conduct or to conform his conduct to the requirements of law was substantially impaired at the time of the crime.

On cross-examination by the prosecutor, Dr. Barnard indicated that at no point in time was Booker insane; that is, Booker did not have a mental disease that prevented him from understanding the difference between right and wrong. Further, Barnard conceded that much of the information he had considered in evaluating Booker was based on Booker's own self-reporting, and that many of Booker's statements to him were inconsistent. Additionally, Barnard testified that individuals who suffer from an antisocial personality disorder, such as Booker, can be expected to lie and malinger in order to gain an advantage in a given situation. He admitted that this fact could call into question the validity of any of the information Booker had provided. Barnard also conceded that he had not performed any psychological tests on Booker. Finally, he testified that, in his various encounters with Booker, he had never seen any manifestation of "Aniel," the alternative personality that allegedly had troubled Booker in the past, and he opined that Booker never suffered from multiple personality disorder.

After presenting the testimony of Dr. Barnard, the defense called six witnesses to expound upon Booker's literary accomplishments during his period of incarceration: Deborah Tall, professor of English at Hobart and William Smith Colleges, as well as editor of *Seneca Review*; Suzanne Tamminen, editor in chief at Wesleyan University Press; Hayden Carruth, professor emeritus at Syracuse University (Carruth testified via videotape); Stuart Lavin, writer and professor of English at Castleton State College; Stuart Friebert, poet and professor of English at Oberlin College; and Willard Spiegelman, professor of English at Southern Methodist University. These witnesses testified that Booker had made substantial contributions in the field of poetry, including being published in numerous well-respected literary journals.

Finally, the defense presented the testimony of Betty Vogh, a Gainesville woman who, along with her husband, had befriended Booker during his period of incarceration, as well as the testimony of Mary Page McKean Zyromski, a great-niece of the murder victim. Both Vogh and Zyromski had helped Booker with his literary endeavors over the years, and Zyromski specifically testified that Booker had assigned to her the royalties generated from the sales of one of his published works.

None of it mattered. Booker's new jury voted for death (the count was eight to four), and the trial judge sentenced him to death. He appealed that judgment to the Florida Supreme Court, which upheld the death sentence in October 2000. Booker's case is now progressing along the capital appeals assembly line all over again.

On the day the Florida Supreme Court affirmed Booker's second death sentence, Booker was forty-seven years old. He had been on death row for twenty-three years. Only 15 of the 372 people on death row had lived there longer than Booker.

Stephen Todd Booker's legal odyssey shows the legal system at its best or its worst, depending on one's perspective. On the one hand, Booker's case might be seen as Exhibit A in support of the proposition that a multilayered system of appellate review is necessary to vindicate the basic constitutional rights that protect us all. If those who would radically limit the appellate and postconviction avenues available to the condemned had had their way in the early stages of Booker's appeals, he would have been dead before the illegality of his death sentence was recognized by the Supreme Court.

On the other hand, Booker can be seen as the poster child for how legal technicalities can thwart essential justice. After Booker had spent years and years on death row, the courts decided that Booker's original jury was misinstructed on the law. That's a pretty technical reason for requiring a new sentencing trial. In Booker's case, the jury instruction didn't matter; the resentencing jury, which was properly instructed on the law, voted for death.

In the end, how one evaluates the Booker case depends on the importance one attaches to the legal error that caused the federal courts to mandate Booker's resentencing. That error—the constitutional issue that bears the name of Jim Hitchcock—is the subject of the next chapter.

9

The Landmark Case:
Jim Hitchcock

We think it could not be clearer that the advisory jury was instructed not to consider . . . evidence of nonstatutory mitigating circumstances, and that the proceedings therefore did not comport with the requirements of [the U.S. Constitution].

—Supreme Court Justice Antonin Scalia, writing for a
unanimous Court in Hitchcock's case

George Washington fought only nine battles in the Revolutionary War, and of those nine, he won only three. But Washington won the war—and we don't all carry British passports today—because he understood that he didn't need to win every battle. What he needed to do, and what he did, was to make his army *survive,* to continue to exist. He fought and lost and rose and fought again. Thus did his scarecrow band of citizen-soldiers whip the most powerful military power of the age. Thus did he beat a king.

Jim Hitchcock's case become a landmark capital decision in the U.S. Supreme Court in 1987. The *Hitchcock* decision removed more people from Florida's death row than any other single case in recent times. Looking back on it now, we all appeared brilliant in Hitchcock's case. Maybe we were; I know we were lucky. I know that Craig Barnard, who served as Hitchcock's lead counsel, was brilliant and tenacious—and lucky.

The idea that capital sentences must be *individualized*—that is, grounded in the particular facts and circumstances of the particular person on trial for his or her life—is central to the American jurisprudence of death. In the case of *Lockett v. Ohio* in 1978, the U.S. Supreme Court ruled that cookie-cutter capital punishment does not pass constitutional muster. People on trial for their lives have a right to present—and to have their juries consider—whatever relevant evidence in mitigation they want to present.

But what about people who were tried and condemned before *Lockett* was decided in 1978? Whether a pre-*Lockett* death sentence was lawful or not depended on whether the particular state where the case was decided had managed to anticipate the rule of *Lockett*. If the state courts had anticipated *Lockett*, then the pre-*Lockett* death sentences were okay; if not, the pre-*Lockett* death sentences were illegal. Florida fell into the second category. Prior to *Lockett*, the Florida courts had utterly failed to require that capital juries be allowed to hear and consider all relevant mitigating evidence.

In 1972, Florida enacted its present-day capital statute. The plain language of this statute confined consideration of mitigating circumstances to a narrow statutory list. In Vernon Cooper's case, for example, Cooper wanted his jury to consider his stable employment record. A good employment record wasn't listed as a mitigating circumstance in the statute, however, so the jury was not permitted to consider Cooper's employment record, and he was sentenced to death.

In 1976, in Cooper's case, the Florida Supreme Court found that the statutory language was clear in using "words of mandatory limitation" to confine the jury's consideration to a nonexpandable "list" of mitigating factors, and thus "other matters have no place in [the capital sentencing] proceeding." The *Cooper* court stressed the clarity of the statutory language restricting consideration of mitigating factors to those "as enumerated" in the statute's list, emphasizing that these were "words of mandatory limitation." Accordingly, the court decided in *Cooper* that "the sole issue in a sentencing hearing is to examine in each case the itemized aggravating and mitigating circumstances. Evidence concerning other matters have [sic] no place in that consideration."

Cooper's case was decided by the Florida Supreme Court in 1976. It was not until the U.S. Supreme Court decided Sandra Lockett's case in 1978 that another view was expressed. Lockett's case posed an obvious problem for the Florida Supreme Court, but the court couldn't admit that some sixty Florida death sentences—all those handed down pre-1978—were illegal. So the justices claimed that Florida law had anticipated *Lockett* and had always been consistent with the rule of *Lockett*.

Instead of admitting that Florida's previous "mandatory limitation" on mitigating circumstances conflicted with *Lockett* and resolving that conflict honestly and forthrightly, the Florida Supreme Court simply denied that there had ever been such a limitation in the statute or in the court's previous judicial decisions. In Carl Songer's case, decided in late 1978, the court said that "obviously" their construction of the capital statute "has been that *all* relevant mitigating circumstances"—statutory and nonstatutory—"may be considered in mitigation." Employing historical revisionism, the court in *Songer* rewrote its prior decisions in Songer's and other cases to make them consistent with the rule of *Lockett*. These cases claimed that Florida's pre-1978 standard jury instructions violated *Lockett*.

Vernon Cooper, Carl Songer, and other condemned prisoners challenged, in federal court, the Florida Supreme Court's revisionist take on *Songer* and other pre-1978 cases, including Cooper's. In 1982, these constitutional challenges reached the U.S. Court of Appeals for the Eleventh Circuit. On February 10, 1983, the Eleventh Circuit ruled that it couldn't say the Florida Supreme Court had been fibbing in Carl Songer's case in 1978: Florida pre-1978 standard jury instructions and other laws had not been inconsistent with the rule established in *Lockett*. The Eleventh Circuit was divided on this issue; Judge Vance cast the deciding vote.

Having lost the standard jury instruction issue in 1983, lawyers for Florida's death row population—led by Craig Barnard—reverted to a more complex claim: that even though the jury instructions didn't violate *Lockett*, defense lawyers *believed* Florida law precluded them from presenting nonstatutory mitigating evidence. If that erroneous belief was unreasonable, then those lawyers rendered ineffective assistance of counsel. If the belief was reasonable, then Florida law violated *Lockett* "as applied."

From 1978 to 1987, the Florida Supreme Court got away with its claim that Florida had anticipated *Lockett*. Craig Barnard, however, never stopped pounding away at the issue. Finally, in 1987, in Jim Hitchcock's case, the U.S. Supreme Court caught the Florida Supreme Court in its lie.

In its U.S. Supreme Court brief in Hitchcock's case, the state of Florida summarized the evidence adduced at Hitchcock's trial in this way: On January 21, 1977, Hitchcock was found guilty of the first-degree murder of Cynthia Ann Driggers. The evidence presented at trial showed that approximately two weeks prior to the murder, Hitchcock, unemployed, ill, and with no place to live, arrived in Winter Garden, Florida, to stay with his brother, Richard. Hitchcock knew that his traveling to Florida was a violation of his Arkansas parole.

Cynthia Ann Driggers, thirteen years old, was Richard Hitchcock's stepdaughter. On the night of the murder, James Hitchcock went out with some friends, drank some beer, and smoked some marijuana. In a statement James Hitchcock gave to the police, he said that upon returning to his brother's house late that night, he went into Cynthia's bedroom. He had sex with Cynthia, and afterward she stated that she was hurt and was going to tell her mother. When Hitchcock told her that she could not, she began to cry out. In his effort to silence her, he picked her up and carried her outside to the yard. He told her that she could not tell her mother, and she began to scream. He grabbed her by the throat and began choking her, and when he released his grip, she again began to scream and cry out. He hit her twice, but she continued to scream, so he choked her and "just kept chokin' and chokin,'" and after she was still, he pushed her body into some bushes in the yard and went back into the house. He then took a shower, washed his shirt, and went into his bedroom and lay down. Medical evidence showed that Cynthia Ann Driggers was, before the incident, a virgin.

When Hitchcock testified at trial, he admitted going into Cynthia's room, but stated that the sex was consensual. He stated that afterward, he was sitting on the bed putting his pants back on when his brother Richard came in, grabbed Cynthia, and pulled her out of the house. He followed and tried to prevent Richard from choking his own stepdaughter. According to James Hitchcock, he could not break his brother's grip, and after a time, it was clear that Cynthia was dead. He then told Richard to go into the house and that he would take care of the matter, and then he put Cynthia's body in the bushes.

During the defense case, Hitchcock's trial counsel introduced the testimony of a number of individuals, including Hitchcock's siblings and his mother, relating to his nonviolent character. In addition, despite the fact that the prosecutor's relevancy objections were in many cases sustained by the court, defense counsel persisted in questioning those witnesses who knew Hitchcock as to his family background, in an attempt to get certain information before the jury: that Hitchcock was one of seven children, that he had been quite young when he left home, that he was very young when his natural father died, that he had never previously exhibited any violence toward children, that his "attitude" toward his mother and family was good, and that he always "minded" his mother and did what he was told. Hitchcock's own trial testimony likewise related numerous aspects of his background for the jury's edification: his childhood poverty, the fact that he left home at the age of thirteen because he could not stand to see his stepfather striking and verbally abusing his mother, that he had been drifting from place to place since then, and that his natural father had died when Hitchcock was only six, leaving his mother to try to support herself and her many children. Furthermore, Hitchcock asserted that the confession he had given the police was motivated by his desire to protect his "crippled" brother Richard, who had helped him and had been like a father to him. He also said that he had confessed because he felt he had nothing else to live for and nowhere else to go.

After the jury returned a verdict of guilty, the advisory sentencing phase of the proceeding was held. Defense counsel again elicited family background information on Hitchcock, similar and in addition to that already submitted at trial, through the testimony of one of Hitchcock's brothers, who noted that Hitchcock's father had died in 1963 after having been bedridden with cancer for eight months, that his father and mother had worked as farm laborers in Arkansas in attempting to support their family of seven children, and that James had "sucked gas" on various occasions when he was five to six years old (and after his father's death), which had seemingly caused his mind to wander at times.

When Craig Barnard walked up to the Supreme Court podium during the *Hitchcock* oral argument, he was prepared to make the complex "as applied" *Lockett/Cooper/Songer* argument. But he was cut off by a justice who asked, somewhat impatiently, whether Florida's pre-1978 standard jury instructions didn't simply violate *Lockett*.

It was one of those rare, defining moments that an experienced oral advocate may encounter only once or twice in a long career. A question from the bench requires you to reevaluate your entire position and decide whether or not you should change it—all within the space of a few heartbeats. You know that the court's center of gravity has just shifted, that you can win the case if you say exactly the right thing in exactly the right way.

Craig hesitated for a moment—knowing that this very jury instruction had been upheld by the Eleventh Circuit in 1983, and that virtually everyone Florida had executed since 1983 had received the same jury instruction—before arguing, somewhat wryly, that it had always seemed to *him* that the jury instruction violated *Lockett*. In the end, a unanimous Supreme Court agreed.

In *Hitchcock*, Justice Scalia, writing for a unanimous U.S. Supreme Court, held:

> We think it could not be clearer that the advisory jury was instructed not to consider, and the sentencing judge refused to consider, evidence of nonstatutory mitigating circumstances, and that the proceedings therefore did not comport with the requirements of [the U.S. Constitution]. [The prosecutor] has made no attempt to argue that this error was harmless, or that it had no effect on the jury or the sentencing judge. In the absence of such a showing our cases hold that the exclusion of mitigating evidence of the sort at issue here renders the death sentence invalid.

For years prior to 1987, the Florida courts and the federal courts had ruled, in case after case, that this jury instruction was constitutional. Men had been executed based on these rulings. Suddenly, in 1987, a unanimous U.S. Supreme Court had decided that "it could not be clearer" that Florida law pre-1978—including the standard jury instruction—was flatly contrary to the rule of *Lockett*. In the wake of *Hitchcock*, the Florida Supreme Court quickly reversed the death sentences of at least eighteen individuals who had been tried before 1978.

In *Among the Lowest of the Dead*, David Von Drehle captures the importance—and the mortal irony—of *Hitchcock*:

> The courts can change their minds very quickly. That was the message of the second death penalty ruling published on that April day in 1986, Hitchcock v. Dugger. Technically, the U.S. Supreme Court had never ruled on whether Florida's death penalty law limited a defendant's right to present evidence in favor of a life sentence. But the Court had been asked repeatedly to take the question under consideration, and repeatedly the Court had refused. And eighteen people went to Old Sparky. That suggests the majority had made up their minds. Now they changed them: The justices ruled unanimously—all of them, the conservatives,

the moderate, the liberals—that the law had been "authoritative-ly interpreted by the Florida Supreme Court" to mean that mitigating evidence was limited.

Craig Barnard was right. The Florida Supreme Court had denied this for some eight years—eighteen executions—but Barnard had kept at it, kept hammering, despite scolding and even ridicule from judges and prosecutors. The public complained bitterly about lawyers like him, with their delaying tactics and technicalities. Politicians had proposed all sorts of bills to limit his access, and the access of his colleagues, to the appellate courts.

Now the U.S. Supreme Court said unanimously that Barnard had been right all along. Justice Scalia, the new conservative tiger, wrote the opinion. "We think it could not be clearer . . . " he intoned, in his confident, definitive way, that the judge and the jury believed they could consider only a few favorable factors. It could not be clearer.

The Court's opinion in Hitchcock was brief, scarcely hinting at the years of litigation that had gone into Barnard's victory. In the end, the subtle shift Barnard had made in his argument was the fig leaf the justices grasped to cover their sudden change of heart. . . .

The opinion was written to make it seem that a very small point had been decided, but Craig Barnard could see that a new generation of appeals had been opened for the men who had been on Florida's death row the longest. What was true for James Hitchcock was at least arguably true for all of them . . . dozens of them, and they were the men closest to Old Sparky. And Hitchcock had an even larger meaning for Barnard. After the ruling, he proudly told his troops: "When people ask why we keep appealing, why we raise these issues over and over, why we never give up fighting . . . tell them to look at Hitchcock."

All of the condemned men whose stories are told in this book were tried and sentenced prior to the *Hitchcock* decision in 1987; virtually all were tried and convicted prior to the *Lockett* decision in 1978. All of their death sentences were unlawful under the *Hitchcock* decision; that is, none of their sentencing juries had been allowed to consider their stories in full.

In the years since *Hitchcock* was decided, more than twenty Florida death row prisoners have won new sentencing trials based on the legal principles set out in the *Hitchcock* decision. Between 1979 and the time *Hitchcock* was decided, eighteen men were killed in Florida's electric chair. Virtually all of these executions were unlawful under the rules set out in *Hitchcock*.

Soon after Jim Hitchcock won in the Supreme Court, he sent me a letter that I still cherish:

To: Michael Mello   6-4-87

Dear Sir:

I just wanted to drop you a line or 2 to say thanks for all your help in my appeal. I know your work rarely shows appreciation. But know your efforts are appreciated deeply by me.

Thanks to you and a lot of other people who worked on my case together you gave me a new lease on life.

Even if I get resentenced to Death—It will have bought me valuable time. Which I was nearly out of. And I hold life precious. And where there's life and time—there's possibility of change and hopes for things to get better.

So thanks—And take care and keep punching.

Sincerely
James Hitchcock

In the end, it was luck that decided who lived and who died. Those still alive when *Hitchcock* was decided would live. Jim Hitchcock's luck continued, at least for a while. A second jury sentenced him to death, and in 1991 the Florida Supreme Court affirmed. A year later the U.S. Supreme Court, in a different case, invalidated Florida's jury instructions on the "heinousness, atrocious and cruel" aggravating circumstance. In light of that decision, the Florida Supreme Court revisited the legality of Jim Hitchcock's reimposed death sentence, and in 1993 it vacated that sentence and remanded the case for a third sentencing trial before a third jury.

The third jury voted unanimously for death. Again the Florida Supreme Court reversed, this time for a variety of errors, including yet another illegal jury instruction.

The fourth jury sentenced Hitchcock to death by a vote of ten to two. On March 23, 2000, the Florida Supreme court affirmed the death sentence. Jim Hitchcock continues to litigate for his life.

10

My Roommate: Joseph Green Brown

Take a good look at me. I *am* capital punishment in Florida.

—Joseph Green Brown, following his release from death row in 1987

Joseph Green Brown was innocent of the murder that sent him to death row. He spent thirteen years on death row and came within fifteen hours of being executed before his attorney obtained a stay from the Eleventh Circuit Court of Appeals. He had eaten his "last meal" and had been measured for the suit of clothes he would have worn for his funeral.

Ultimately, the Eleventh Circuit overturned Brown's conviction based on prosecutorial misconduct. This result occurred due to the hard work and commitment of Brown's pro bono lawyers, Richard Blumenthal and David Reiser. In ordering that Brown's habeas petition be granted, the Eleventh Circuit found that the prosecutor knowingly allowed and exploited perjured testimony from the state's star witness.

The issue of prosecutorial withholding of information made national headlines in May 2001 when, less than a week before the scheduled execution of convicted Oklahoma City bomber Timothy McVeigh, the FBI revealed that it had failed to disclose three thousand pages of documents to McVeigh's lawyer. The government maintained that the failure had been unintentional, the result of human error, and that, given the overwhelming nature of the evidence of McVeigh's guilt, the undisclosed information would not have led a reasonable jury to acquit McVeigh.

McVeigh's was the most high-profile capital case in recent memory.

The FBI's effort in the case cost $82 million and at one time occupied half the agents in the entire bureau. The government knew that all its actions would be scrutinized by press and public, yet even so the FBI, America's premier law enforcement agency, committed a colossal blunder. Clearly, if such errors (or misconduct) can happen in such a high-profile case, they can happen in run-of-the-mill capital prosecutions. Columbia Law School Professor James Liebman and his colleagues, in a troubling report titled "A Broken System," note that important suppressed evidence has led to dismissal of one in five capital cases since 1973.

The materials not disclosed in the McVeigh case probably would not have made any difference to McVeigh's jury. In Joseph Green Brown's case, however, prosecutorial withholding of exculpatory evidence led to a wrongful conviction and very nearly to the execution of an innocent man.

Brown was twenty-four years old in 1974 when he was convicted of the rape, robbery, and murder of Earlene Barksdale, a Tampa, Florida, shop owner. He was sentenced to death for the murder. Brown is African American. His alleged victim was white.

The state's case against Brown hinged on the testimony of Ronald Floyd, the only witness who placed Brown at the crime scene and the only witness to testify to Brown's alleged admission that he had committed the rape and murder. According to Floyd's testimony, Floyd, Brown, and a man identified as Poochie (who was never located) drove to Barksdale's shop; Brown and Poochie entered the shop while Floyd waited in the car outside. Floyd testified that he did not know what Brown and Poochie intended to do once they were inside the shop. He said that he did not see a gun, but he did notice a bulge under Brown's shirt that looked like a gun. Floyd testified that after waiting in the car for fifteen minutes, he went to the shop door to look in, heard a shot, entered the store, and saw the foot of a body lying inside. He said that Brown and Poochie then emerged from the shop, and all three men got into the car and drove away. In the car, Floyd testified, Poochie told Brown, "Man, you didn't have to do that." Floyd also said that the next day, he, Brown, and another man were together and heard a radio broadcast about the Barksdale murder. He said that Brown subsequently admitted to him that he had killed the woman.

On the evening after the murder, Brown and Floyd robbed a couple at a Holiday Inn. Brown also tried to sexually assault the woman, but stopped and fled. After the robbery, Brown, not yet a suspect in Barksdale's murder, turned himself in to the police and implicated Floyd as his accomplice in the motel robbery. Noting similarities between the Barksdale and Holiday Inn crimes—timing, location, robbery, and sexual assaults—the police offered Brown immunity if he would testify against Floyd. Brown refused, saying he knew nothing about the Barksdale crime. When Floyd was arrested and heard that Brown had implicated him in the Holiday Inn robbery, he implicated Brown in Barksdale's murder.

Floyd's testimony was the key to the state's case. As the Eleventh Circuit opinion noted, other than his testimony, there was little evidence linking Brown to the rape and murder, "possibly not even sufficient evidence to submit the case to the jury." During the trial, Brown's attorney attempted to impeach Floyd's testimony by casting doubt on Floyd's credibility. The attorney questioned Floyd on whether he had entered into a plea agreement with the state that was beneficial to him. Floyd testified that he had not entered into any plea agreement, nor was he promised immunity or leniency with regard to either the Barksdale case or the Holiday Inn case. In his closing argument to the jury, the prosecutor used Floyd's denial of any promises to bolster Floyd's testimony: "I submit that there have been no promises made to Ronald Floyd for his testifying in this case. . . . He has absolutely nothing to gain by testifying against this particular individual."

The only other evidence linking Brown to the murder was a .38 Smith & Wesson revolver, allegedly the murder weapon, which had been traced to Brown. In fact, however, Brown's weapon had not been fired, and the prosecutor knew it. The prosecutor deliberately led the jury to believe that the gun Brown had used during the Holiday Inn robbery was the murder weapon, even though he knew that Brown's gun could not chamber or fire the .38 "Special" bullet that had killed Earlene Barksdale. The FBI ballistics report conclusively ruled out Brown's .38 Smith & Wesson as the murder weapon. Nevertheless, the prosecutor deliberately misled the jury in his opening and closing statements, implying that Brown's gun was the one used to kill Barksdale.

The prosecutor had included the FBI agent who prepared the ballistics report on his pretrial list of witnesses, and because the agent was already listed as a witness, Brown's attorney did not himself subpoena the agent. However, the prosecutor never called the agent to the stand. On the last day of the trial, and without notifying Brown's attorney, the prosecutor released the agent, who went back to the vacation he had been summoned from, in a location where he could not be reached on short notice. Brown's attorney requested a continuance so that he could locate and subpoena the agent, but his request was refused.

The prosecutor's statement that Floyd had cut no deals with the state was also untrue. Agreements had been reached between Floyd and prosecutors on both the Holiday Inn robbery and the Barksdale murder prior to Floyd's testifying at Brown's trial. Floyd was never indicted for the Barksdale murder, and he received probation for the Holiday Inn robbery. The Eleventh Circuit directed that the habeas writ be granted "because the prosecution knowingly allowed material false testimony to be introduced at trial, failed to step forward and make the falsity known, and knowingly exploited the false testimony in its closing argument to the jury."

The prosecutors decided not to retry the case, primarily because by that time Floyd had recanted his trial testimony, and without it the state had virtually no evidence with which to make a case against Brown. Floyd first tried to retract his trial testimony two weeks after the trial ended, when he signed an affidavit saying he had lied in his trial testimony. At a subsequent hearing, the judge and prosecutor warned Floyd about perjury, incorrectly informing him that the sentence for perjury was life in prison. Floyd backed down from his recantation. During the course of Brown's postconviction litigation, Floyd came forward again and, in a videotaped sworn statement, testified that police had put him under pressure to testify against Brown at trial, that detectives showed him pictures of the murder scene before he agreed to testify, and that he had been promised probation in the Holiday Inn case if he agreed to testify against Brown in the murder case. He further testified that he agreed to testify against Brown in part because he was angry at Brown for implicating him in the motel robbery, that he had invented "Poochie" because police told him a third assailant was involved in the crime, and that he had retracted his 1975 recantation because the judge and prosecutor threatened him with perjury charges. Brown was released from prison in March 1987, after spending thirteen years on death row and coming within fifteen hours of being executed for a murder he most likely did not commit.

The Brown case and the cases of other innocent persons wrongly convicted of capital crimes raise an interesting question: Does the release of the wrongly convicted from death row suggest that "the system works"? In Illinois, it was a group of undergraduate journalism students who proved the innocence of Anthony Porter (who came within forty-eight hours of execution) and others. Can we seriously contend that such cases show that the judicial system is working? In evaluating whether or not the system is working, we should focus not on the reasons innocent men and women have been able to prove their innocence before they could be executed by the state, but on why they were sent to death row in the first place.

Innocent people don't end up sentenced to death because police and prosecutors wake up in the morning and decide, "Today I think I'll frame an innocent person for capital murder." Judges don't affirm the death sentences of people they believe to be innocent. Governors don't sign death warrants on people they know to be innocent. Rather, innocent people are sometimes found guilty because of factors that blind these professionals to the facts of innocence that are right in front of them. Part of it is psychological inertia: once the police decide someone is guilty—and often they decide this very early on—they go about building a case against that person. They tend to minimize or disregard altogether any evidence that is inconsistent with the person's presumed guilt and to magnify any evidence that supports it. Much of this process is subtle and unconscious. We all superimpose order and logic upon a chaotic world of indeterminate and often conflicting facts. Police and prosecutors apply their own logic as they make judgment calls about which witnesses to believe and which facts are important.

By the time a capital case comes to trial, the police and prosecutors believe the defendant is guilty. Once a jury has found the defendant guilty, the assumption of guilt becomes etched in granite. From that point on, the police and prosecutors have a huge stake—professional, emotional, and political—in defending that verdict against all assaults by appellate and postconviction defense counsel.

Subsequent reviewing courts also have a stake in refusing to second-guess the jury's finding of guilt. Procedural errors, yes. Legal errors, yes. Constitutional errors, yes. But rarely will appellate courts seriously question the factual question of guilt that has been determined by a jury.

By the time a case is in appeals, everyone is fighting over the *law,* and often the question of innocence gets lost in the noise and smoke of the legal battle. Innocence becomes just another legalistic argument, or, worse, it becomes considerably less than that. The U.S. Supreme Court held in 1993 that innocence is not in and of itself a reason for voiding a death sentence: unless it is tied to a constitutional violation, the fact of a defendant's innocence is constitutionally irrelevant.

Sometimes the legal system is forced to catch its mistakes before an innocent person is executed. That happened in the case of Joseph Green Brown. Sometimes, however, the legal system ignores its actors' errors, and innocent people die.

When Joseph Green Brown was released from prison in 1987, it was important for him to get out of Florida, so I invited him to stay with me in my small apartment in Washington, D.C., where I was practicing law at the time. He stayed with me for a few weeks, until he got back on his feet, and I will never forget his quiet intensity—and his lack of malice toward those who had framed him for capital murder. He was a delightful houseguest. We had many long talks, but we seldom talked about his time on death row. Once, though, he looked me in the eye and said the words that begin this chapter.

In addition to practicing law, I was teaching a seminar on capital punishment at the University of Maryland Law School during the time Brown stayed with me, and I asked him to be a guest speaker for one of the classes. He began the class by placing strips of masking tape on the floor of the classroom to illustrate the dimensions of his death row cell. Then he talked to the students about life on the row, and he answered their questions. His guest appearance was one of the most extraordinary experiences I've ever had in a law school classroom. For me—and for many of my students—Joseph Green Brown gave capital punishment a human face.

In legal lore, however, Brown's case isn't famous because Brown was innocent. It is famous for a fib told in the 1970s by the Florida Supreme Court. Actually, there were two fibs: one had to do with an issue in the Hitchcock case (discussed in chapter 9) and one concerned an issue in the Brown case. Both issues reached the Eleventh Circuit in an early incarnation of Alvin Ford's case (discussed in chapter 4).

The full Eleventh Circuit noted that it took Ford's case in 1982 to resolve "several important issues that repeatedly arise in capital cases." One such issue was the so-called *Brown* claim: a constitutional challenge to the Florida Supreme Court's secret, ex parte solicitation of psychological screening reports on Florida death row prisoners. The reports, prepared by the Florida prison system as part of its routine procedures for handling new prisoners, wound up in the Florida Supreme Court files of at least twenty-five capital inmates between 1976 and 1978. The information had not been disclosed to the prisoners' defense attorneys, who were appealing the inmates' convictions and sentences to the Florida Supreme Court.

Soon after the court's secret practice came to light—fortuitously during an oral argument before the Florida Supreme Court in Paul Magill's case (discussed in chapter 7)—all 123 inmates then on Florida's death row, at various stages of their appeals and postconviction proceedings, filed a class action petition for habeas corpus in the Florida Supreme Court. Prisoners who were able to prove that information in their cases had in fact been secretly solicited relied upon a case that recognized a defendant's right to see and challenge information used against him or her in capital sentencing proceedings. Inmates who could not demonstrate that secret information had actually been obtained by the Florida Supreme Court in their cases argued that the use of the screening reports in some cases tainted the overall fairness of capital sentencing and required the invalidation of all death sentences in Florida. Since Joseph Green Brown was first on the alphabetical list of class members, the case became styled *Brown v. Wainwright,* and the claim became known as the *Brown* issue.

The Supreme Court of Florida denied the habeas petition on its merits, as a matter of law. The court stated that "the doctrines of constitutional law here argued are singularly unpersuasive." Moreover, the court held that "even if petitioners' most serious charges were accepted as true," that would not change the court's decision: "As a matter of law our view of the non-record information petitioners have identified is totally irrelevant either to our appellate function in capital cases as it bears on the operation of the statute, or as to the validity of any individual death sentence." Drawing a distinction between sentence "review" and sentence "imposition," the court concluded that "since we do not 'impose' sentences in capital cases, *Gardner* presents no impediment to the advertent or inadvertent receipt of some non-record information. . . . non-record information we have seen, even though never presented to or considered by the [trial] judge, the jury, or counsel, plays no role in capital sentence 'review.'" Accordingly, "as we view the case . . . appellate review can never be compromised . . . by the receipt of any quantity of non-record information." All relief was denied to each petitioner.

Because Governor Robert Graham signed his death warrant, Alvin Ford became the first member of the *Brown* class to reach the Eleventh Circuit. By a narrow vote of six to five, with Judge Vance casting the decisive vote, the en banc Eleventh Circuit found Florida's procedure constitutionally tolerable. The court based that determination on the convoluted reasoning that the Florida Supreme Court deliberately and regularly obtained ex parte information of an important nature, but then failed to "use" it.

The majority view was expressed in two opinions. The plurality opinion assumed that resort by an appellate court to secret materials in reviewing capital sentences would violate the U.S. Constitution. However, the plurality read the *Brown* opinion as a statement that the Florida Supreme Court did not "use" the materials it had solicited. Judge Tjoflat concurred specially. He determined that the Florida court had read the materials but had not relied on them. The concurring opinion then noted that the outcome might have been different had Ford separately alleged that "as a matter of federal constitutional law, members of the Florida Supreme Court should be forced to step down in this situation on the ground of appearance of impropriety."

I find Judge Vance's decisive vote for the plurality opinion curious, not only because that opinion cannot withstand analysis, but because it defies the common sense that I generally found to typify Judge Vance's jurisprudence. This view is grounded in my belief that the logic of the plurality would be laughable were it not so vitally important to the lives of some sixty human beings. At least twenty members of the *Brown* class have since been executed, and at least twenty-one others remain under sentence of death without an intervening resentencing proceeding.

The *Ford* plurality's major premise was that the Florida Supreme Court did not "use" the ex parte materials that it had solicited. But, as Justice Marshall wondered in his dissent from the denial of plenary review of the *Brown* issue, "if the [Florida Supreme] Court does not use the disputed nonrecord information in performing its appellate function, why has it systematically sought the information?" Further, the

Florida Supreme Court in *Brown* did not quite say otherwise. Eleventh Circuit Chief Judge Godbold noted (charitably) "the intractable ambiguity" of the Florida court's *Brown* opinion. He observed that a majority of Eleventh Circuit judges inferred that the Florida Supreme Court had not used the secret material, another circuit judge said the Florida court "actually did consider" the material, and still another said the *Brown* opinion raised a "presumption" that the material had been used.

The secret practice itself betrays the hollowness of the plurality's semantic distinction between "use" on the one hand and "solicit," "receive," "see," "read," "review," and "consider" on the other. Word games aside, the six to five majority's conclusion in *Ford* that the Florida Supreme Court did not "use" the materials was belied by actual experience.

The oral argument before the Florida Supreme Court in the capital case that inadvertently revealed the practice to the outside world made the point. Paul Magill had been sentenced to death. At oral argument on direct appeal before the Florida Supreme Court, Magill's attorney urged that a life sentence should have been imposed. She relied, in part, upon psychiatric information presented to the trial court. She was then questioned by a Florida Supreme Court justice about an inconsistent extrarecord psychological evaluation that the Florida Supreme Court had secretly obtained from the prison. That, it appears to me, is "use" of the materials.

But maybe not. The U.S. Supreme Court did, after all, deny full review of the *Brown* issue. We outsiders do not know why. Maybe the Court denied plenary review in part because the justices relied upon the Eleventh Circuit's local understanding of the Florida practice. We do know that the death sentences of all the members of the *Brown* class were tainted with constitutional error, and that the Florida Supreme Court was less than forthright in dealing with that error. I believe that the federal courts shied away from recognizing the error out of reluctance to call the state judges liars. Those 123 death row prisoners lost because the federal courts were simply too polite to acknowledge that the state judges had been less than forthright.

The Innocent Man: Bennie Demps

Bennie Demps, 49, was executed last June for the 1976 murder of a fellow inmate at Florida State Prison. But ask the investigator on the case just how the murder happened and who was involved, and his answer is that he doesn't know for sure.

—Steve Mills, Maurice Passley, and Ken Armstrong, "Shadows of Doubt Haunt Executions," *Chicago Tribune,* December 17, 2000

I let Bennie Demps down. When I was his lawyer, in the 1980s, Demps always adamantly maintained his innocence. I didn't really listen; I was too enamored of the constitutional issues in his case.

The U.S. Supreme Court has made some hideous rulings in capital cases. Some of the worst involve innocence. In 1993, the Court held that innocence, in and of itself, is an insufficient constitutional reason to void a death sentence or delay an execution. A few years earlier, the lawyer for a condemned prisoner with a strong innocence claim filed the prisoner's brief one day late; the Supreme Court decided that the late filing was enough to preclude the federal courts from reviewing the constitutional claims; the Court cleared the way for the execution, and the man was executed.

Demps, an African American, served in the military during the Vietnam era. After suffering a racially motivated beating, Demps began getting into trouble. He received a dishonorable discharge, which was later upgraded to a general discharge.

Demps was first sentenced to death in 1971 for a double murder. R. N. Brinkworth and Celia Puhlick were inspecting land when they came upon Demps in a citrus grove, where Demps was hiding with a safe he had stolen. Surprised by the couple, Demps shot and killed them.

After Demps had been on death row less than a year, the U.S. Supreme Court, in *Furman v. Georgia,* invalidated all extant death sentences in the United States. The *Furman* decision resulted in the commutation of all ninety-eight death sentences in Florida, including Demps's. In December 1972, the Florida legislature enacted a revised capital statute, and the U.S. Supreme Court upheld the new statute's constitutionality in July 1976. Two months later, on September 6, 1976, a prison inmate named Alfred Sturgis was stabbed to death in a fight with several other prisoners. Demps was convicted of the crime and once again sentenced to death.

While I was Demps's lawyer, we concentrated on two main issues. The first was that the prosecutor had improperly withheld exculpatory evidence from Demps's trial lawyer; the second was *Hitchcock.*

Demps was convicted and sentenced to death for his alleged role in the murder of Alfred Sturgis. The victim and the three accused perpetrators—Harry Mungin, James Jackson, and Demps—were all inmates at the Florida State Prison at the time of the crime; the three accused were codefendants at trial. According to the prosecution's theory of the crime, an inmate witness, Larry Hathaway, saw the three codefendants assaulting the victim in his cell. Prior to the killing, Hathaway said, Mungin had told him that "he [Mungin] was fixing to get rid of a snitch." Hathaway testified that Demps held the victim while Jackson lunged at and beat the victim. Correctional Officer A. V. Rhoden testified that the deceased told him in a dying declaration, "You have to get Mungin and Demps, they held me and Jackson stabbed me." All three were convicted. Jackson and Mungin were sentenced to life. Demps was sentenced to death.

Two types of testimony convicted Demps: (1) inmate Hathaway's "eyewitness" testimony, and (2) Officer Rhoden's testimony that the victim had identified Demps in a dying declaration. Had the state revealed what it actually knew about and how it obtained Hathaway's testimony, there is a reasonable probability that the result in this case would have been different.

Hathaway testified at trial that he had been promised nothing but protection in return for his testimony. The following is excerpted from

Hathaway's testimony about the actual offense. Hathaway was examined by the state's prosecutor, Tom Elwell.

ELWELL: Where was the first opportunity you had to see the defendant, Harry Mungin?

HATHAWAY: In front of his cell.

ELWELL: All right. What cell was that?

HATHAWAY: He lived in the first cell on the north side third floor.

ELWELL: Tell the jury what you observed of him?

HATHAWAY: I come out of my cell to go downstairs to the second floor and as I approached Inmate Mungin's cell he stepped out and I stopped and he asked me if there was anybody else on the floor besides me.

ELWELL: At that time was there anybody else on the floor?

HATHAWAY: No, sir, except for two inmates who lived across from me. They were inside their cell, and other than that I didn't know of anybody else up there.

ELWELL: How long had the wing call gone out for the evening meal before the time you're now testifying to?

HATHAWAY: Probably three or four minutes.

ELWELL: And was the defendant, Harry Mungin, at that time by himself or with others?

HATHAWAY: He was by himself.

ELWELL: What did he say to you?

HATHAWAY: He asked me if there was anybody else on the floor besides me that I knew of and I told him no. He told me to go downstairs and stay downstairs.

ELWELL: Did he tell you why?

HATHAWAY: Yes, he said he was fixing to get rid of a snitch.

ELWELL: All right. What did you do?

HATHAWAY: I went downstairs.

Hathaway further testified that he then returned to the area, and he saw Mungin in Sturgis's cell; he also saw Jackson striking the victim while Demps held the victim.

The duty of a prosecutor is not to win as many cases and to obtain as many convictions as possible. The duty of a prosecutor is to do justice. For this reason, the U.S. Constitution requires prosecutors to turn over to the defense any material evidence that tends to exculpate the defendant.

Prosecutors not infrequently ignore the duty to disclose exculpatory evidence to the defense. The conduct of the FBI in the Timothy McVeigh case is perhaps the most famous. The problem is pervasive, however. As I mentioned in chapter 10, James Liebman and his colleagues found that vital hidden evidence of innocence has led to the invalidation of one in five capital cases since 1973.

Another study, reported in January 1999 in the *Chicago Tribune,* found that 381 murder convictions—including 67 capital convictions—had been thrown out because of prosecutorial misconduct in concealing evidence suggesting innocence or presenting evidence the prosecutors knew to be false. The *Tribune* observed that prosecutors "have prosecuted black men, hiding evidence the real killers were white. They have prosecuted a wife, hiding evidence her husband committed suicide. They have prosecuted parents, hiding evidence their daughter was killed by wild dogs." I am not talking about legal technicalities here. This is evidence of *innocence.*

Such prosecutorial sandbagging is a large part of the reason so many innocent people have been sentenced to death under the modern capital punishment statutes. As of this writing, one hundred condemned people have been exonerated and released since 1973 under current death penalty statutes. During that same time, 777 people have been executed. Thus, nationally, one innocent person has been released as innocent for every eight executed—*one in eight.*

In Florida the numbers are even worse. Florida has freed eighteen for the fifty-one it has put to death. Eighteen for fifty-one; that's *one in three.*

On Christmas Day 1998, retiring Florida Supreme Court Chief Justice Gerald Kogan was quoted in the *Washington Post* as saying he had "grave doubts" about the guilt of some of the people executed in Florida in recent years. He stated, "There are several cases where I had grave doubts as to the guilt of a particular person." Chief Justice Kogan did not name names. Bennie Demps could not have been one of the cases the chief justice had in mind, given that he had not yet been executed as of the time Kogan made his statement. I do know that *I* have grave doubts about Demps's guilt. I also know that the prosecutors withheld exculpatory evidence from Demps's lawyers.

Hathaway's testimony was highly impeachable for a number of reasons known to Elwell, but the prosecutor concealed that information from defense counsel. For example, soon after Sturgis's murder, David Beardsley, a prison inspector, wrote an "addendum report" regarding his investigation of the crime. This report was provided to Elwell, but not to defense counsel. In the report, Beardsley gave the following account of what Hathaway had told Beardsley concerning the initial Mungin contact:

> That he was standing in front of his cell door on the third tier of W wing around 4:30 in the afternoon on the 6th of September, 1976, when he was approached by inmate Harry Mungin. Mungin asked him if there was anyone on the third floor besides him. Hathaway states that he replied to Mungin that he didn't know and was told by Mungin to check and if there was no one that was visible, he was to walk down the stairs. He says he told Mungin, "Sure," and then he looked around and at that time Mungin looked at him and said, "We're fixing to kill a snitch," Hathaway will say that he then went down the stairs.

This reveals that Hathaway was an accomplice to the murder—a lookout. He was asked to check to see if anyone might be around and give an "all clear" signal so that the murder could take place, and he did so. Yet he testified at trial simply that he told Mungin what Mungin purportedly already knew—no one was around. The suppressed report reveals that Hathaway looked around and then gave the signal by walking down the stairs. Defense counsel was not provided this information, which implicated Hathaway and differed from his trial testimony. There were further inconsistencies between Hathaway's pretrial statements and his testimony. For example, according to the report, Hathaway told Beardsley that Mungin was not just in the doorway of Sturgis's cell, but rather that Mungin was "holding on to Sturgis." Hathaway's testimony was that Mungin was in the doorway.

When Hathaway testified at trial, he expected that Elwell and Beardsley would try to help him to obtain parole afterward, because Elwell and Beardsley had told him they would. And they did indeed help him. In a letter to Elwell dated May 17, 1978, one month after trial, Hathaway reminded Elwell of his promise: "You said if I told the truth and the trial turned out alright you'd try and help me." Elwell's promise to help Hathaway had never been disclosed to the defense. The only help Hathaway was supposedly to be given was protection. A few months later, Beardsley wrote a letter to Louie Wainwright, secretary of the Florida Department of Corrections, on Hathaway's behalf. Beardsley asked Wainwright to present Hathaway's "very special case" to the Parole Commission and mentioned that Elwell would also "give any help he can to parole consideration for inmate Hathaway." Wainwright, in turn, wrote to the Parole Commission:

September 12, 1978

Mr. Maurice G. Crockett, Chairman
Florida Parole and Probation Commission
1309 Winewood Boulevard
Tallahassee, Florida 32301
Re: Larry Hathaway, #040479

Dear Chairman Crockett:
    Mr. Bill Beardsley, Prison Inspector, has requested in his letter of August 31, 1978, "special parole consideration for inmate Hathaway." Mr. Beardsley goes into facts that henceforth had not been presented in writing. He has also acquired a progress report from the Northern Nevada Correctional Center where Inmate Hathaway is presently housed. This report also goes into additional depths detailing the special nature of his confinement.
    It would be most appreciated by Mr. Beardsley and the Department if the Commission would review Inmate Hathaway's file with consideration being given for possible parole action.

Sincerely,
Louie L. Wainwright, Secretary

Beardsley continued to assist Hathaway. As postconviction proceedings in Demps's case (and the need for more Hathaway testimony) neared, Hathaway was promised a "small camp" assignment in west Florida. Prior defense counsel John Carroll wished to depose Hathaway, but the state officials were squeamish:

DATE: December 3, 1982
FROM: Joyce C. Bruce
TO: Mr. Charles H. Lawson
    Tallahassee
RE: HATHAWAY

At your request I met with Dave Bachman, Beardsley, and Russell Smith on December 2nd.

The outcome of the discussion was that Bill Beardsley would discuss Hathaway's situation with Phil Welch, have Phil review entire file, make a classification determination, at which time a better idea would be had of what type facility Hathaway could be placed into in Florida. Mr. Beardsley would then write to Hathaway regarding the type facility he would be placed into and obtain a response from him regarding whether or not it is still his desire to return to Florida. . . .

If subject is returned to Florida, Beardsley said it would be best to have the deposition delayed until his return since he felt the need to talk to him personally, and possibly have him meet and talk with Tom Elwell before the deposition is taken by Mr. Carroll to be sure his story is the same.

As the time for Hathaway's testimony in postconviction proceedings grew still nearer, new "help" came from Beardsley and Elwell:

DATE: March 21, 1983
FROM: Bill Beardsley, Inspector
TO: Department of Corrections Admission and Release Authority
ATTN: Liz White
RE: Larry Hathaway #040479

Attached are two letters I have received pertaining to the parole plan of Larry Hathaway. Request they be placed in his file so they might come to the attention of the Parole Examiner.

In 1978, I placed a letter in Hathaway's file recommending parole considerations based on his assistance to our Department and the State Attorney. Request those facts again be presented to the Parole Examiner.

As I've noted, defense counsel was not aware of any of the promises made to Hathaway, and, consequently, the jury was not made aware of

Hathaway's expectations. Demps did not unearth this information until long after his trial. His defense attorney did not unreasonably fail to discover this information—it had been hidden by the government.

In fact, Hathaway was a crazed murderer himself, and the state knew him to be a liar. Beardsley himself at one point said that he could never "be sure his [Hathaway's] story is the same."

Hathaway had been a witness/suspect regarding another inmate stabbing, that of Gary Herndon. Beardsley had investigated the Herndon crime, and his description of Hathaway's informing—a year before Demps's case—is telling:

> As you will remember our only conversation concerning the stabbing of inmate Herndon resulted in your fabrication of the true events which have now been determined through lengthy investigation.

Defense attorney was not informed of Hathaway's history of fabrication.

Hathaway lied in his trial testimony about his prior record. He testified:

Q. Have you ever been convicted of a crime?

A. Yes, sir, I have.

Q. How many times?

A. Three times.

Three times a year would have been closer to the truth. Hathaway's adult record, known to the state at the time of trial, reads as follows:

Date	Place	Charge	Disposition
2/14/63	PD Tulsa, Okla.	Forgery	Probation
7/17/63	PD Tulsa, Okla.	Petit Larceny Shoplifting	$16 fine pluc cc
7/20/63	PD Tulsa, Okla.	Violation of probation	2 months county jail (unverified)
11/16/63	SO Tulsa, Okla.	Grand larceny	1 year county jail
3/18/64	PD Tulsa, Okla.	Attempted armed robbery by fear	Turned over to Tulsa County
5/21/64	SPen McAlester, Okla.	Attempted robbery by fear	1 to 3 years

6/26/64	SRef Granite, Okla.	Attempted robbery by fear	1 to 3 years
8/20/65	PD Tulsa, Okla.	Voluntary registration as ex-con	Liberty
10/19/65	PD Phoenix, Ariz.	Defrauding innkeeper	$50 fine
6/12/66	PD Las Vegas, Nev.	Vag. Fug. Arizona	10 days
6/25/66	PD Elroy, Ariz.	Party to exceeding the posted speed limit and no operator's license	Suspended sentence Placed on probation
7/25/66	PD Phoenix, Ariz.	Burglary first degree	Rel to SO Phoenix
7/25/66	SO Phoenix, Ariz.	Burglary	2 to 4 years
10/21/66	PD Phoenix, Ariz.	Grand theft	Rel to SO Phoenix
10/21/66	SO Phoenix, Ariz.	Burglary Ct. I	2 to 4 years state prison
	Florence, Ariz.	Grand theft Ct. II	
5/5/69	PD Phoenix, Ariz.	Convict registration	Liberty
5/20/69	PD Tulsa, Okla.	Voluntary registration as ex-con	Liberty
11/6/69	PD Tulsa, Okla.	Reckless driving	unknown
11/15/69	PD Tulsa, Okla.	Forgery	unknown
1/23/71	PD Phoenix, Ariz.	Forgery, credit cards	JP court order of Rel $3,300
1/27/71	PD Phoenix, Ariz.	Forgery, credit cards	1 year county jail (unverified)
3/5/71	PD Phoenix, Ariz.	Burglary	Rel to SO Phoenix
3/11/71	SO Phoenix, Ariz.	Burglary, ran stop sign	unknown
4/22/71	PO Phoenix, Ariz.	Forgery C/C 3 counts	Rel to SO Phoenix
4/22/71	SO Phoenix, Ariz.	Forg C/C; Forg C/C Pled to Forg. C/C 2 Ct. Forg C/C 3 Ct.	4 to 5 years Arizona state prison
11/12/71	SPr Florence, Ariz.	Forg. C/C	4 to 5 years
10/7/72	Deuel Voctl. Inst. Rec. Guidance Ctr. Tracy, Calif.	Forg. C/C	Received for 5 to 6 years, housing only under Sec. 11190PCC
8/9/73	Palm Beach	First degree murder	Second degree—99 yrs.

Further, prison records not released to Demps's counsel until long after trial revealed Hathaway's chronic mental illness, instability, and habit of dissembling. This person who "needed protection" described himself much differently in 1974. As a prison psychiatric report revealed, this man was seriously mentally ill:

> This is a 28 year old, white, blond, male individual, who was seen today at DeSoto Correctional Institution where he is serving a 99 year sentence for murder. He states that he killed, not only a 23 year old girl whose body was found in a ditch, but also a 25 year old man who was with her at the time, and whose body has never been found. He said that at the time, he was pushing drugs and he was very involved in a deal that was going on with these 2 particular individuals, who turned out to be undercovers. Inasmuch as they did not produce the money, he "eliminated" them. In reviewing his record, it is noted that he denied the offense at the time that he was arrested and gave a completely different history. During the interview today, he said that he has committed murder before and that he had been arrested twice for the same thing, but there was not enough evidence, and consequently he was released, and that he had been under suspicion 7 times total. He says that on 2 occasions, he got paid $2500.00 for killing, which he did and the other times, he just did it for "no reason"—"It just occurred." He states that in 1966, he committed murder and did not know that he had done it, that he was just in the kitchen of a house and he stabbed this man to death and just stood there and his brother shook him up, slapped him, and he didn't even move. The same thing happened in 1971. He indicated that he did not care and that whoever is in his path, he would eliminate without second thoughts, without guilt or remorse. However, he contradicts himself by then saying that he is now concerned about what he is going to do because he has been unable to sleep and remains awake all the time thinking and thinking, his mind constantly working, has become completely paranoid, not wanting to be around people, being scared of everybody, and this is exactly the way that he has felt in the past when he had committed murder.
>
> Mr. Hathaway indicates that he has had problems with the law on many previous occasions, starting when he was 13 years of age when he had an argument in a nightclub and shot an individual 4 times, but was not incarcerated because he was a juvenile. In reviewing his FBI record, it is noted that his long career of crime started in 1963 when he was 17 years of age. . . .

He talks about those "trances" but his reliability is questionable. Mental status examination reveals a 28 year old, white male individual, who appears in no acute distress. He is extremely manipulative. He wants to be transferred to Lake Butler so that he could be "helped." He contradicts himself by saying that he did not care about killing and doesn't care about doing the same if somebody bothers him, and later in the next breath by stating that he is now begging for professional help so that he would not kill again. He also contradicts himself by stating that the so-called trances happened with no warning but later stating that he right now feels exactly the same way (meaning restless, unable to sleep, etc., etc.) as in the past when he had committed murder for no reason or provocation. His speech was relevant and coherent. There is no disorganization of thought processes. No delusional material can be elicited. He denies hallucinations. He is considered to be unreliable.

Diagnostic Impression: Personality Disorder, Anti-social

Antisocial personality has as its paramount characteristic persistent lying—a characteristic singularly relevant to impeachment.

When Hathaway first entered Florida State Prison, he was diagnosed as schizophrenic. Since then, he had been repeatedly diagnosed as mentally ill. A prison mental health report about him dated November 20, 1974, describes him as "a very unstable individual" who "needs observation over a long period of time." Another, dated October 10, 1975, calls him "a young man who apparently has no real insight [and] is in serious need . . . of psychiatric and psychological assistance. . . . A dangerous individual, one who certainly must remain incarcerated." In a prison mental health report written a week after Hathaway purportedly saw Sturgis's killing, the examiner noted information "as to his tales he gave to the psychologist about killing people and things of that sort." And a couple of months before Hathaway's trial testimony, Beardsley stated in a report, "This man still has some medical problems and is currently on medication."

When it came time for Hathaway to testify in Demps's postconviction proceedings in federal court in 1983, he was once again being diagnosed as mentally unstable. As noted above, Beardsley and Elwell arranged to speak with Hathaway before his deposition to ensure his "story was the same." Before he returned to testify, Hathaway "was involved with a narcotics smuggling operation," according to an Eleventh Circuit brief.

On February 8, 1983, Hathaway was deposed by Demps's defense counsel. On December 14, 1983, he testified in state postconviction proceedings. On March 30, 1983, Hathaway was seen to be acting in a bizarre manner. In an Eleventh Circuit brief, Prison Lieutenant B. Weeks described his encounter with Hathaway this way:

On March 30, 1983, at approximately 11:00 AM, Capt. Harrell called me, B. Weeks, to his office. Sgt. Hearn told me and Capt. Harrell that Inmate HATHAWAY, Larry, W/M, DC 040479, was acting very strange. Capt. Harrell told me to go talk with inmate Hathaway. I had inmate Hathaway brought to the all purpose room. I sat on one side of the desk and inmate Hathaway sat on the other side. I asked inmate Hathaway what was wrong with him. He started talking very low where I couldn't hear him. I told him to speak up so I could hear him. He then started talking in Spanish or something. I told him I didn't know what he was talking about. I had my arms lying on the desk and he reached across the desk and grabbed me by both wrists and stated, "you know what I mean" and made a very sneering face. I twist my hands around and grabbed him by both wrists and held him. I told him to cool it, that I was trying to help him.

Weeks summoned Dr. Robert Kirkland, a psychiatrist, who observed Hathaway that same day. Kirkland gave this account:

On Wednesday, March 30, 1983, I was at Okaloosa Correctional Institution interviewing an inmate when Lt. B. Weeks requested that I assist him observing an inmate's behavior. The Lieutenant and the inmate were in a room next to the Confinement area. When I entered the room, Lt. Weeks introduced the inmate name as Larry Hathaway, number unknown. Inmate HATHAWAY looked at me and told Lt. Weeks he knew who I was and began talking in a language unknown to me. Inmate HATHAWAY appeared disoriented as to time and date and made some remarks about inflicting physical damage to his body. In my opinion, inmate HATHAWAY needed to be examined by a doctor as soon as possible, and I asked Lt. Weeks to step out.

I caught inmate HATHAWAY by his arms with both of my

hands and pushed him away from me. I let go of him and continued with the conversation. He continued to sit and talk with me. I realized he was high on some type of drug or he had lost his mind. Mr. Carl W. Kirkland [no relation to Dr. Robert Kirkland] was at the prison and I had him talk with inmate Hathaway. Mr. Kirkland came to the same conclusion as I did. Mr. Kirkland advised us to transfer inmate Hathaway to R.M.C. [the prison medical center] as soon as possible. Inmate Hathaway was transferred to R.M.C. that day.

Hathaway is today diagnosed as psychotic, schizophrenic, paranoid (chronic in remission), and antisocial personality. He requires psychotropic medication. This is the witness who, more than any other, sent Demps to death row.

Then there was *Hitchcock*. At every stage of Demps's trial, the members of the advisory sentencing jury were told unequivocally that in recommending a sentence for Demps they could consider only the mitigating factors set out in Florida's capital statute. That message was hammered home by the judge and the prosecutor. As a consequence, although substantial nonstatutory mitigating evidence was introduced at Demps's trial, the jury considered that evidence only as relevant to the statutory factors.

The limitation condemned in *Hitchcock* clearly occurred in this case. A unanimous Florida Supreme Court correctly found that the sentencing-phase jury instructions in this case were indistinguishable from the jury instructions invalidated in *Hitchcock*. During voir dire, the prosecutor told the jury that the court would "set out guidelines for you." The prosecutor exacted a promise from the prospective jurors that they would "operate under the guidelines that the Court has talked about." The prosecutor told the jurors that they "would have to follow the guidelines of the Court." And: "Now, the court will give you guidelines—which the court has already told you—that after you first determine guilt or innocence of these defendants that the second step will be your opportunity to hear those facts which show it's an aggravated case or these facts to show they are not aggravating, in helping you make a recommendation. With that guideline in mind, would you be able to follow the Court's instructions?"

The judge impressed upon the jurors the same requirement to follow the guidelines discussed previously, asking at least one prospective juror directly, "If you were selected as a juror in this case would you follow the Court's instructions on all matters of law and apply that law to the facts as you find them from the evidence?" All of the jurors promised the judge and the prosecutor that they would follow and apply only the law that the judge told them to follow, "without any regard to any beliefs you might have as to whether it's a good law or a bad law." The jurors were not to substitute their own beliefs for the law as instructed. The judge addressed the jurors:

> You heard the Court's explanation of the nature of this case, as far as it could result in two proceedings, the initial proceeding would be that of guilt or innocence and that verdict would have to be unanimous, but should your verdict as to any defendant be guilty as charged in the bifurcation section where you would both hear mitigating and aggravating circumstances for the purpose of rendering an advisory sentence to the Court, keeping in mind that the Court would not be bound by the advisory sentence, the final decision would rest with the Court as to what disposition would be made of the case. Would that prevent any of you from listening to any of the evidence in this case and applying the law as the Court tells you the law is and would you follow that law without any regard to any beliefs you might have as to whether it's a good law or bad law? Would you be bound by that law as the Court would instruct you?

All of the jurors answered in the affirmative.

Defense counsel requested that the jurors be instructed that they could consider nonstatutory mitigating evidence, but the trial court refused to give the instruction. The judge himself recognized that nonstatutory mitigating evidence was relevant to sentencing, but he viewed Florida's standard jury instructions—incorrectly, in light of *Hitchcock*— as sufficient to apprise the jury of that fact. He responded to defense counsel:

> Mr. Carroll, our Supreme Court has said that judges don't vary from the charges that we have approved for the jury unless you can show stood cause why you did. You have read that portion in there and I'm going to stick with the charge that is recommended by the Supreme Court in these cases.

The jury therefore was instructed in the way later invalidated by *Hitchcock*. Just before the jury was presented with evidence at sentencing, the trial judge instructed them, "At the conclusion of the taking of the evidence and after argument of counsel you will be instructed on the factors in aggravation and mitigation you may consider."

Evidence and argument were presented, and then the jury was instructed: "It is your duty to follow the law which will now be given you by the Court. . . . The aggravating circumstances which you may consider are limited to such of the following as may be established by the evidence." The judge then read to the jury the statutory list of aggravating circumstances. He then went on: "The mitigating circumstances you may consider if established by the evidence are as follows," and he read to the jury the items on that statutory list.

Substantial nonstatutory mitigating evidence was presented to Demps's jury, as the Florida Supreme Court later recognized. Defense counsel argued to the jury:

> [Demps's] record also shows that from 1958 [*sic*] to 1971 he was in the United States Marine Corps . . . and that when he returned to the States he committed the crime. It also shows that when he was admitted into the correctional system that he was addicted to narcotics. I ask you to put yourself where he was in 1971—not excuse this crime in any way, shape or form, but think about what may have motivated it. I ask you to consider further that for seven years he existed at Florida State Prison with no problem.

Defense counsel also argued that the prison environment within which the crime had occurred was itself a mitigating circumstance.

The jury also knew, but was precluded by the court's instructions from considering, that the state was not seeking the death penalty for Demps's codefendant Harry Mungin, one of the accomplices who was equally as, if not more culpable than Demps. Mungin, from the record, was the motivating force behind the crime. According to the trial testimony, Mungin had said that "he was fixing to get rid of a snitch"—not "we," but "he." Whatever was done was done at Mungin's request and for his benefit. In addition, Mungin physically participated in the actual homicide. According to the trial testimony, he was either immediately inside the victim's cell while the killing took place or he was holding the victim while Jackson stabbed him. The record is also unequivocal that

Jackson was the person who actually stabbed Sturgis. Both key state's witnesses, inmate Hathaway and Officer Rhoden, pointed to Jackson as being the killer. The record is devoid of any evidence that Demps planned the homicide or dominated anyone. Taken at its absolute worst, the trial testimony shows that Demps held the victim while Jackson killed him. Mungin planned the homicide and Jackson executed it, yet they were sentenced to life and Demps was sentenced to death.

The Florida Supreme Court agreed that *Hitchcock* error occurred in Demps's case. The majority dismissed the error as "harmless," but two judges dissented. Leander Shaw, one of the dissenting judges, wrote:

> There is no debate over whether there was error at the sentencing phase of Demps' trial. As the state and the majority concede, the instruction given to the jury is identical to that given in *Hitchcock*. That instruction expressly restricted what evidence in mitigation the jury may consider in rendering its advisory sentence. As has been clarified in *Hitchcock*, such limitation on the jury's role is impermissible. The majority today concedes this error, but labels it harmless error, reasoning that, even though the jury was misdirected, the true sentencer, the judge, did appear to consider nonstatutory mitigating evidence. Because this holding is contrary to the United States Supreme Court, as well as several of our own holdings, I dissent.
>
> Any time a court delves into the speculative area of harmless error, a complete, extensive review of the record is necessary. The time should be taken to do so for the simple reason that harmless error, by its very nature, requires a complete reweighing of the evidence by the appellate court. To hold that an error is harmless beyond a reasonable doubt presumes that there is nothing in the record which would raise any reasonable doubt as to that conclusion.
>
> Under the standards established by this court, a jury's recommendation must be given great weight. The majority's disposition of the *Hitchcock* error in this case relegates the jury's role to one of minimal weight, rather than great weight. Had the jury been permitted to consider everything in mitigation, it cannot be said beyond a reasonable doubt that the jury would have recommended death. And if the jury had returned with an advisory

sentence of life, that recommendation would be entitled to great weight. Such a jury recommendation could only be overridden upon a clear and convincing showing that virtually no reasonable person could differ from a death recommendation.

At the sentencing proceeding, Demps offered evidence that, upon his return from Viet Nam, he was an alcoholic and drug dependent, caused by the stress of combat in the far east. Had the jury been permitted to consider this, as well as the fact that the state was not asking for the death penalty for one of Demps' accomplices who was equally or more culpable than he, it cannot be said beyond a reasonable doubt that the jury would not have returned a life sentence recommendation. And, had the jury returned such an advisory sentence, it would be entitled to great weight.

Far more evidence of nonstatutory mitigating circumstances existed and could have been presented in Demps's case. Demps's 1987 post-conviction counsel conducted an investigation into Demps's background and obtained affidavits from family members and friends. A good summary of their proffered testimony is contained in a report prepared by Dr. Brad Fisher, a clinical forensic psychologist. Fisher performed tests upon Demps and examined his life history, which is pertinent to a proper mental health diagnosis. Dr. Fisher's cogent recitation of Demps's background has independent mitigating weight; I include it here as a synopsis of what more trial counsel could have presented in mitigation of punishment:

Bennie Eddie Demps was born in Orange County, Florida, on June 17, 1950, at his grandmother's home, with a midwife assisting. His natural father, Porter Williams, was shot and killed in Atlanta, Georgia, during the summer of the child's birth. His mother, Inez Demps Riley, married Isaac Riley when the subject was four years old. Isaac Riley died three months after the marriage after being struck by lightning while harvesting oranges in the groves. The mother, who was born and raised in Shortis, Alabama (a rural area near Montgomery), was fifteen years old at the time of Mr. Demps' birth. The mother's immediate family included 16 siblings, five of whom died in infancy. This large family worked the fields in Alabama, picking cotton.

Mr. Demps' early childhood years are characterized by abject poverty (no indoor plumbing, shotgun-type houses) and the virtual absence of parental supervision. Mr. Demps was apparently left to fend for himself for extended periods of time. While there are no indications that Mr. Demps presented a serious disciplinary problem, what discipline there was took the form of corporal punishment with belts and hard leather. The family, including the children, were migrant, seasonal workers who traveled as necessary, a practice which led to Mr. Demps' absence from and failing in school. Moreover, Mr. Demps experienced several instances of sexual trauma as a child, and experienced fear of the dark and bedwetting. At age 15 or 16, Mr. Demps was the victim of homosexual rape. The severity of this incident was compounded by extremely insensitive handling by police who simply put the boy on a bus and sent him home, and by his mother's refusal to press charges against the perpetrator. There are indications of Bennie's attempts to cope with his overall undesirable situation by becoming active at a very early age in the Pentecostal church, which was opposed and ultimately halted by his family, and later, by his school sports activity.

With adequate background information and the assistance of a competent mental health expert, Demps's trial counsel could have demonstrated a plethora of mental health mitigating circumstances. Dr. Fisher reported on his testing and diagnosis:

The most outstanding dynamic was apparent in those tests which are geared, in part, toward determining the presence of organic deficit. Specifically, these tests include the drawing test, the Bender Visual Motor Gestalt, and the WAIS. The Bender test, for example, showed significant indicators of organic brain impairment, demonstrated through extensive perseveration, figure rotation, and lack of figure closure. These results and indications were further supported by significant subtests scatter on the WAIS. Finally, these results were once again supported in deficits noted on the mental status interview for short and intermediate recall capabilities.

A second dynamic apparent from both projective results and interview data, was that Demps had an underlying high level of stress and anxiety which he attributed to the extreme duress and danger of the prison environment that he had experienced, primarily between 1975 and 1978. It appears from his projective test responses that the memories of this constant threat, and danger, during that time remain with him and are a source for current underlying anxiety.

Dr. Fisher concluded:

Organic brain damage can cause impulsivity and abnormal behavior. The brain is simply not intact, which naturally alters an individual's capacity to act "normally." Consequently, mitigating circumstances arise that pertain to the ability to understand conduct and its consequences, the ability to control conduct and actions, and the ability to react to situations and events, especially stressful situations, in a rational manner. Such a defect, in combination with a stressful maximum security, violent prison setting, could inherently lead to sudden violent behavior.

Other mitigation was available. Investigation into prison violence would have revealed the seething hell within which the crime in this case occurred. An understanding of the Florida prison system in the late 1970s, and how violence was a way of life in that subculture, was essential for an individualized sentencing determination in this case. Defense counsel, through guards and inmates, could have revealed to the jury the true picture of the tragic condition in Florida's prisons that led to, encouraged, and virtually required the violence that occurred in this case.

The prosecutor argued that any *Hitchcock* error was harmless and that the conduct of the government in withholding evidence of enormous impeachment value regarding its star witness, Larry Hathaway—that he was crazy and the state knew it, that he was a liar (especially about prison stabbings) and the state knew it, that according to his statements to the police he served as lookout for this killing, and that the prosecutor and police promised him help on parole in return for his testimony—had been found too late by Demps's counsel.

The prosecutor's claim that Demps's lawyers should have raised the exculpatory evidence sooner was disingenuous. Demps's attorneys could not have raised the claim sooner because the truth was hidden by the state, despite the attorneys' repeated requests for the information. Demps's trial attorney would have testified at an evidentiary hearing that he asked for this very information and was told it did not exist. As Demps's postconviction counsel, I finally obtained the information only after invoking the Florida Public Records Act.

I argued before the Eleventh Circuit that the state ought not be permitted to conceal facts and then to penalize condemned inmates for failing to unearth the hidden facts earlier. Because Demps's failure to raise the claim earlier was attributable to the state and not to Demps, there should be no bar to his representation of the issue. The Eleventh Circuit disagreed, ruling that Demps's lawyers should have raised the exculpatory evidence claim sooner. The court's disposition of the *Hitchcock* issue was more complicated.

I was counting on the *Hitchcock* issue to win a new sentencing trial for Bennie Demps, and it nearly happened. All three Eleventh Circuit judges on the panel wrote separate opinions. All three judges found that the *Hitchcock* error had occurred. Judge Fay wrote an opinion explaining why he thought the error was harmless. Judge Johnson dissented and wrote an opinion asserting that the *Hitchcock* error rendered Demps's death sentence unconstitutional.

My role in the Demps case was over. Bill Salmon and George Schaefer took over as counsel and conducted their own investigation of the case. They found yet more evidence pointing to Demps's innocence. For example, according to an article published in the *Chicago Tribune* on December 17, 2001:

> Lawyers also were never given a copy of a one-page report from chief inspector Cecil Sewell that was written the day after Sturgis died and sent to Secretary of Corrections Louie Wainwright. It said that "before Sturgis died, he named James Jackson, B/M, #029667, as his assailant." Demps and Mungin are not named in the report, which surfaced 20 years after the murder.
>
> In an interview with the Tribune, Wainwright, who retired in 1986 after 24 years as secretary, said the report was meant to apprize him, in detail, of incidents at the state's prisons. "It should have been fairly detailed," Wainwright said. "It should have had all three inmates."

Bennie Demps survived three death warrants. He lived on death row for twenty-nine years. He was executed on June 7, 2000. According to an Associated Press article written by reporter Ron Word, Demps was "served his last meal of barbecue chicken and beef, french fries and dinner salad, Spanish rice, rolls, cherry vanilla and butter pecan ice cream, a mango, banana pudding and Pepsi. He only ate half of the meal." His wife "sat in a car outside the prison before the execution was scheduled to take place."

Demps outlived Florida's electric chair, but his execution proved that even lethal injections can be botched. He was the third Florida prisoner to be killed by lethal injection. The new, more "humane" method of execution did not run smoothly. Rick Bragg reported in the *New York Times*:

> Bennie Demps, a three-time convicted killer sentenced to die by lethal injection on Wednesday, was strapped to a gurney for 33 minutes. While he said his final words, technicians at the Florida State Prison struggled to insert the lethal intravenous drip into a vein.
>
> When the procedure to insert the intravenous drip, which normally takes a few minutes, was completed and the curtain between the execution chamber and witnesses was opened, Mr. Demps pleaded with his lawyer to investigate the way the state's executioners had handled him.
>
> "They butchered me back there," Mr. Demps said from the gurney. "I was in a lot of pain. They cut me in the groin; they cut me in the leg. I was bleeding profusely." . . .
>
> Mr. Demps said the technicians twice sliced painfully into his body, and had stitched up one wound before taking him into the execution chamber.
>
> Prison officials said that the delay was partly because the state was awaiting word from the United States Supreme Court on a last-minute appeal.
>
> But Mr. Demps's lawyer, George F. Schaefer, told The Miami Herald that the court had notified the warden by 5:30 p.m. that it would not act on the case.
>
> Mr. Demps was pronounced dead at 6:53 p.m., his lawyer said in a written statement.

Innocent people are sentenced to death and executed in the United States. It's as inevitable as the law of averages and the fallibility of human institutions. I believe Bennie Demps was innocent of the crime for which he was executed, and he was not the first innocent person executed by the state of Florida in modern times.

Most people on America's death rows are guilty—factually, legally, and morally. Capital punishment opponents must acknowledge this simple reality: most people on death row are guilty of the crimes of which they have been convicted. Likewise, supporters of capital punishment must acknowledge that some percentage of the roughly thirty-six hundred people currently on death row in America are totally factually innocent. To believe that any government is perfectly infallible in this particular area of human endeavor is to deny human nature and human experience.

Capital punishment as a legal system is utterly dependent on the human beings who run it. And human beings make mistakes. Because governments are made up of human beings, governments make mistakes as well.

In February 2000, the governor of Illinois, a conservative Republican and a strong supporter of capital punishment, declared a moratorium on executions because the state of Illinois had freed thirteen wrongfully condemned prisoners in the previous twenty-one years—one more than the state had put to death. Governor Ryan appointed a commission to study ways to make the capital punishment system more reliable, and four months into the moratorium, he told the press he would not "go ahead with executions unless the panel can give him 'a 100 percent guarantee' against any mistaken convictions. 'I don't know if we'll ever go back to the death penalty as we knew it, as long as I'm governor.'"

Governor Ryan recognized what some other prominent conservatives across the nation are beginning to understand: (1) that *supporters* of the death penalty have the strongest stake in ensuring that innocent people are not sentenced to death and executed, and (2) that the large numbers of miscarriages of justice discovered in recent years suggest that the system is not working. Conservative columnist George Will has addressed the "catalog of appalling miscarriages of justice, some of them nearly lethal. Their cumulative weight compels the conclusion that many innocent people are in prison, and some innocent people have been executed." Televangelist Pat Robertson agrees. He also has called for a moratorium on executions, noting that the death penalty is handed down disproportionately to minority group members and poor people who can't afford competent counsel. And recently, Senator Patrick Leahy of Vermont introduced a bill into the U.S. Senate that would give death row prisoners access to DNA technology if they are fighting to prove their innocence.

As I have noted previously, capital punishment as a legal system is extremely expensive. One way some may be tempted to cut the costs is by limiting the appeals and the resources necessary to guarantee (to the extent that humans are capable of guaranteeing) that innocent people are not sentenced to death and executed. However, it is those who favor death as a punishment who ought to fight the hardest to prevent capital justice from being provided on the cheap. The supporters of capital punishment should be pressing for the most reliable system of deciding who dies, even though such reliability comes at a high price. Supporters of capital punishment should be clamoring for the most exacting review of death cases that human minds can conceive and human pocketbooks can fund. I say this because nothing will end capital punishment in the United States sooner—as it ended capital punishment in England in the 1950s—than if the American public were to become convinced that there is a genuine likelihood that totally innocent Americans are being sentenced to death and executed.

Executing the wrong person—executing one person for another person's crimes—comes perilously close to simple murder. Americans will not tolerate murder done in their name by their government.

12

Missing in Action:
David Funchess

In a war without aim, you tend not to aim. You close your eyes, close
your heart. The consequences become hit or miss in the most literal
sense. . . . I have done bad things for love, bad things to stay loved. Kate
is one case. Vietnam is another.

—Tim O'Brien, "The Vietnam inside Me," *New York Times,*
October 2, 1994

Capital punishment in our time has always reminded me of the Vietnam war. "Certain blood for uncertain reasons," as Tim O'Brien wrote
of his war. The only measure of success was the body count. No front
lines, and no rear areas. No epic battles, only a series of brutal firefights
against a largely invisible enemy. No lasting victories. Only casualties.

David Funchess was a war hero. For his service in combat in Vietnam he received the Purple Heart, the Vietnam Service Medal, and the
Republic of Vietnam Campaign Medal (with device). The Vietnam War
also destroyed David Funchess. He was the first Vietnam veteran executed in America.

The War

I was cocounsel for David Funchess. Through his case I first learned
about a then little understood psychiatric disorder called post traumatic
stress disorder, or PTSD. At the time of Funchess's capital murder trial
in the mid-1970s, the American Psychiatric Association had not yet recognized PTSD as a diagnosable disorder. By the time Funchess was
scheduled to die, in the spring of 1986, there was much more public

awareness of PTSD and greater understanding of the disorder among mental health professionals. We tried to tell that to the courts, but they refused to listen, telling us we should have raised the issue of PTSD at the time of Funchess's trial.

David Funchess was on death row for a botched robbery of a liquor store in Jacksonville, Florida, that left two people, Anna Waldrop and Clayton Ragan, dead and a third person in a coma. The judge, in sentencing Funchess to death, explained:

> The robbery and the murders committed by the Defendant were premeditated. The Defendant selected the place for a robbery and like a cobra, he carefully chose the time to strike while casually drinking a cup of coffee across the street from the scene of the crimes. The State has proven beyond a reasonable doubt that the robbery and the murders were premeditated. The objective of the Defendant was to obtain money and he was willing to take the lives of others in order to do so. By stabbing and cutting throats, he killed two people and pitifully mangled a third person who, at this writing, has not recovered consciousness and after seven months, remains in a coma hardly more than a vegetable. The victims were all practically twice the age of the Defendant and two of the victims were women, one of whom was left gasping for breath at the scene of the crimes. These are truly some of the most senseless, heinous and horrible murders that have ever taken place in the City of Jacksonville.

Florida's Governor Bob Graham signed Funchess's death warrant on March 20, 1986. Funchess had already been through one full round of appellate and postconviction litigation, state and federal. To stop the execution this time, Funchess's lawyers, led by Mark Olive, and his investigators, led by Scharlette Holdman, would need to come up with some pretty powerful new evidence to show why Funchess did not deserve to die for his crimes.

Olive, Holdman, and their colleagues *did* uncover powerful new information. Part of it came in the form of statements from people who knew Funchess before his service in Vietnam. They described a quiet, intelligent, and caring person who was in no way headed toward a life of crime. Nolan Wilkerson, an associate minister at a Baptist church in Jacksonville, stated:

I met David Funchess when we were both in seventh grade together at Matthew Gilbert School in 1959. David and I did lots of activities together. We studied and did science projects together. I used to come over to David's house after school.

David was a smart kid. He didn't have to study. He had a natural gift to retain things. School was easy for him. David was always a quiet person, he was never rowdy. In those days, we didn't know anything about drugs. High school students didn't even drink in those days. We were never into anything of that nature.

Fred Hendon, who had been Funchess's high school biology teacher, made this statement:

I have known David Funchess all his life. David grew up in this neighborhood, less than a block from my house. I taught at Matthew Gilbert High School at the time David attended that school.

I never knew David to cause any trouble. He was a normal student. He was always quiet and respectful. He was a regular American kid; there wasn't anything about him that stood out. He didn't leave a mark; you hardly knew he was around. Whenever I saw him, he was mannerable and respectful.

A more personal portrait came from Funchess's close childhood friend Lawrence Holmes:

David's heart was unique. He was so easygoing. He would take anything and not react violently.

Before he went to Viet Nam, David was easygoing and freehearted. He was never in trouble. My father watched over all of us really close. David didn't hang out in the streets back then and none of us knew anything about drugs. David went to school and stayed out of trouble. David was smart and he was a good student. We would talk all day long sometimes, about history and all sorts of things. We would talk and figure out life.

The worst thing I ever knew David to do was actually an ingenious plan that he never carried out. It was our graduation time and all the kids were sending out their invitations to graduation. David's father wouldn't give him any money to pay the postage to send out his invitations. Most of the other parents were encouraging their accomplishments in graduation from high school, but David's father wouldn't even help him buy the postage stamps for his invitations. So David thought up a way to get them mailed anyway. He said he would address them all to himself and put the return address as the person's he wanted it to go to. Since he couldn't put a stamp on the envelope, the post office would return the envelope to the sender which would be where he wanted it to go anyway. He never did that, but I'm just recalling the incident as the worst thing I ever knew David to think of and it really wasn't that bad.

From another of Funchess's childhood friends, Leonard Holmes, Lawrence's twin brother:

David was very smart. He could read anything, could figure anything out. He liked music, and would study listening to Beethoven. I have never seen and I can't even imagine David being mean. There was nothing I could do to make him angry. He never would get upset or mad.

David Funchess apparently turned out to be a fine young man despite the triple disadvantages of being poor, black, and a victim of childhood abuse. His sister Mary made this statement:

When most children got spankings when they misbehaved, we got "killings." We would have been glad to have been hit with just a hand or a belt, but it was usually with fists, sticks, extension cords or a piece of water hose. Often we didn't even know why we were being hit.

Funchess did well in high school, graduating in 1965 with a rank of 47 out of 167 in his class. He had no criminal record, worked hard, and was well on his way to transcending the barriers that his race, class, and family problems had put in his way. All indications were that he was well on his way to entering Florida's middle class.

Funchess embraced the traditional American value of patriotism, and upon his graduation from high school he enlisted in the U.S. Marine Corps. He was subsequently sent to Vietnam, where he was immediately thrust into intense combat. In addition to the horrors of jungle combat, Funchess was exposed to the herbicide Agent Orange, which has since been linked to a wide range of serious health damage in Vietnam veterans. Among the common symptoms are a recurring whole-body skin rash, which Funchess's prison health records clearly reflect. Another symptom among many Vietnam veterans has been neuropsychological damage.

While in Vietnam, Funchess had four particular experiences that were to bear heavily upon his life when he returned from the war. The first occurred immediately after Funchess had arrived in Vietnam. He was on patrol when the Marine who was in front of him had his head blown off by a rocket. According to a medical evaluation of Funchess:

> He relates this memory with the puzzled comment that he can only remember the action occurring in a central focus of intense and vivid color with a dull and blurred gray periphery. He then notes that his memory of this event is totally without sound.
>
> In the incident, Mr. Funchess is walking on patrol several paces behind the point man. The blurred form of a rocket emerges from the right periphery, striking the point man in the head and blowing his head completely off. Then, in astonishment, he describes the body continuing to walk, carrying the rifle for several steps while headless, before collapsing. Mr. Funchess described himself as being numb and fascinated rather than shocked or surprised. He then reports watching, as if from a distance, while ants began swarming over the body.

In the second incident, Funchess was literally thrown through the air by the blast of an incoming mortar explosion. The medical evaluation quoted above notes:

> During the summer of 1967, the Marines at Con Thien took a great deal of incoming artillery fire. Often the fire was timed to coincide with the times when the Marines were leaving their bunkers to eat their meals. Mr. Funchess describes often taking two plates of food so that when they got hit he had a 50% chance of saving his meal.
>
> On the day of this incident, he was out in the open, crossing the compound, about 10 or 12 feet from a large drainage pipe, when the mortars began hitting around him. As in the earlier incident, he describes his behavior in terms consistent with a dissociative

episode. "It's as if it wasn't real," said Mr. Funchess in our interview. "The colors got real vivid and it seemed like I flew through the air backwards ten or twelve feet into the drain pipe. Again, there was no sound and it's as if it were in slow motion."

Third, David experienced forms of "military action" that caused him great distress. He was able to mention these incidents to his sister, Queenie, upon occasion in the early years after his return, but he has since blocked all such memories out of his mind in a manner characteristic of those suffering from PTSD. His sister remembered:

> We could be at the table eating, carrying on a conversation, and David would go blank. He would stare straight ahead and I could wave my hand in front of his face and he wouldn't even blink. I could reach over and touch his arm and say, "David," and he would not respond at all. After a few minutes, he would come back.
>
> They trained David to be a soldier. He never used weapons or violence before. When he came back, he had terrible nightmares. He would hear people screaming. He told me that he had had to kill innocent Vietnamese civilians because he was ordered to. They were people who were no threat at all, but just because they were Vietnamese, David had to kill them. Innocent unarmed civilians. He would remember the people screaming. It bothered him all the time. I don't think he talked to many people about this because it upset him so much. He would describe women, children and wrinkled old men, all harmless people that he was told to kill because they were "the enemy." He told me about one old man who had on pajamas. He could hardly walk, much less run. He was totally harmless. He couldn't have done anything to anyone, but David had to shoot him down in cold blood. It killed David to have to do that. When I would get up to check on my children during the night, I would hear David crying in his room. Sometimes he would talk about it, but most of the time he wouldn't.

The same medical report cited earlier describes the fourth war experience that had bearing on Funchess's later life:

> [It] occurred near the Demilitarized Zone. It was on this operation that Mr. Funchess was wounded. And, again, his description and

experience of the event was dissociated. Mr. Funchess described himself with his unit walking on patrol in a valley with ten or fifteen men ahead of him. He heard the explosion and again the colors became quite vivid. "The colors were intense," he said in the interview, "like just after a hard rain." He knew he was wounded. In the interview, he remarked, "I told myself, 'Oh, my God, the bastard got me.' Time was distorted. I knew it was me, but it just seemed like it was something that happened. Everything was clear. I remember then calling in a Med Evac. It just didn't seem real."

Mr. Funchess had shrapnel lodged in his left ankle and right leg. He was evacuated from Dong Ha to Phu Bai and on to a naval hospital in Japan for three months. The next thing he remembered was being admitted to Ward 3B at the Naval Hospital in Norfolk, Virginia. He was stunned to discover he was on a psychiatric ward with a diagnosis of Psychoneurotic Depressive Reaction. [Prior to the introduction of post traumatic stress disorder in the third edition of the American Psychiatric Association's *Diagnostic and Statistical Manual of Mental Disorders (DSM-III)* in 1980, many cases of this disorder were classified as psychoneurotic depressive reaction.) After thirty days, he was released and returned to duty.

For his service in Vietnam, David Funchess received excellent ratings for proficiency and conduct. As noted earlier, he also received several military decorations.

After his return from Vietnam, Funchess was a deeply disturbed and confused young man. Compounding these problems, the medication he was receiving for his painful leg wounds eventually led him into a debilitating heroin habit. His sister Mary described his bizarre behavior:

David was as crazy as a bed bug when he came home from Viet Nam. You could look at him and see something was wrong. My mother told me that he dug holes and would put newspaper in them and would sleep there at night. This is not normal behavior. My mother said he often woke up screaming. On many occasions he would lock himself in a garage apartment behind my grandfather's house and stay in there by himself for long periods of time with no lights on. My mother would call me and ask me to come see about him and talk to him. When I would go to see about him, this place where he was would be absolutely filthy. One time he drew a strange picture over an entire wall. He had drawn this picture with either a black piece of chalk or some charcoal.

I remember a man in the picture. This man had a bizarre looking face. There was a large wood cook stove in the room. David had even taken time to go behind the stove and complete the picture on the wall. No one really wanted to admit that there was something wrong with David's mind. It was just not something you did in the "ghetto." You did not admit to the fact that your child, friend or brother had a brilliant mind, was a Viet Nam veteran and now his mind was gone. I called the outreach veteran clinic on many occasions to try and get help for David. They told me he had to come in on his own. I mentioned to him that he should go and talk with a counselor. He said he would.

His sister Queenie gave this statement to his postconviction attorneys:

After David came back from Viet Nam, he stayed with me for long periods of time. He was a changed person. Before, he was always easygoing, quiet, and very particular about his appearance. When he came back, it wasn't the same David. I was working and David was not contributing anything to the finances. He couldn't work. He was very jittery and jumpy. It was like when a person has a hangover. He couldn't tolerate loud or sudden noises and it seemed like even the slightest noise seemed loud to him. When I would go to work, he would be there and when I got home he would be there. He never went anywhere. He was acting crazy all the time. I would tell him he was "shell-shocked."

Whenever David would come in the house, he would crouch down like he had a rifle or a big gun in his hands and he would search the house. Sometimes he would think he saw or heard something, but there was no one there. It would scare me when he would act like that because I had small children. One time he kicked open the back door and acted as though he had a machine gun in his hands shooting. My kids would ask why Uncle David was shooting up the yard. He did this a lot. You could call his name and he would not hear or respond. It was like he wasn't really there at all. He wouldn't even know who I was.

Funchess, in behavior consistent with PTSD, tried to suppress his memories of Vietnam and the effect they had on his behavior. Unfortunately, the only tool he had with which to numb himself was heroin. Ferntanzy Brown, a fellow heroin addict, described Funchess's drug habit and his deterioration:

David was not involved with drugs before he went to Viet Nam. After the war, he couldn't get through a day without drugs. I know that David had a heavy drug habit because we used to shoot drugs together and do drugs. We would shoot up first at about 8 or 9 in the morning, and looking for ways to get more drugs.

I know that David was on drugs the whole time between 1969 and 1974. Before his arrest, his appearance was going down. His hair was nappy. He didn't take care of himself. His clothes were dirty and smelly. People started backing off from him, he was so far down. I would look at him and tell myself I would never let myself get like that.

Funchess's sister Mary described his condition in 1973:

He was living . . . in my grandfather's old house. I went over there to clean it up for him. It was absolutely filthy inside. I had to wear gloves to clean, it was so nasty. I threw away most of the bed-clothes and linens. David never would have lived like that before.

Funchess's rationality eventually deteriorated to such a degree that in 1973 he almost got himself killed. His friend Eugene Frazier described the incident:

An example of how crazy David acted on drugs was the time he got shot. I saw it. A guy we called "Willie Albert" and David were having an argument down on Florida Avenue. It had something to do with David's wife. The guy pulled a gun and told David to go on, but David just kept walking toward him. He was in a daze, like he didn't hear the guy or see the gun. Willie Albert shot at David, emptying the gun, but hitting him only once and David never stopped. He still kept walking up on the gun. His sister Queenie came there finally and got David to the hospital.

By the time of the crime for which Funchess was convicted and condemned to die, his Vietnam experiences and subsequent PTSD had made him a tragedy waiting to happen. One doctor noted:

> The result was a prolonged episode of cognitive confusion and dissociation, during which the crimes occurred. . . .
>
> . . . We can only surmise that the ill-fated robbery provoked a heated confrontation for Mr. Funchess with individuals who had been his former accusers and had fired him. As Dr. Miller notes, the likely use of narcotics undoubtedly enabled the release of long controlled anger and rage. This overcontrol and release of anger under extraordinary stress, especially with drug or alcohol usage, are typical of stress disorder cases. Individuals with a pattern of unconscious flashback and the dissociative coping pattern noted previously in Mr. Funchess also are likely to exhibit this pattern of overcontrol and episodic anger.

David Funchess never intended to commit the murders that occurred on December 16, 1974. When they occurred, he went into a dissociative state similar to what he had experienced in combat.

All U.S. veterans who fought in Vietnam had challenges to overcome when they tried to readjust to civilian life; some met these challenges more ably than others. The damage that the war did to David Funchess, and to too many other soldiers, made his transition to civilian life extremely difficult. In addition to the effects of their time in combat, Vietnam veterans had to contend with the negative reception many Americans gave the returning soldiers. The American public was sharply divided over the country's involvement in Vietnam, and U.S. soldiers suffered greatly from this division. The unpopularity of the war carried over into many Americans' attitudes toward returning Vietnam veterans. Not only did they receive little recognition for having served their country, many were overtly ostracized upon their return to the United States. As of mid-1971, six months after David Funchess was discharged from the service, the unemployment rate for Vietnam veterans ages twenty to twenty-four was 12.4 percent; for African American and disabled veterans it was 25 percent. Many people viewed the veterans as either violent or drug addicts, or both. In 1975, the *New York Times* reported on a study of Vietnam veterans conducted by a congressional committee. Among the study's findings were the following:

> Of those veterans who had been married before they went to Vietnam, 38 percent were separated or divorced within six months of their return.
>
> Approximately half a million Vietnam veterans had attempted suicide after being discharged from the military, either directly or by putting themselves in harm's way.
>
> As of 1975, 13,167 Vietnam veterans had been classified as 100 percent disabled because of psychological and neurological problems.

In 1980, the U.S. Congress finally began to be more responsive to the needs of Vietnam veterans. On January 25, 1980, Senator Alan Cranston of California opened special hearings of the Senate Committee on Veterans' Affairs by noting that the needs of Vietnam veterans had been neglected throughout the 1970s:

> Some Vietnam veterans, particularly those who are educationally disadvantaged, disabled, or members of minority groups, have had a very difficult time trying to straighten out their lives and their thinking, their view of the world, their view of themselves. We really do not yet know precisely the depth and scope of their problems nor the best ways to address their needs.
>
> Often, [efforts to provide better services for veterans] were not well supported and many initiatives took far too many years to get through the Congress. For too long, many in the country were too involved debating the merits of the Vietnam war to focus on those who had served in that war.

The shift in thinking that these Senate committee meetings represented was most dramatically illustrated in the growing recognition that Vietnam veterans faced problems specific to their experience, both in Vietnam and upon their return home. A study commissioned by Congress and presented in January 1972 had focused on only two areas thought to be of concern for the returning veteran: employment and drug use. By the end of the decade, another study greatly expanded the areas of concern to include mental/emotional problems, being frightened by memories of death or dying, employment problems, drug abuse and drinking, discrimination because of military service, health problems, problems with insufficient benefits, money problems, family problems, education problems, and confusion about life. More important, the later study found that the vast majority of both veterans and the American public in general believed that military service directly "caused" or "heavily contributed" to these problems.

When Senator Cranston convened the special hearings of the Senate Committee on Veteran's Affairs, Americans were just beginning to recognize the specificity of Vietnam veterans' problems and were hearing for the first time in an official forum about the studies identifying one particular problem: post traumatic stress disorder. At that point, David Funchess had already been on death row for five years. Numerous researchers and scholars who testified before the Senate committee described PTSD as a clinically identifiable disorder with symptoms directly attributable to the Vietnam experience. Dr. John P. Wilson eloquently explained why experience in Vietnam could not help but produce such problems:

> While it is true that all wars are stressful, indeed catastrophically stressful, few have ever had the long-term guerrilla nature or psychological elements of the Vietnam War. The typical combatant in Vietnam fought in a maximally stressful environment; one in which it was impossible, short of delusion, to have had some sense of control or predictability over events. In its most obvious form it was almost always difficult to: (1) know for certain who the enemy really was . . . ; (2) trust the A.R.V.N. as a reliable Army prepared to fight; (3) know for certain that the women, children and elderly were not Viet Cong; (4) know for certain that there were not land mines or other booby-traps implanted throughout the jungles, rice-paddies or mountains; (5) know with reasonable certainty whether or not an attack or ambush was forthcoming; (6) know for certain that the war was worth one's life and whether or not one would return home alive; and (7) know for certain that orders were tactically proper and effective for the mission objective.

Thus, these and other stressful events served to characterize the typical psychological milieu of the combatant. And while many men found ways to survive and cope with these experiences there was often the gnawing sense that it "was all for nothing" and that the stated purpose of the war was false. . . . Thus, the typical combatant had to face twin sets of stressors: those indigenous to the guerrilla war and those generated by the dissonance produced by ideological warfare. Stated simply, we can say that in any war it is difficult to "lay one's life-on-the-line" but it becomes doubly difficult to do so when faced with the existential task of creating meaning in an environment of seemingly "meaningless death."

Add the unique stresses of reentering American society during the Vietnam era to the stress of the war itself, Wilson noted, and the damaging effects were compounded. His testimony continued:

If you were daemonic and powerful enough to want to make someone "crazy" following a war like Vietnam, how would you do it? . . . What would be the worst set of social, economic, political and psychological conditions you could create for the returnee?

First, you would send a young man fresh out of high school to an unpopular, controversial guerrilla war far away from home. In that war you would expose him to a high level of intensely stressful events, some so horrible that it would be impossible to really talk about them later to anyone else except fellow survivors. However, to insure maximal stress you would create a one year tour of duty during which the combatant flies to and from the war zone singly, without a cohesive, intact and emotionally supportive unit with high morale. You would also create the one-year rotation to instill a "survivor mentality" which would undercut the process of ideological commitment to winning the war and seeing it as a noble cause. Then . . . you return him to his front porch without an opportunity to sort out the meaning of the experiences with the men in his unit. . . . No decompression. No deprogramming. No homecoming welcome or victory parades. Ah, but yes, since you are daemonic enough to make sure that the veteran is stigmatized in society as a "drug-crazed psychopathic killer" with no morals or impulse control over aggressive feelings . . . you would want him to feel isolated, stigmatized, unappreciated and exploited for volunteering to serve his country. . . . Tragically, of course, this scenario is not fiction; it was the homecoming for most Vietnam veterans.

Wilson explained that all of the stressors he had mentioned "impacted on the process of identity formation and the process of adaptation to the various stressful events," resulting in PTSD, "a dynamic survivor response to the catastrophic stressors experienced in the war and to the intense social stressors after it."

Another witness before the committee, Dr. Charles R. Figley, reported that the American Psychiatric Association would soon, in *DSM-III,* "for the first time introduce a category on 'stress disorders,' and would give PTSD an officially recognized clinical definition." According to *DSM-III,* PTSD is characterized by the following symptoms:

> Symptoms of depression and anxiety are common, and in some instances may be sufficiently severe to be diagnosed as an Anxiety or Depressive Disorder. Increased irritability may be associated with sporadic and unpredictable explosions of aggressive behavior, upon even minimal or no provocation. The latter symptom has been reported to be particularly characteristic of war veterans with this disorder.

In a 1982 psychological report, John Smith, one of the country's top experts on PTSD, stated that such a diagnosis was consistent with the psychological data collected by the clinicians who had previously examined David Funchess. Smith also noted that Funchess could be expected to respond extremely well to treatment specifically designed to combat this disorder. According to Michael Hahn, executive director of the Florida Commission on Veterans Affairs, about half of the eighty thousand Floridians who saw combat duty in Vietnam have shown signs of having mental or emotional problems.

The Last Full Measure of Devotion

Governor Bob Graham signed David Funchess's death warrant in February 1986. CCR took the lead in litigating the claim that Funchess deserved a new trial because PTSD was not recognized at the time of

Funchess's original trial, and because Funchess's moral blameworthiness for the murders could not be fairly judged without reference to PTSD. The procedural barriers made such an argument futile, however.

Funchess's best chance was clemency, because the clemency process is not burdened with the legal technicalities that exist in the appellate courts. Governor Graham was free to consider Funchess's PTSD, and he had said some things that indicated he was sympathetic to the problems of Vietnam veterans. Governor Graham denied clemency, however, at 6:30 P.M. on Monday, March 21, 1986, with Funchess's execution scheduled to take place at 7:00 the next morning. Now it was up to the courts.

CCR's offices were only a few blocks from Florida's then-new Vietnam War Memorial. In the days and nights before Funchess's scheduled execution, his fellow Vietnam vets stood around-the-clock vigil at the memorial. Taking shifts, they stood at attention, day and night, rain or shine. Whenever we at CCR had a lull in our battle to keep Funchess alive, we would leave our offices and walk to the war memorial. Although the memorial is in the heart of downtown Tallahassee, what I remember most about being there was the silence of the place. It was as though the quiet dignity of all those vets absorbed the city noises of Tallahassee, creating a sort of a black hole for sound. Nothing loud could enter the perimeter of their vigil for David Funchess.

About an hour after Governor Graham denied clemency, Mark Olive called CCR from the federal district court in Jacksonville to tell us that no decision on our stay application was expected until 8:30 or 9:00 P.M. At 8:00, I left the CCR office for the vigil, where I stayed for about an hour. Some religious leaders had joined the Vietnam vets, including Tom Horkin, director of the Florida Catholic Conference.

At 10:30 that night, Mark called again from Jacksonville. The federal trial court had denied everything, including permission to appeal. He read us the judge's opinion over the phone, and it was a killer: procedural technicality piled upon procedural technicality. There are bad ways of losing a capital case in court, and there are worse ways—this was the worst way.

I delivered the bad news to the folks standing vigil. When I told them that Funchess's hopes of a stay were dead, their response was silence and sadness. There was no surprise.

At midnight, Mark called to chat, and after our conversation, as soon as I hung up the phone, it rang again. It was a clerk for the U.S. Supreme Court calling: "Have you heard? Did the Eleventh Circuit tell you what they did?" I said no. "Then I'd better let them tell you. Call 'em now." I tried, but I got a busy signal. Finally, at 12:55 A.M. I got through to the Eleventh Circuit clerk's office and found out that the court had granted a stay until noon on Tuesday; in effect, a five-hour stay. The stay had been granted because an Eleventh Circuit judge had asked for a poll of all the judges on the court, to see if there were enough votes to take Funchess's case en banc, that is, to have it heard by the full Eleventh Circuit.

At 1:00 A.M. Mark called again from Jacksonville to let me know he was heading back to Tallahassee and to ask me to start drafting some additional papers we needed to file in the U.S. Supreme Court. At 1:50 A.M., the Eleventh Circuit's death clerk called to read me the Eleventh Circuit's opinion: the judges had voted against a review by the full court. I continued to work on the draft for the Supreme Court, and then at 5:00 A.M. I returned to the vigil. The morning drizzle had ripened into a downpour, though, and I stayed for only a few minutes.

I returned to the office and a morning of long stretches of waiting interspersed with intervals of frenetic activity: drafting, dictating, editing. At 10:10 A.M.—one hour and fifty minutes before the stay was scheduled to expire and David Funchess would be electrocuted—the U.S. Supreme Court's clerk called. The Court had extended the stay for five more hours, until 5:00 P.M. The prison rescheduled the execution for 5:01 P.M. We continued to wait.

The news from Washington came at 3:25 P.M. The Court had denied any additional stay by a vote of seven to two, with Justices Brennan and Marshall dissenting. It was over. At 4:30 I went to join the vigil one last time; at 5:01, I laid a flower at the base of the Vietnam War Memorial.

A reporter accurately described the scene at the Florida veterans' memorial the evening David Funchess was executed:

At the late afternoon vigil, people looked at their watches. It was 5:20. "It must be over by now," one woman told another. Others held each other and wept. Still others stared at the color photograph of Funchess in his Marine uniform placed atop a basket of flowers. The group formed a circle in between the two huge granite columns that form the war monument.

Rev. Jim Hardison, coordinator of the death penalty project for Florida IMPACT—an interfaith lobby group for social justice issues—said he was angered not by capital punishment per se but by the way the state administers it.

"Again, we've taken a poor, penniless, minority person who was mentally ill and executed him," Hardison said.

Others present said they felt compelled to speak.

"We're really appalled by your callous indifference toward David Funchess," said Linda Reynolds, Director of the Florida Clearinghouse on Criminal Justice, referring to the governor. "Viet Nam veterans will not forget what you've done today."

"David Funchess was killed twice by society," Reynolds said. "Once in Viet Nam and once today."

Later, from Jim Thompson, David's friend and fellow Vietnam veteran, who had witnessed the killing, I learned that, at the end, "David was free, from the first burst of electricity." We, Funchess's lawyers and investigators and paralegals and secretaries and support staff, were not fine. We went out to a dinner of steak and red wine, something of a CCR ritual when our clients were executed. That night at dinner we cried. We all cried, Scharlette and I included. For the rest of the night, I slept on Mark Olive's couch at CCR. For some reason, going home to my clean bed and orderly house would have felt like treason.

David Funchess was buried on Florida land owned by Jim Thompson.

David Funchess was killed on a legal technicality. The courts in 1986 refused to consider PTSD because, they said, Funchess's lawyers should have raised it at trial; because they had not, it was too late for us to raise it in 1986. But PTSD was not recognized at the time of David's 1976 trial. There is a catch-22 quality to the courts' deadly game of "gotcha" here: How can trial lawyers in 1976 be blamed for not raising a claim that did not exist in 1976? How can courts in 1986 use that prior failure as a basis for refusing to consider powerful evidence of PTSD? And the ultimate question: Why should a condemned person have to pay with his life for the mistakes of his lawyers?

Actually, David Funchess was killed by two legal technicalities. One was the you-found-the-evidence-too-late rule. The other was *Hitchcock*.

David Funchess was executed in May 1986. The next year, a unanimous U.S. Supreme Court decided Jim Hitchcock's case. David Funchess's jury received the same jury instruction later invalidated by the Supreme Court in Hitchcock's case. Thus Funchess's death sentence was as unconstitutional as Hitchcock's. Of course, the *Hitchcock* decision came too late for David Funchess. David was already dead.

Remembering David Funchess's case always makes me think about walls. In 1995, nine years after David was executed, I visited, for the first time, the powerfully moving Vietnam War Memorial in Washington, D.C.—the most visited site in a city full of memorials. I looked for David's name on the wall, even though I knew it wouldn't be there.

David Funchess was the first Vietnam veteran executed by Florida or any other state. He was not the last. In 1993, Larry Joe Johnson was killed in Florida's electric chair for the 1979 robbery and beating death of a sixty-five-year-old man. Johnson's death row nickname was "Timebomb." Indeed. Johnson joined the Navy and served two tours of duty in Vietnam. He witnessed the horrors of combat firsthand, including the sight of a close friend being blown apart—beyond recognition—by a land mine. Johnson was honorably discharged in 1977. Then he was on his own. Two years after his discharge, Johnson committed capital murder.

As we had done in David Funchess' case, Johnson's lawyers argued that the same government that sent this man to a war that destroyed his mind ought now take what was the rest of his life. The state and federal courts refused to stay the execution, and Governor Lawton Chiles denied clemency. Johnson was executed on May 8, 1993.

David Funchess was African American. Did I mention that?

13

Poorhouse Justice:
David Washington

An omnipresent feature of the Supreme Court's decisions vacating stays of executions is their tone of rage. The supporting opinions are uniformly marked by petulance, impatience and wrath.

—Anthony Amsterdam, "Selling a Quick Fix for Boot Hill," 1999

David Leroy Washington's case resulted in a seminal U.S. Supreme Court decision on the quality of counsel guaranteed to indigent defendants by the Constitution. I was involved along the edges of the case from before it reached the Supreme Court until the day of Washington's execution.

Lawyers for the Poor

The Eleventh Circuit's landmark attempt to deal with the problem of ineffective assistance of trial counsel in criminal cases occurred in the capital case of David Leroy Washington. Judge Vance's opinion for the en banc court in *Washington* was a commonsense attempt to craft a workable doctrinal solution to a very real practical problem. The U.S. Supreme Court's reversal in *Washington* can be characterized fairly as a denial of reality.

Justice Sandra Day O'Connor has breezily remarked that "ineffective-assistance-of-counsel claims are becoming as much a part of state and federal habeas corpus proceedings as the bailiffs' call to order in those courts." This is particularly true in capital cases, and it is true for two principal reasons trivialized by O'Connor. First, many capital defendants receive terrible representation at trial. Second, this occurs because capital trial lawyers often have extraordinarily limited resources with which to work.

It is a commonplace that the adversarial judicial system that exists in the United States is premised on the idea that justice is best served when all sides in a dispute are represented zealously and competently. Effective counsel ensures that the judicial system works properly.

The right to effective assistance of counsel is no technicality. It has been called the "most pervasive right" because it defines an individual's ability to assert any other rights. Competent counsel serves to ensure the operation of procedural and constitutional protections guaranteed to a criminal defendant. The Supreme Court recognized more than half a century ago in the Scottsboro case that without counsel capital defendants face conviction and condemnation not because they may be guilty, but because they lack the tools to prove their innocence. This is especially so when defendants are ignorant, illiterate, of feeble intellect, or on trial for their lives.

The right to counsel is not simply a supplemental right; because it cuts to the heart of our judicial system, the right to counsel deserves protection proportional to its stature. That protection is not always forthcoming, however. Notwithstanding the ringing aspirational rhetoric of the Scottsboro case and its progeny, such as *Gideon v. Wainwright,* and notwithstanding the functional importance of the right to counsel, violations of the right are routine if not assumed (albeit not admitted) as a matter of course. In the years leading up to the *Washington* decisions, there was a clear recognition that a problem existed.

The judicial system often forces defendants (in both capital and noncapital cases) into the legal arena with the severe handicap of having no way to ensure the protection of their constitutional right to effective assistance. Indeed, as Vivian Berger has observed, it is probably reasonable to assume that most capital defendants receive ineffective assistance of counsel. Judge Vance seemed to understand this, and his en banc opinion in *Washington* reflects that recognition. Justice O'Connor, on the other hand, has appeared unwilling to accept that a real problem exists and that a real solution is needed in the form of a pragmatic and usable standard for protecting the Sixth Amendment right to effective assistance of counsel for *all* defendants.

To the Supreme Court

David Leroy Washington's case was an unfortunate vehicle through which to try to resolve the issue of what standards should govern claims of ineffective assistance of trial counsel in criminal prosecutions. Many of the systemic problems described above were not present in Washington's trial. Yet the doctrinal standards articulated by the Supreme Court in his case now control claims of ineffective assistance in all cases, capital and noncapital alike.

Washington's case became a landmark by accident. The issue the case presented just happened to reach the federal court of appeals at the precise time the judges had realized that there was a need for some definitive standards for measuring unconstitutional ineffectiveness of counsel. They had been swamped with death cases raising claims of ineffective assistance, and Washington's case just happened to reach the court just when the judges' patience with the issue had reached critical mass.

In *Among the Lowest of the Dead,* David Von Drehle, the leading historian of Florida's modern experience with capital punishment, describes Washington and his crimes:

> David Washington was death row's beautiful athlete, quick, lithe, and graceful. When he wasn't in the exercise yard, he could often be heard weeping in his cell. True remorse is rare on the row—most of the men there have nothing but empty space where their conscience should be. But even hardened observers tended to agree that Washington's remorse was real and gut-wrenching. He had a wife and a baby in a Miami slum when, in September 1976, he lost his job and fell completely, violently, to pieces. Washington was in a laundromat one day, worried about being evicted, when a man approached and identified himself as a minister. The minister suggested they might get together for a date, suggested there might be a little money in it for handsome David Washington. So Washington went to the man's house. The minister proposed that Washington strip and straddle his face.
>
> "I just stabbed him with a knife," Washington later told an interviewer. "I stabbed him about five times. The only thing going through my mind, I said, 'Here I am out here trying to get some money to feed my family, and here go a minister, supposed to be a minister in the church, running about doing stuff like this.'"

Tragically, once he snapped he stayed broken. In the span of a week, David Washington killed three times. He barged into the home of some old ladies in the neighborhood—he believed they ran a fencing operation, though newspapers reported only that the old women "ran frequent yard sales." Washington brandished a gun and began tying them up. One of the women rose from her chair, and Washington started firing wildly. Blood everywhere, one woman dead. Next, Washington kidnaped a student from the University of Miami, robbed him of eighty dollars, and considered holding him for ransom. Instead—as the young man recited the Lord's Prayer—Washington stabbed him to death.

He waived a jury trial, confessed everything to the judge, and received a death sentence. Until they paved the dirt football field in the death row exercise yard, Washington juked and glided through the defense like a gazelle. He spent most of his time admitting and apologizing for what he'd done, which made many of the other men on the row uneasy.

Washington had surrendered to police after his two accomplices were arrested for one of the murders. He gave the police a lengthy confession to one of the murders, and an experienced Miami criminal defense lawyer was subsequently appointed to be his attorney. Acting against his lawyer's advice, Washington subsequently confessed to the other two murders. As Von Drehle notes, Washington waived his right to a jury trial and, again contrary to the advice of his attorney, pleaded guilty to the three killings and accepted responsibility for his crimes. His attorney advised him to invoke his right under Florida law to an advisory jury at his capital sentencing hearing, but he rejected the advice. He chose instead to be sentenced by the trial judge without a jury recommendation. The judge sentenced Washington to death on each of the three counts of first-degree murder.

The U.S. Supreme Court later found that Washington's trial attorney conducted only minimal investigation into the existence of possible mitigating evidence. Although "counsel spoke with [Washington] about his background" and had telephone conversations with Washington's wife and mother, "he did not follow up on the one unsuccessful effort to meet with them. He did not otherwise seek out character witnesses. . . . Nor did he request a psychiatric examination." At the sentencing hearing, "counsel decided not to present and hence not to look further for evidence concerning [Washington's] character and emotional state." The Court noted: "That decision reflected trial counsel's sense of hopelessness about overcoming the evidentiary effect of [Washington's] confessions to the gruesome crimes. It also reflected the judgment that it was advisable to rely on the plea colloquy for evidence about [Washington's] background and about his claim of emotional stress." Counsel's dependence on the plea colloquy was due at least in part to a statement made by the trial judge that he had "a great deal of respect for people who are willing to step forward and admit their responsibility."

Washington claimed in collateral proceedings that his lawyer rendered ineffective assistance because he failed to conduct a meaningful investigation into Washington's background and character. The state courts and federal district court rejected Washington's claims, but a panel of the Eleventh Circuit Court of Appeals ordered the case remanded for an evidentiary hearing. The en banc court decided that the case was worthy of review.

In his opinion for the en banc court in *Washington,* Judge Vance attempted to elucidate the proper standards for evaluating claims of ineffective assistance of counsel based upon allegations of inadequate trial preparation. In addressing Washington's principal contention, that his trial attorney's assistance was not reasonably effective because counsel breached his duty to investigate mitigating circumstances, Judge Vance agreed with Washington that the Sixth Amendment imposes on counsel a duty to investigate. Reasonably effective assistance must be based on informed professional deliberation, and a person can make informed legal choices only after investigating the options. Recognizing that "the amount of pretrial investigation that is reasonable defies precise measurement," Judge Vance set forth in his opinion a typology of cases presenting issues concerning the scope of counsel's duty to investigate before proceeding to trial.

Judge Vance reasoned that if there is only one plausible line of defense, trial counsel must conduct a "reasonably substantial investigation" into that line of defense, because there can be no strategic choice that renders such an investigation unnecessary. The same duty exists if counsel relies at trial on only one line of defense although others were available. In either case, the investigation need not be exhaustive. Although the scope of counsel's duty depends on such facts as the strength of the government's case and the likelihood that pursuing certain leads may prove more harmful than helpful, it must at a minimum include "an independent examination of the facts, circumstances, pleadings and laws involved."

In cases where more than one possible line of defense exists, counsel ideally should investigate each one substantially before making a strategic decision about which defenses to raise at trial. If the attorney conducts such an investigation, the strategic choice made as a result would "seldom if ever" be found to be the result of ineffective assistance of counsel. Given that legal advocacy is more art than science, and given that the adversarial system requires deference to the informed tactical decisions of attorneys, strategic choices must be respected in these circumstances if they are based on reasonable professional judgment. If counsel does not conduct a substantial investigation into each of several plausible lines of defense, however, assistance may nonetheless be considered effective if the lawyer excludes certain lines of defense only for strategic reasons. Financial and caseload limitations may force an attorney to make early strategic choices, often based solely on conversations with the client and review of the prosecutor's evidence.

These strategic choices about which lines of defense to pursue would receive deference only to the extent to which they were reasonable. Thus, Judge Vance's opinion states, "when counsel's assumptions are reasonable given the totality of the circumstances and when counsel's strategy represents a reasonable choice based upon those assumptions, counsel need not investigate lines of defense that he has chosen not to employ at trial." Factors relevant to deciding whether particular strategic choices are reasonable would include the experience of the attorney, the inconsistency of unpursued and pursued lines of defense, and the potential for prejudice from taking an unpursued line of defense.

Judge Vance's opinion also addresses the prejudice to the defense that must be shown before counsel's errors would be held to justify invalidation of the conviction or sentence. A special showing of prejudice would be required except in cases of outright denial of counsel, of affirmative government interference in the representation process, or of inherently prejudicial conflicts of interest. For cases of deficient performance by counsel when the government is not directly responsible for the deficiencies and when evidence of deficiency may be more accessible to the defense than to the prosecution, a prisoner must show that counsel's errors "resulted in actual and substantial disadvantage to the course of his defense." The requisite showing of prejudice would result in reversal of the judgment, Judge Vance reasoned, unless the prosecution could show that the constitutionally deficient performance, in light of all of the evidence, was harmless beyond a reasonable doubt. A majority of the Eleventh Circuit judges sitting en banc agreed that David Washington's case should be remanded to the district court for application of the newly announced standards governing ineffective assistance of counsel.

The Supreme Court granted review. Writing for seven members of the Court, Justice O'Connor noted at the outset that no special standards apply in determining ineffective assistance of counsel claims in capital cases such as the one before it. As Judge Vance had done, the Supreme Court treated the punishment that the defendant faces as merely one factor in the totality of circumstances to be considered in determining whether counsel was reasonably effective. The lawyer in a capital sentencing proceeding occupies a place "comparable" to that at trial. "The benchmark for judging any claim of ineffectiveness must be whether counsel's conduct so undermined the proper functioning of the adversarial process that the [proceeding] cannot be relied on as having produced a just result."

The Supreme Court held that to prevail on a claim of constitutionally ineffective assistance of counsel, a prisoner must make a two-pronged showing. First, he or she must establish that counsel's performance was deficient. To do this, a claimant must prove that the lawyer's representation fell below an objective standard of reasonableness, measured by "prevailing professional norms." Critically, Justice O'Connor exhorted reviewing courts to adhere to a standard "that counsel is strongly presumed to have rendered" constitutionally adequate assistance.

In addition to showing substandard performance, a claimant must show that counsel's deficient performance caused prejudice. For O'Connor, prejudice requires a demonstration that the attorney's errors were "so serious as to deprive the defendant of a fair trial, a trial whose result is reliable." It is not enough to show that counsel's defective performance "had some conceivable effect on the outcome of the proceeding." Conversely, a petitioner need not demonstrate that counsel's substandard performance "more likely than not altered the outcome in the case." Rather, the Court articulated what it viewed as an intermediate standard: "The defendant must show that there is a reasonable probability that, but for counsel's unprofessional errors, the result of the proceeding would have been different. A reasonable probability is a probability sufficient to undermine confidence in the outcome."

Applying this two-pronged standard to the facts of David Washington's case, the Court concluded that Washington's trial lawyer passed muster under both criteria in his representation of Washington at the sentencing hearing. According to the Court, counsel's "tactical" choices fell within the range of reasonableness, and the omitted mitigating evidence would not by any reasonable probability have changed the sentence due to the aggravating factors in the case. David Leroy Washington was executed several months after the Court issued its opinion in his case.

Justice O'Connor's opinion in *Washington* has been criticized generally by commentators, but I will not undertake such a general critique here. Rather, I want to compare Vance's approach in *Washington* to O'Connor's approach in *Washington*. There are three central differences between the two opinions: (1) O'Connor's strong presumption of attorney competence; (2) O'Connor's generalized "reasonableness" standard governing determinations of substandard performance, instead of Vance's more structured inquiry; and (3) O'Connor's stricter requirement of prejudice.

Perhaps the most pernicious aspect of the constitutional standard adopted by Justice O'Connor in *Washington* was her strong presumption in favor of attorney competence. Her opinion established the standard of "reasonably effective assistance," assumed reasonable performance by the defense attorney, and required a showing of clear prejudice to the defendant. At the same time—and again unlike Judge Vance—Justice O'Connor gave virtually no guidelines, beyond the opaque requirement of "reasonableness," for determining what an attorney must do to be considered effective. Further, Justice O'Connor's prejudice standard requires too much: "This is far less a standard for effective assistance of counsel than a standard for disposing of effective assistance of counsel claims." As Yale Kamisar has observed, applying Justice O'Connor's prejudice test to capital sentencing proceedings, when juries are called upon to make the highly subjective determination of whether a fellow human being has lost the moral entitlement to live, is "particularly anomalous—almost bizarre."

Two weeks after the high court ruled in Washington's case, I spoke at length with Judge Vance. Among other topics, we talked about the vagueness of the legal standard set out by the U.S. Supreme Court in *Washington*. I firmly believe that Judge Vance's approach had been both more concrete and more attuned to the real world. Unclear as the

Supreme Court's legal formula was, however, the message the justices sent in reversing *Washington* was clear as a bell. Judge Vance put it to me with typical directness: "The message to us is to stop finding ineffective assistance of trial counsel in death cases."

Virtually everyone involved in the legal machinery of death—nationally, not just in Florida—was waiting for the Supreme Court to issue its landmark opinion in *Washington*. When the opinion came, the postmortem analyses and chess playing began in Florida and every other state with a working death penalty.

Everyone in the legal world knew that Washington had lost in the Supreme Court, so when Governor Graham signed Washington's final death warrant, none of us had much hope. Our best chance was to raise the issue of Gross and Mauro's statistical study on race discrimination in sentencing (discussed in chapter 5). Washington was African American, and his victims were white. Further, the trial prosecutor had suggested, prior to sentencing, that the lives of the victims were worth more than Washington's.

It was a thin claim, but we got a hopeful sign when the state trial judge requested that we draft an order issuing a stay. We did, and the judge took it and went further. He not only stayed the execution, he threw out the death sentence. We had been down this road before, though, and so had the prosecutor and the Florida Supreme Court. The prosecutor appealed, the Florida Supreme Court reversed, and the execution was back on.

My job was to craft the arguments around the minefield of procedural technicalities we would encounter in federal court. But it was no use—the federal trial court denied the stay, and the Eleventh Circuit and U.S. Supreme Court did the same.

David Leroy Washington was executed on schedule. He was thirty-four years old. He was survived by his wife and twelve-year-old daughter.

Soon after Washington's execution, the federal courts began to deal seriously with the *Hitchcock* issue (discussed in chapter 9). Washington's case was tainted by *Hitchcock* error, but he was long dead by the time the courts began grappling with Hitchcock's case.

14

Killed by a Legal Technicality: Ronald Straight

Q: [Justice Powell, would you change your vote in any case, now that you have retired from the U.S. Supreme Court?]

A: . . . I would vote the other way in any capital case.

Q: In *any* capital case?

A: Yes . . . I have come to think that capital punishment should be abolished.

—Retired U.S. Supreme Court Justice Lewis F. Powell Jr.,
in a 1991 interview, as quoted in John C. Jeffries Jr.,
Justice Lewis F. Powell, Jr., 1994

I have never witnessed an execution, although I have had many opportunities (if that's the right word for it) to do so. When I was a Florida capital public defender in the 1980s, my colleagues and I decided that we should send a lawyer from our office to witness the execution of any of our clients. We felt that it was important that the client see at least one friendly face among the designated witnesses (who include reporters, police, prison personnel, and victims' family members). We discussed at length which of us should go: should it be the frontline litigator who knew the client best or the office's chief administrator? After agonizing discussions, we decided that litigators should not have to witness the execution of their clients—that might be emotionally devastating. So the administrator went, because he could afford to be adversely affected by the task for a few weeks or months.

The closest I came to violating this office policy came in 1986, in the case of Ronnie Straight. Straight was a con's con, a stone killer; his *nom de row* was Frog, because he was always jumping on people. Straight and I became close in the two weeks before his scheduled execution. Days before his time, when we both knew a stay was unlikely, he asked me to witness it. He wanted me to—desperately—but then he changed his mind and told me not to come, because "It would fuck you up, and other guys need you." We agreed that I wouldn't witness Ronnie's execution, but I would attend his funeral; I would be there for his mother.

I was assigned to Ronnie Straight's case my very first day of work at CCR, the day the office opened its doors, October 1, 1985. Straight's case was nearing the end of the first round of appeals; he had just lost in the Eleventh Circuit, and the next piece of work was to file a motion for rehearing. That first day, I saw at once that Straight's case had one of the strongest *Hitchcock* claims I'd ever encountered. The work I'd put into Jim Hitchcock's case would pay off handsomely now. Still, the obstacles were many, beginning with the crime itself.

Ronnie Straight was a violent man, and his reputation stood out even against the background of Florida's condemned population. His violence could be casual and random, and he romanticized danger.

On July 30, 1976, Straight, who had been serving time for robbery, received a mandatory conditional parole from the Florida Parole and Probation Commission. By early September, he had drifted to Jacksonville, where he moved into an apartment occupied by Timothy Palmes, Jane Albert, and Albert's seven-year-old daughter. Jane Albert worked as a secretary for James Stone, who owned a furniture store. After discussing Stone's business with Albert, Straight and Palmes proposed that they would collect old debts owed by some of Stone's customers in exchange for 40 percent of the monies collected. Stone rejected their offer because he understood that they contemplated using violence against any uncooperative debtors. But Stone did offer to give Straight one hundred dollars to buy some new clothes, and he told Palmes there might soon be a full-time job opening in the store.

By late September, Stone had decided not to employ Palmes, who then told Straight and another, "You know, I'm going to kill him." Straight replied that he should have the opportunity of killing Stone because Stone's offer of money was insulting. Palmes and Straight agreed to wait until after the first of October, when customers' monthly credit account payments would be in the store. On Sunday, October 3, 1976, Straight, Palmes, and Albert purchased lumber, cement, metal supports, and screws, which they used to construct a heavily weighted coffin. The next morning, Albert lured Stone from the store to her apartment, where her daughter told him to go to the back bedroom. Straight and Palmes were waiting for him and there struck him with a hammer, bound his hands and feet with wire, and placed him in the box. For approximately thirty minutes, they beat him, amputated several of his fingers, and otherwise tortured him. During this time Stone repeatedly begged for his life. Finally, with a machete and butcher knife, Straight and Palmes stabbed Stone eighteen times, eventually killing him. They took his watch, money, and car. Meanwhile, Albert took twenty-eight hundred dollars from the store. Straight and Palmes dumped the weighted coffin, with Stone's corpse inside, into the St. Johns River. Palmes and Straight then left for California with Albert and her daughter. When police there apprehended them, Straight resisted arrest by firing a weapon at the officers. Albert was granted immunity from prosecution by the state in exchange for her testimony as a witness. Palmes confessed, and the coffin was recovered from the river. Tried separately, Palmes and Straight were both convicted of first-degree murder and sentenced to death. Palmes was executed in 1984, and Straight two years later.

During the period when Straight's trial took place, there was ambiguity concerning the *Hitchcock* issue of the admissibility of mitigating evidence outside the statutory list. During that period, it was reasonable to interpret the law as explicitly limiting the consideration of mitigating factors to only those set out in the statute.

The jury in Straight's case was told by the judge, at the beginning of the penalty phase, that it would later be instructed on "the factors in aggravation and mitigation that you may consider." The prosecutor argued to the penalty-phase jury:

> Now, the Court will talk to you at some length later on and I'll talk to you now and I know [defense attorney] Fallin will, too, about how you are supposed to determine when death is the appropriate recommendation. The law doesn't leave it up to your own good graces or your gut feelings or your reactions. It spells out in, I think, pretty clear and unmistakable terms the criteria

which you are to use in order to determine whether or not death is an appropriate recommendation to the Court. In other words, you're going to have a guideline and all you have got to do is look at the guideline and see how the facts of this case or the background of that man fit those guidelines in order to determine what your recommendation should be.

Before getting to the specifics of the case itself, I'd like to look a little bit with you at the law concerning the death penalty. Now, the Florida Statute sets out a list of what is called aggravating and mitigating circumstances as you heard the Court mention a moment ago and the Court will go into some length about it, but there are eight aggravating circumstances and there are seven mitigating circumstances and it's pretty much your job to determine which aggravating, if any, and which mitigating, if any apply and then to determine, which is the balancing or the weighing process, which outweighs the other in deciding what your recommendation should be. And I'm going to, as Mr. Fallin will, to discuss with you the aggravating and mitigating circumstances and talk with you about what I think you will find the aggravating circumstances are and what the mitigating, if any, I think you will find. . . .

As I said before, the law doesn't leave the recommendation of life or death to your speculation or your whim. It sets out very clear guidelines by which you are to follow and the Court will give you a copy of them and you can read them over and I submit to you, Ladies and Gentlemen, that given the facts of this case, his prior record and the aggravating and mitigating circumstances that will be set out to you by the Court and which you can take with you into the Jury Room, there is no recommendation you can make but that that man should die in the electric chair and I ask you to do just that.

In his final jury instructions, the judge told the jury that "the aggravating circumstances are limited to such as the following as may be established by the evidence," and then read the list of statutory aggravating circumstances. Then, in strikingly parallel language, he instructed the jury that "the mitigating circumstances which you may consider, if established by the evidence, are these," and he read the statutory mitigating circumstances. At no point in the instructions did the judge tell the jurors that they could legitimately consider any relevant mitigating circumstance in addition to the mitigating circumstances specified in the instructions. It was Jim Hitchcock's case all over again, but better. There were procedural problems with Jim Hitchcock's claim, but there were none in Straight's case.

I drafted a motion for rehearing in the Eleventh Circuit in one night, but the following morning brought trouble. Straight's volunteer lawyer had also written and sent a rehearing petition to the Eleventh Circuit in Atlanta. His cover letter told the Court to withdraw his motion if ours arrived first. For ours to arrive first, we would need to throw it together in three hours and put it on a plane to Atlanta. We got the petition done by 9:30 P.M., but then the flight to Atlanta was canceled. We knew that the next flight might not get the papers there in time, but we had to take a chance on it anyway.

I actually don't know whose *Straight* rehearing motion reached the court first. I was on a plane to Miami myself, to work on a CCR death warrant case. Between the warrant case and the "brain snatchers" incident, I lost track of *Straight*. On Sunday, October 6, 1985, the *Miami Herald* broke a story on a practice I'd known about for some months previously. It seemed that the brains of executed death row prisoners in Florida were being extracted from their bodies (without the prisoners' prior consent or the consent of their families), sent to the medical school of the University of Florida, and used for medical experiments. For a few days we were abuzz with the possibilities of using this macabre practice as a legal claim, but we couldn't find a way to make it work. The practice did stop, however.

From the Miami warrant, I headed to St. Petersburg on another warrant case. Then Joe Spaziano got a death warrant, and I dove back into his case. Then it was on to Paul Magill and the issue of executing juveniles.

By mid-January 1986, Ronnie Straight's case was out of the Eleventh Circuit. I wrote a petition seeking U.S. Supreme Court review in his case. The argument was pretty straightforward: this big *Hitchcock* case is coming your way, and Ronnie Straight has the identical constitutional issue.

I finished the petition on Thursday, January 23, and the next day I drove to the prison to meet with two old clients and one new one,

Ronnie Straight. Straight and I went over the petition together, and he seemed to be very appreciative of our work for him. I found Straight to be smart, articulate, and in tune with the legal arguments we would be making. He asked me some hard questions about his chances, and he seemed glad when I gave him frank replies. Three days later, he wrote me a very warm thank-you letter. I'm ashamed to admit that I didn't find the time to answer that letter or the next three I received from Straight. Warrant followed warrant, including one in Ted Bundy's case.

We got stays in every single one of those cases, because the U.S. Supreme Court had given us a gift. The court had granted review in a case challenging the way juries were selected in capital cases. The jury-selection procedure at issue in that case was similar to the procedure used in virtually every Florida capital case; a win in that case would have cleared death row in Florida. In the meantime, we convinced the U.S. Supreme Court to stay every Florida execution in which that jury-selection process was used—which was almost every Florida case. So long as the jury-selection case remained pending in the U.S. Supreme Court, we had a moratorium on executions in Florida. I told Straight that, as long as this situation continued, I would get him a stay if the governor signed his warrant. We exchanged letters throughout February and March.

On April Fools' Day, the U.S. Supreme Court denied the petition I had filed in Straight's case. It wasn't a total loss; Justice Blackmun had joined with Justices Brennan and Marshall in dissenting from denial of full review. I called Straight with the news. He was calm, but he expected his death warrant would be signed soon. So did I. A conversation I'd had with Governor Graham's clemency aide had led me to believe that the governor had his eye on Ronnie Straight.

We still had the jury-selection issue, we thought, but then, suddenly, we didn't. The big jury-selection case was still pending in the Supreme Court but, on April 11, the Court denied stays in several other cases with no explanation. The moratorium on executions was over.

I didn't know what to tell Straight about the jury-selection case, because I didn't know for sure what the Supreme Court's actions meant. The big jury-selection case was still pending, so maybe the stay denials in other cases meant that we were going to lose the big case. Or maybe the justices had found the other cases distinguishable from the big case.

Or maybe the stay denials were clerical errors; after all, no one had actually been executed yet.

Four days later, someone was executed: Dan Thomas, another of our clients, was put to death. That day, Straight wrote me a letter that began: "I know you and the others are feeling very bad. My heart goes out to Dan's loved ones. I knew him well, and we were friends." Then he wrote of his fear of a warrant. "I sit here day after day, waiting for them to come and take me back to deathwatch. I'll level with you, Mike, it's a terrible feeling. Especially after what happened to Dan."

Governor Graham signed Straight's death warrant on April 18. Straight called me right after they had read him the warrant. He seemed okay, and we talked mostly about the jury-selection case, even though we urgently needed a Plan B. I didn't have time to come up with one then, however. David Funchess was scheduled to die in ninety hours, and we were scrambling. The day after Funchess was executed, I turned full-time to Ronnie Straight's case. If we were going to win a stay, it would have to be through *Hitchcock,* even though the Supreme Court had already denied review on the *Hitchcock* claim in Straight's case.

Two days after his death warrant was signed, Ronnie Straight wrote me a letter from his deathwatch cell, only a short walk from the electric chair. He thanked me for my work on his case and on other cases. He wrote: "I know you always give it your very best. From what I see of you in the short period of time we've been friends, you always give not only me but all of us 100%. You are a very dedicated young man." Then, this man whose life I held in my hands wrote that he understood why I had not yet pursued some of the factual leads he had given me. "I know you're so busy. The fact of the matter is you're a human being and not a robot who keeps going on a battery charge (excuse the word 'charge'; just making a little humor, buddy)."

A pattern evolved over the next weeks. I would work on the case all day, and at night—often very late—Ronnie would phone from his cell on deathwatch and we would talk, some about his chances and issues, but mostly he would talk about his mother's worrying about him.

On May 5, we lost—really lost—the big jury-selection case in the U.S. Supreme Court on a vote of six to three. Ronnie took it hard, becoming very depressed. I think my faith in the *Hitchcock* issue cheered him up a bit, but not much.

That's how things went. I spent the days writing and the nights talking with Ronnie. I filed papers in courts and lodged papers in other courts. The state trial court ruled against us at 6:10 P.M. on the Friday before the scheduled Tuesday morning execution. That night I worked late and slept in the office. When I woke up at 1:00 P.M. on Saturday, I finalized the papers for the Florida Supreme Court. I was missing some documents from the trial file, though, and the only place I could get them was from the file in the Florida Supreme Court. The court was closed for the weekend, but one of my colleagues convinced a justice to provide me with the documents I needed. I worked until 2:30 Sunday morning.

On Sunday I wrote all day and caught a nap in the late afternoon. At midnight I began crafting the oral argument I would deliver in the Florida Supreme Court on Monday morning. I finally gave up at 3:00 A.M. and crashed on the couch in my office. A phone call from Ronnie Straight woke me up at 4:30 A.M. He had called to wish me luck on the oral argument. As it turned out, that call was the high point of the day. The oral argument did not go well at all. In my diary that day, I called it "slaughter: everyone was hostile . . . ; I got buried in poison; [two of my colleagues] marveled that the justices could be so savage."

The Florida Supreme Court didn't take long to decide; by 11:40 we found out the court had ruled against us, unanimously. I called Ronnie, and he asked me to call his mom with the news. When I told her, she burst into tears.

We filed papers in the federal trial court. Oral argument was at 5:00 P.M., and the federal trial judge denied us at 7:40 P.M. Again I called Ronnie's mom, who cried and cried, and thanked us.

Mark Olive had spoken with Ronnie, and said that he seemed to be calm. Ronnie was preparing himself to die, and in this he had counseling. We called it "white-lightning" a condemned soul.

We were now in the Eleventh Circuit. Our panel consisted of Judges Vance, Fay, and Clark. At 8:30 P.M., the order was issued. Any real stay was denied, unanimously. However, the court had given a temporary stay, until noon on Tuesday. On to the U.S. Supreme Court. I called the Supreme Court's death clerk and activated the papers we had lodged previously.

At the time, the U.S. Supreme Court had under consideration another Florida capital case, *Darden v. Wainwright*; the Court also was deciding whether to grant plenary review in *Hitchcock*. I filed, on Straight's behalf, a petition for writ of habeas corpus claiming that, at the time of his trial, Florida's capital sentencing procedure was constitutionally defective. We asserted that this claim was also presented in *Darden* and asked the Court to stay Straight's execution pending the decision in that case (a stay requires five votes). We also petitioned for plenary review of his case, or certiorari (certiorari requires four votes). Finally, we asked for a "hold" until the Court could decide *Darden,* or at least until the Court could decide whether to decide *Hitchcock* (at that time, a "hold" required three votes).

My papers in the U.S. Supreme Court stressed that the *Hitchcock* case had been decided by the full Eleventh Circuit; Straight's case presented the identical issue, and the fact that the full Eleventh Circuit found the claim worthy of its time in *Hitchcock* suggested that the Supreme Court itself might later grant review to *Hitchcock* (which, of course, it later did).

On May 16, 1986, Supreme Court Justice Lewis F. Powell Jr. wrote two internal memos to the other justices. The first memo summarized the history of Straight's case. The second articulated Powell's reasons for his vote to deny a stay: "The Florida Supreme Court found that Straight is procedurally barred from raising his *[Hitchcock]* claim . . . I accordingly vote to deny both the stay application and the [petition] seeking full review in the Supreme Court."

The day before Straight was scheduled for execution, the other votes trickled in. Justice Byron White wrote, "My vote in this case is the same as Lewis Powell's—deny." That was two votes to zero for a stay. Justice Thurgood Marshall was next: "I vote to grant the stay and hold this case pending disposition of *Darden*; if the stay is not granted, I will write [an opinion]." That made the vote two to one. Justice Brennan weighed in next: "I vote to grant the petition for [full review] and the stay in this case." We were tied at two to two. Chief Justice Warren Burger broke the tie: "I vote to deny the . . . stay." And Justice Sandra Day O'Connor wrote, "I vote to deny the stay in this case." That made the vote four to two against us. Justice John Paul Stevens wrote, "I vote to grant the stay and hold the [case] for *Darden*," and Justice Harry Blackmun wrote, "My vote is to grant the stay and hold the [case] for *Darden*." We were tied again at four to four. Justice William Rehnquist cast the swing vote: "My vote is to deny."

Another series of internal memos made the rounds of the Court the next day, May 20. The initial memo, written by Justice Powell, explained that "the [Eleventh Circuit] Court of Appeals stayed the execution in this case only until noon today. As several Justices apparently have not been available this morning, including the Chief Justice, I have entered an order . . . extending the stay of execution until 5:00 p.m. this afternoon."

Justice Brennan was working on the Straight case, however. He wrote a two-paragraph memorandum setting out why the Straight case should be held (and Straight's execution stayed) pending *Hitchcock* and *Darden*.

Justice Powell responded with a two-page memo that boiled over with his frustration with Straight's lawyer (that is, me). Powell argued that Straight's constitutional claims were barred by multiple procedural rules: "Straight has been relying on various versions of his *[Hitchcock]* argument since 1981. He and his lawyers have been fully aware of that argument's significance. The Court has repeatedly stated that it will not tolerate this kind of sandbagging of the judiciary in capital cases." He concluded: "This is not a hold for *Darden* or *Hitchcock*, or for any other pending case. My vote therefore is to deny the application for a stay. If the case is held [for *Hitchcock* or *Darden*], I will write [an opinion]."

Justices Brennan and Marshall circulated draft opinions dissenting from denial of the stay. Justice Powell circulated a proposed opinion concurring in the denial of the stay. In his book *Closed Chambers,* Edward Lazarus, who was a U.S. Supreme Court clerk at the time, describes the night before Straight's execution as a "night of hair-tearing fury" for Justice Brennan, who was "straining to find language sufficient to his outrage."

By a five-to-four vote, the Court denied Straight's application for a stay. Justice Powell filed an opinion concurring in the denial of the stay, which was joined by Chief Justice Burger and Justices Rehnquist and O'Connor. Justice Brennan dissented in an opinion joined by Justices Marshall and Blackmun. Both the concurrence and the dissent addressed the question of the Court's obligation to stay an execution where the petition for certiorari presents an issue on which certiorari has already been granted and on which decision is pending. Justice Brennan's dissent revealed that "four Justices have voted to 'hold'

Straight's petition because they believe that it presents an issue suffi-ciently similar to *Darden* to warrant delaying disposition of Straight's case until a decision is reached in that case." If the Court had actually granted full review in *Straight,* the posture of the case would have been identical to that of *Darden* and the central question on the stay appli-cation would have been, as it was in *Darden,* whether the fact that four justices had voted for plenary review triggers a duty for the remaining justices to vote for a stay in order to preserve the Court's jurisdiction. Here, however, the vote of the four justices was not for full review, but to postpone consideration of the petition until after a decision could be rendered on the merits of Darden's claims. The question before the Court, then, was whether this difference was relevant for the purpose of determining whether the execution should be stayed.

Justice Brennan viewed *Darden* and *Straight* as similar cases in all relevant respects. He argued that, for purposes of staying an execution, a vote to hold should be treated no differently than a vote to grant ple-nary review:

> A "hold" is analogous to a decision to grant a petition for certio-rari. The Court's "hold" policy represents the conviction that like cases must be treated alike. Like the Rule of Four, it grants to a minority of the Court the power to prevent the majority from denying a petition for certiorari when the minority is per-suaded that the issues or questions presented in the case to be held are similar to a case that the Court is to decide. The prin-ciple is apparent: whether an individual obtains relief should not turn on the fortuity of whether his papers were the first, the sec-ond or the tenth to reach the Court. What counts is the merits. A vote to "hold" is a statement by a number of Justices that the disposition of the granted case may have an effect on the merits of the case which is to be held. The fact that a majority of the Justices disagree with the decision to "hold" does not warrant subversion of the "hold" rule any more than does disagreement by five with the decision to grant a petition for certiorari justify departure from the Rule of Four.

Apparently referring to the Court's disposition of the stay applica-tion in *Darden* earlier that term, he added: "It is unthinkable to me that the practice that four votes to grant certiorari trigger an 'automatic' fifth vote to stay an execution should not apply to a 'hold' when a man's life is in the balance." For the dissenters, then, the requirement that held cases be treated identically to granted cases arises from the ancient common-law principle that "like cases be treated alike." Generalizing from the particular context of *Straight*, if the Court has granted certiorari in one case to resolve a particular issue, and, before it has reached a decision on the merits of that case, the same issue is presented in a second certiorari petition, the latter petition must be held pending the adjudication of the first case to enable both petitioners to be treated alike. Otherwise, the treatment of the two petitioners will depend on the "fortuity" of who filed first. In capital cases, this would mean that one petitioner would live and the other would die.

Justice Powell, joined by Chief Justice Burger and Justices Rehnquist and O'Connor, strongly disagreed with the claim that because the Court issues stays when four justices have voted to grant certiorari, it must also do so when three (or four) have voted to hold. This conclusion rested on two arguments. First, Justice Powell stated that a vote to grant certiorari reflects a decision that the case raises an issue worthy of plenary consideration and creates the possibility that the petitioner will obtain a favorable outcome. Thus the petitioner in a granted case has been found, in a sense, to "merit" the Court's consideration. In contrast, according to Justice Powell, a decision to hold may not reflect any such opinion regarding the "merit" of the petitioners' claims: "The Court often 'holds' cases for reasons that have nothing to do with the merits of the cases being held, as when we wish not to 'tip our hand' in advance of an opinion's announcement." Justice Powell's second reason for treating held cases differently from granted cases is no more persuasive. Turning to the merits of Straight's particular claims, Justice Powell stated: "In this case, my vote to deny Straight's petition for certiorari—and therefore not to hold the petition for *Darden*[—] reflects my view that *no matter how Darden* is resolved, the judgment [in *Straight*] will be unaffected." This rationale fully and properly explains why Justice Powell voted against holding the petition in *Straight*. That, however, was not the issue to which his opinion was supposed to be addressed. Instead, the question before the Court was whether the five justices who voted against holding nevertheless had an independent duty to protect the Court's jurisdiction once their colleagues invoked the hold rule.

The opinions published by the Supreme Court in *Straight* provided only a glimpse of the battle within the Court. The rest of the picture came out years later.

Three weeks after Straight was executed, the Supreme Court granted plenary review in *Hitchcock*. Although Straight's jury had received instructions all but identical to those at issue in *Hitchcock*, I had been unable to persuade the Supreme Court to consider the issue in Straight's case. When the Court finally considered the claim in *Hitchcock*, Justice Scalia, the Court's archconservative, wrote for a unanimous Court: "We think it could not be clearer" that Hitchcock's judge and jury believed they could consider only a few favorable facts, that the Florida standard jury instructions given in *Hitchcock* (and *Straight*) violated the same constitutional issue in both cases: the jury instruction on consideration of favorable evidence. *Hitchcock* and *Straight* raised the same issue in the same procedural posture: the issue was properly before the federal courts on a first habeas petition (in *Straight*, the Florida Supreme Court had decided the issue on its merits, thus requiring the federal courts to do so as well—a fact we tried our best to make clear to the U.S. Supreme Court).

The Court issued its unanimous opinion in *Hitchcock* in the spring of 1987. I learned about the *Hitchcock* decision exactly one year to the day after Ronald Straight was executed. None of our attempts to raise the *Hitchcock* jury instruction issue in *Straight* had mattered. In one of the memos quoted briefly above, Justice Powell wrote of the *Straight* case:

> To the extent that Straight is repeating arguments made in his first habeas petition, there have been no changed circumstances that would justify rehearing and deciding those arguments again. (I note that we denied cert on Straight's *Lockett* claim only six weeks ago. No. 80-6264, cert. Denied 3/31/86.) And to the extent he is adding new arguments, this is plainly an abuse of the writ. Straight has been relying on various versions of his *Lockett* argument since 1981. He and his lawyers have been fully aware of that argument's significance. The Court has repeatedly stated that it will not tolerate this kind of sandbagging of the judiciary in capital cases.
>
> For the reasons stated above, this is not a hold for *Darden* or *Hitchcock*, or of any other pending case. My vote therefore is to

deny the application for a stay. If the case is held, I will write [an opinion in dissent].

The memo's dismissive and exasperated tone, its bloodless, legalistic content, and the sense of vanity and moral cowardice it conveys evince Justice Powell's belief that Ronald Straight (meaning Straight's lawyer, meaning *me*) had strategically withheld potentially winning issues until the eleventh hour. Stay denied. Thus did Justice Powell elide responsibility and absolve himself of responsibility for the execution of Ronald Straight.

Powell's memos in *Straight* reveal his belief in what Anthony Amsterdam has called "the myth of the death penalty defense lawyers' conspiracy." That myth provides justices like Powell with important psychological comfort. Amsterdam writes:

> This imaginative universe was one in which the Justices could develop a comfortable habit of killing. The habit itself was bound to harden. For once a judge has sent some people to their deaths after struggling with uncertain questions whether that is constitutional, the judge must kill and kill again—first to insist that his or her struggle be taken seriously, then to ratify that those already dead died rightly. But *comfort* with the habit also had to be achieved.
>
> And the myth of the Death Penalty Defense Lawyers' Conspiracy provided that comfort, in three important ways.
>
> First, it gave the Justices somebody to be mad at. Killing is easier if you are angry. These lawyers really are insufferable. They won't allow the Justices to do the work of justice at a decent distance from the stench of death. They insist on dragging the courts into the very countdown. They are always filing pleadings with labels like: DEATH CASE—EXECUTION IMMINENT. And even when a Justice thinks that he or she has finally managed to kill a particular prisoner once, here it is to do all over again. These cruel and unusual lawyers are imposing double jeopardy on the Justices. So damn them anyway—they and their damned clients.
>
> Second, the Lawyers' Conspiracy made it possible for the Justices to deny that many of the issues which they and the lower courts were deciding in death cases were close judgment calls. Close judgment calls are discomforting reminders of one's fallibili-

ty. But even seemingly plausible lawyer's arguments can be dismissed without accepting the risk of deciding them wrong if they can be viewed as mere delaying tactics, ruses, wiles—doubtless all the more specious for being ingenious, since they are the instruments of deliberate deceivers.

Third, the Conspiracy explained why so few death sentences were being carried out in a nation that supposedly embraced the death penalty as a fit and proper punishment for crime. Even after the Supreme Court had taken on itself the task of flogging the lower federal courts into speeding executions, an embarrassingly small number of people were getting killed. Why? Because a tiny but immensely powerful cabal of schemers had succeeded in bringing this country of 240 million people to its knees. That *had* to be the explanation, because otherwise the explanation might be that this country of 240 million people is so conflicted and agonized about the death penalty that—unlike any other criminal penalty on the books—we almost never can enforce it in the concrete, however much we may swear by it in the abstract. But this latter explanation would mean that, when the Supreme Court sustained capital punishment as consistent with contemporary standards of decency in 1976, the Justices got those standards wrong. And *that* would mean that maybe—just maybe—they have killed and killed again to buy themselves false comfort.

Even assuming that Powell was correct, and that I was as clever as he suggested I was, his *Straight* memos evince a coldness of heart and barrenness of soul that is extraordinary. It beggars the imagination to think that a Supreme Court justice would vote to send a man to his death because the justice disapproves of the actions of the man's lawyer.

It was more than that, of course. The legalistically arid affect and tone of the Supreme Court's internal memoranda in *Straight* do not obscure the essential narrative theme; Justice Powell's subtext all but says, "This guy's lawyer is sandbagging us. We're the highest court in the most powerful nation on Earth; we're the Supreme Court, and we will not be trifled with. We'll show that uppity attorney we mean business. We'll kill his client."

Thus did Justice Powell turn the prose of law poisonous. Not only was there no poetry, but there was no visible trace of humanity in

Powell's imperious pronouncements. In a different, less mortal context, the words of this justice might appear comic, or at least ironic.

To Lewis Powell, Ronnie Straight was nothing more than a stranger's name on a case file. All Powell knew about Straight was his crime. He did not know Ronnie Straight. I did know Ronnie Straight. I had sat in a cramped prison visiting room with him. I knew his crime, but I also knew that there was more to the man than his crime. But I wasn't good enough to save Ronald Straight, or the other Florida prisoners executed prior to *Hitchcock* in 1987.

So James Hitchcock wins a unanimous decision in the U.S. Supreme Court and lives while Ronald Straight, who had the identical issue, is electrocuted. I raised the same issue in both cases in virtually identical language; were the mortally different outcomes caused by my failings as a defense lawyer? Or was it just pure, dumb luck? The legal issues were everywhere; the constitutional basis necessary to craft those legal issues into winning constitutional claims was there all along in both cases.

While the internal memos were flying in the Supreme Court on the last night of Ronnie Straight's life, we waited. Shortly before filing, at around 9:00 P.M., I called Ronnie, and we continued a conversation we'd been having over the past few days, about whether or not I would witness his execution. We ultimately reached agreement that I would not, in part because of Ronnie's concern about how it would affect me. I did agree to attend his funeral, to be there for his mom.

The Eleventh Circuit's temporary stay was set to expire at noon, and the prison scheduled the execution for 12:01. When I woke up at 6:30 that morning, that seemed like a lot of time. However, as the hours dragged on with no word from the Supreme Court, my sense of doom increased. At 10:15 A.M., the Court clerk told me that we wouldn't hear anything from the justices until "around noon." I pointed out that the execution would be carried out at one minute past noon, and that the prison took such timetables seriously. Forty-five minutes later, the clerk called me back. The stay had been extended for another five hours. I phoned Ronnie's mother, and she broke down in tears. She said that these short stays—"baby stays," we called them—were nothing short of "torture." I agreed.

We waited all afternoon, and at 4:53 I could stand the wait no longer. I called the Court and was told the obvious: no word yet.

As the 5:00 P.M. deadline approached, the Supreme Court issued a series of five-minute stays. Then at 5:10 we got the news: no stay, by a vote of five to four. It was too late for me to talk to Ronnie; he was already strapped into the electric chair.

The moment when I was told that Ronnie Straight had lost by a single vote is etched into my memory. At that moment there was no time to assimilate the reality of our razor-thin loss with the granite finality that there was nothing more I or any lawyer could do for Straight now.

I will never forget the waves of helpless rage that washed over me as the Supreme Court's clerk read to me the orders denying the stay. It would have been easy—too easy—to blame the Court as an institution, the five justices who voted to deny the stay, or the one justice who could have switched his or her vote and saved Straight's life. I found that the real target of my rage was myself: a participant in the system of legal homicide. At that moment the seed of my decision, made ten years later, to become a conscientious objector in the death wars was planted.

I learned later that Ronnie Straight was at peace when he died, in large measure because he was able to confess to his priest shortly before the killing took place. This was difficult to accomplish, because in the final stages of deathwatch, all of a prisoner's visits are monitored by prison guards. To allow Straight a modicum of privacy during his last confession, two of his final visitors broke into spontaneous song, providing enough cover that the guards were unable to hear the confession; by the time they figured out what was happening, it was over. Straight's visitors also brought him a bouquet of gardenias. Unable to find a place to buy flowers on Route 121, the visitors picked a handful of gardenias from a local garden ("Now, remember, if someone calls the law, you're a nun"—which was true; and they *did* knock on the front door before liberating the flowers).

The grief took me by the throat and wouldn't let go. I was the little boy in Lincoln's graceful story, who stubbed his toe and said he was too old to cry and it hurt too much to laugh. Throughout all of this my office door remained closed. I felt ruined. My CCR colleagues—people I loved, like Mark Olive, Scharlette Holdman, David Reiser—would not see how hard this had hit me. We would not discuss it—not that day, not that night, not ever.

The day after her son was executed, Ronnie Straight's mother called to thank me and to tell me that the funeral would be in two days. The services were held at Evergreen Cemetery in Gainesville. I arrived late, but I was able to stand beside Mrs. Straight at the grave. Her sobs were like nothing I've ever heard, a one-voice choir of despair and regret.

Conclusion

After twenty years on the high court, I have to acknowledge that serious questions are being raised about whether the death penalty is being fairly administered in this country.

—U.S. Supreme Court Justice Sandra Day O'Connor, in a speech before the Minnesota Women Lawyers, Minneapolis, July 2001

The issues raised about capital punishment in the stories told in this book matter to all of us. The late Supreme Court Justice William Brennan perhaps said it best, in one of his last dissenting opinions before retiring from the court: "It is tempting to pretend that minorities on death row share a fate in no way connected to our own, that our treatment of them sounds no echoes beyond the chambers in which they die. Such an illusion is ultimately corrosive, for the reverberations of injustice are not so easily confined." To the contrary, "the way in which we choose those who will die reveals the depth of moral commitment among the living."

I oppose capital punishment as it exists—and as it will continue to exist for the foreseeable future, regardless of what some politicians claim—*as a legal system* in America today. America's modern experience with capital punishment has taught us that it is a rigged lottery, skewed by matters of politics, class, race, geography, and, most important, the quality of the defense lawyer at trial. The death penalty is not reserved for the worst murderers; it is reserved for the murderers with the worst lawyers at trial.

It isn't even reserved for those who are guilty. Innocent people are sentenced to death and executed in America. As I've said, it's as inevitable as the law of averages and the fallibility of legal institutions devised and administered by humans. No matter how careful we are, no matter how much money we spend to provide the best defense for people on trial for their lives, no matter what we do, innocent people continue to be—as they always have been—sentenced to death and executed.

There is a moment toward the end of Pat Barker's novel *The Ghost Road,* the final volume of her World War I trilogy, that captures the nature of my argument. The time is late August 1918, near the end of the war and shortly before the battlefield death of Wilfred Owen, one of the novel's principal protagonists. For the moment, the war has forgotten Owen and his three comrades, Billy Prior—who, like Owen, had already survived the horrors of the war—and Hallet and Potts, newcomers to the fight. The men have temporarily "created a fragile civilization, a fellowship on the brink of disaster."

They have time and wine, and they argue about the war. "The two new recruits debated whether the war was being fought for Belgium neutrality or for access to the oil wells of Mesopotamia. Billy Prior's silence irritated the two newcomers who pressed him for his thoughts on the matter—he and Owen, after all, had already fought. The others had not."

Prior says: "What do I think? I think what you're saying is basically a conspiracy theory, and like all conspiracy theories it's optimistic. What you're saying is, OK, the war isn't being fought for the reasons we're told, but it *is* being fought for a reason. It's not benefitting the people it's supposed to be benefitting, but it *is* benefitting somebody." But in fact things are much worse than that, because "there isn't any kind of rational justification left. It's become a self-perpetuating system. Nobody benefits. Nobody's in control. Nobody knows how to stop."

After a while, Wilfred Owen speaks slowly: "You say we kill the beast. I say we fight because men lost their bearings in the night."

In time, we have come to see World War I as pointless slaughter. In time, I believe, we will come to see capital punishment the same way. Until then, the body count will continue to increase.

As of this writing, that body count is at 777 nationally, 52 in Florida. And rising.

Index

Michael Mello is professor of law at Vermont Law School. He is the author of *The Wrong Man: A True Story of Innocence on Death Row* (Minnesota, 2001), *The United States of America versus Theodore Kaczynski, Dead Wrong,* and *Against the Death Penalty.* He has worked on several high-profile cases, including those of Ted Bundy, Theodore Kaczynski, Elizabeth Morgan, and "Crazy Joe" Spaziano.

Mark E. Olive is an attorney in private practice in Tallahassee, Florida. He represents only persons who have been sentenced to death and is a nationally recognized expert on capital postconviction proceedings.